THE GUN DIGEST BOOK OF THE .45

By Dean A. Grennell

DBI BOOKS, INC.

ABOUT THE COVER

Brand new and just in time to appear on our front cover is Colt's first-ever double-action auto, the Series 90 Double Eagle .45 ACP pistol.

Made entirely of stainless steel, this big-bore auto has a decocking lever which permits the hammer to be lowered from the full-cock position without squeezing the trigger. It has a five-inch barrel, an eight-shot magazine capacity and a three-dot sight system that is quite popular with combat shooters. The rear sight is a square notch that is drift-adjustable for windage and has two white dots flanking the notch; the blade front has a single white dot and together they give a 6½-inch sight radius. For greater visibility, both front and rear sights are blued.

The stocks are of a moulded black composition plastic, deeply checkered for a good grip, and have the Colt logo on each side. As is standard practice with Colt, the magazine catch button is on the left side of the frame. The hooked trigger guard offers the shooter good control should he care to use it, while a flat, checkered mainspring housing is included.

On the back cover you'll see the redoubtable Colt Government Model .45 ACP in blue finish with checkered walnut stocks. Also available in 9mm Parabellum and 38 Super, the Government Model has a seven-shot magazine, five-inch barrel and weighs thirty-eight ounces. It has both grip and thumb safeties and internal firing pin safety, grooved trigger, arched mainspring housing and Colt's Accurizor barrel and bushing. This seems to be the .45 auto by which all others are judged, and with good reason.

Also on the back cover is the Colt Combat Elite in .45 ACP only. This popular auto has a stainless steel frame, ordnance steel slide and internal parts, and high-profile three-dot sight system. The extended grip safety, beveled magazine well and stippled rubber combat stocks complete the outfit to make it a very popular choice among today's top shooters.

Photos by John Hanusin.

Produced by

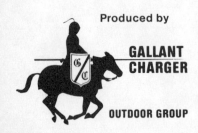

GALLANT CHARGER

OUTDOOR GROUP

EDITORIAL DIRECTOR
Jack Lewis

PRODUCTION DIRECTOR
Sonya Kaiser

ART DIRECTOR
Kristy Bunn

ARTISTS
Denise Comiskey
Gary Duck
Rueselle Gilbert
Eric Kincel

PRODUCTION COORDINATOR
Nadine Symons

COPY EDITOR
David Rodriguez

PHOTO SERVICES
C'est DAGuerre Labs

LITHOGRAPHIC SERVICES
Gallant Graphics

PUBLISHER
Sheldon Factor

ISBN: 0-87349-043-6   Library of Congress Catalog Card Number: 89-05035

CONTENTS

ACKNOWLEDGEMENTS

Getting a book such as this completed, with no empty pages, is a project of fairly Augean stature and the helpful efforts of a lot of people go into it, apart from the nominal writer. The book at hand — informally known as "BOFF" among the production crew — certainly is no exception.

Jack Lewis edited the copy for Pepper Federici, David Rodriguez, Nadine Symons and Rene Riley to set. The galleys of type, along with sheafs of photos from C'est DAGuerre Labs, landed on Kristy Bunn's desk and she composed them to final format, with help from Gary Duck, Denise Comiskey, Rueselle Gilbert, Eric Kincel, and Sonya Kaiser.

Back at DBI Books, Sheldon Factor and Pam Johnson scanned the layout proofs. I am aware there are people who find their keenest delight in spotting typographical errors or "literals," as our British friends like to say. I have not included any such deliberately but, if there are none in the entire book, I shall be pleasantly astounded and grateful.

I had a lot of help from people within the firearms industry, including John Nassif and Stan Newman at Colt; Sherry A. Collins at Smith & Wesson; Bob Grueskin at Springfield Armory; Steve Hornady and Dick Placzek of Hornady; Bob Nosler of Nosler Bullets; Jim Hull and Bob Ellison of Sierra Bullets; Thanos Polyzos at Para-Ordnance; Dave Zeigler of Browning; Tony Aeschliman at Marlin; Doc and De Carlson of Carlson's Trading Post; Dick Dietz of Remington; Mike Jordan of Winchester; Marty Liggins of Accurate Arms; R.E., J.B. and Bruce Hodgdon of Hodgdon Powder; Allan Jones, Scot Heter, Dave Andrews, Jay Postman and Bill Keyes of Omark; Dave Corbin of Corbin Manufacturing; Joe Zambone of MagSafe Ammo; Rudy Herman of Safariland; Dick Lee of Lee Precision; Mike Bussard of Federal Cartridge; Evan Whildin of Action Arms Ltd.; Bob Olsen of Olsen Development Labs; Will Moore and Linda Zachow of Wildey; Warren Center, Ken French, Bob Gustafson and Tim Pancurak at Thompson/Center; Bill Ruger, Tom Ruger, Jim Triggs and Steve Vogel of Sturm, Ruger & Co.; Joe Wright of Thompson/Center Association; Richard C. Davis of Second Chance; Pete Dickey of the National Rifle Association; Stan Kaswer of Pin Grabber; Mike Dillon of Dillon Precision Products and especially those not mentioned who richly deserve to be listed, but weren't. I'm sure I left out some names and I'm equally certain I did not intend doing so.

In addition, many friends contributed helpfully: Jim and Joanne Andrews; Terry Tussey; Tom Ferguson; Colonel Claud S. Hamilton; Ernie Marrs; Jack Kendall; Gene Spenser, Ace Hindman and James E. Clark, to name but a few.

Last but far from least, was my wife by my first marriage, Jean, who has been puttting up with me since May of 1945, including those interludes when I'm doing books.

Many thanks, also, to all you book-buying .45 buffs, without whom none of this would be possible. May your tribe increase!

Cordially/gratefully,

Dean A. Grennell

CHAPTER 1

AN OLD GUN, FROM AN OLD WAR

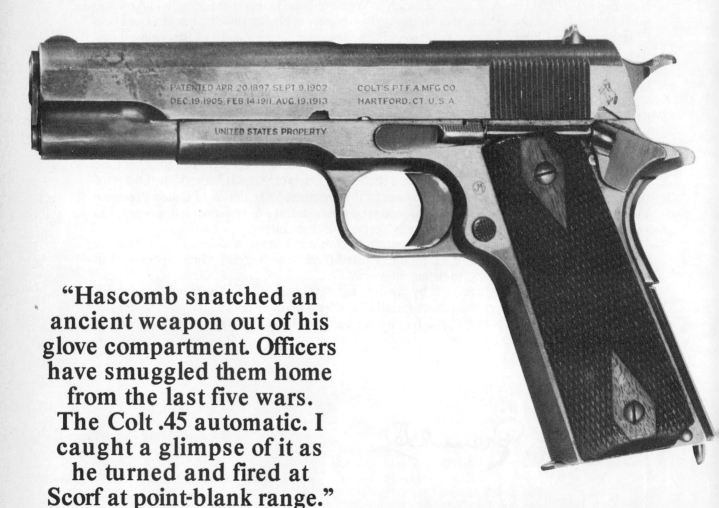

"Hascomb snatched an ancient weapon out of his glove compartment. Officers have smuggled them home from the last five wars. The Colt .45 automatic. I caught a glimpse of it as he turned and fired at Scorf at point-blank range."

Strictly as issued, back in 1917 or 1918, this old Colt Model 1911 remains absolutely unmodified in any way. It is rather unusual to encounter one that is true, as most of them have been improved somewhat.

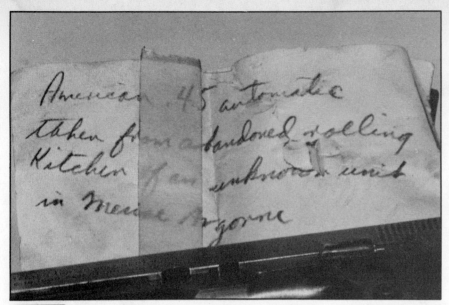

This is the note tucked into the flap of the GI holster by the soldier who brought the old Colt back as a souvenir of World War I.

THE QUOTED passage on the opposite page, occurs on page 266 of the paper-back edition of *The Dreadful Lemon Sky,* the sixteenth episode in the saga of Travis D. McGee, as crafted onto paper by the late John Dann MacDonald, himself a lieutenant colonel in the Army, CBI Theater, during WWII. That particular manuscript was copyrighted in 1974 and I'll admit I've been puzzled to account for all five of the specified wars. Be that as it may, enlisted men have smuggled them home, also.

Accompanying photographs illustrate numerous details on one such pistol, fetched home from the first — or, perhaps, the second — of JDM's five wars, if you count the Mexican pacification as the first. The smuggler, in this instance, was not an officer; not even a non-commissioned one. He was a private first class by name of Leo A. Ihli, 147th Field Artillery, doing duty as a horse-mounted scout/courier in that first of all global conflicts. He had been issued a sidearm in the form of what has come to be known as a Model 1917 revolver — Colt or Smith &

Wesson? The only available information doesn't recall and the revolver was duly turned back in to the quartermaster, ordnance officer — or whatever the original issuing agency may have been — sometime after November 11, 1918.

A slightly battered note, tucked beneath the flap of the government issue holster that encases an old auto reads, "American .45 automatic taken from abandoned rolling kitchen of an unknown unit at Meuse-Argonne."

This book is getting under way in September 1988, precisely seventy years after the Meuse-Argonne engagement; a notably bloody campaign. The 1968 edition of the *World Book* encyclopedia, volume 20, page 376, states, "About 1,200,000 Americans fought in the Battle of the Meuse-Argonne. About one of every ten was killed or wounded." It was not, however, a vain expenditure of lives, precious though they may have seemed to the owners thereof. Two more months and the entire messy business was over — at least until the next one began, in early September 1939.

Wars, somewhat in the manner of earthquakes, result

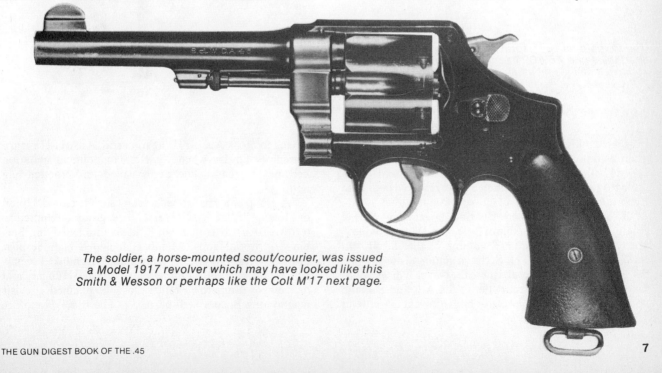

The soldier, a horse-mounted scout/courier, was issued a Model 1917 revolver which may have looked like this Smith & Wesson or perhaps like the Colt M'17 next page.

The Colt Model 1917, top, compared to the M'17 Smith & Wesson. Both revolvers fired the same .45 ACP cartridge used in the Model 1911 Colt autoloader and had to have small steel half-moon clips for easy ejection of the rimless cartridges.

from accumulating strains and tensions, triggered — as often as not — by failure of some small segment of the opposed masses. In the instance of WWI, the initial touch-off factor seems to have stemmed from resented complexity in marketing pork, of all unlikely commodities.

"The conflicts between Austria-Hungary and Serbia chiefly concerned ownership of Bosnia and Hercegovina," notes the previously quoted volume of the '68 *World Book,* on page 369."The Serbs, a nationalistic people, believed they had a natural right to the two provinces. With them, Serbia had a direct outlet to the Adriatic Sea and could ship products, especially hogs, to market without

having to cross Austro-Hungarian soil. Austria-Hungary closed its border whenever Serbian political agitation became too tense. The Serbs called this practice 'pig politics.'

"A group of Serbs formed a secret society called 'Union or Death,' or 'the Black Hand.' This group attempted to terrorize Austro-Hungarian officials into satisfying Serbia's territorial aims. Members included high Serbian army officers. The society learned that Archduke Francis Ferdinand, heir to the thrones of Austria and Hungary and nephew of Emperor Francis Joseph, planned to visit neighboring Bosnia in June, 1914. The Black Hand de-

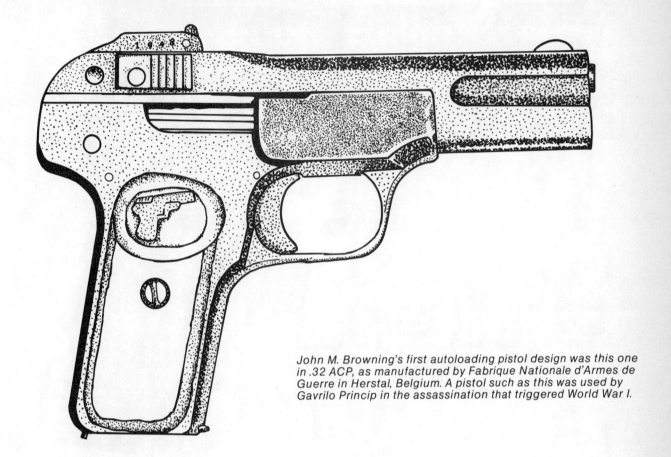

John M. Browning's first autoloading pistol design was this one in .32 ACP, as manufactured by Fabrique Nationale d'Armes de Guerre in Herstal, Belgium. A pistol such as this was used by Gavrilo Princip in the assassination that triggered World War I.

cided to kill him. Some young Bosnian revolutionaries were living in Serbia, because the Austro-Hungarian government had exiled them as undesirable. They received training in assassination.

"As Ferdinand and his wife rode through Sarajevo, a Bosnian revolutionary threw a bomb at their car. The bomb exploded in the roadway behind the automobile. Later that day, Gavrilo Princip, another of the trained assassins, jumped on the running board and fired the shots that touched off World War I."

Curiously enough, the weapon used by Princip was a 7.65mm (.32 ACP) autoloading pistol, manufactured by *Fabrique Nationale d'Armes de Guerre,* (customarily termed FN), in Belgium and designed by John M. Browning. Browning also designed the pistol officially termed Model of 1911, U.S. Army: PFC Ihli's souvenir.

The Ihli Colt is a remarkable artifact in this day and age, because it remains absolutely unmodified in any way from the day it emerged from beneath the Onion Dome at Hartford, Connecticut, to be shipped overseas for issue to the mess sergeant who presumably ran the rolling kitchen of the unknown unit at the Meuse-Argonne. What happened to the original issuee is anyone's guess and a matter for speculative conjecture.

Speaking personally, I own a Model 1911 Colt that was acquired by paying its asking price — $25 — to a gun store in Lomira, Wisconsin, early in the Sixties. Today, getting a working M1911 for such a price would be viewed as tantamount to stealing it, but the world of the early Sixties was a different place, as you may or may not recall.

Originally, in my unlettered innocence, I thought I'd bought a Remington-Rand, because that was the name of

This is my M1911 Colt with its somewhat deceptive slide rollmarked Remington-Rand, purchased for a fast $25 in the early Sixties. I had it fitted with the target sights and reblued, but years of happy shooting wore the bluing away, as is all too apparent. The stocks are homemade set in burl-grained teak and the entire pistol has been retrofitted to Model 1911A1 configuration, except for the crescent shaped cuts behind the trigger. More changes were to come...

the maker rollmarked into the left side of the slide. The Model 1911 Colt and its successor, the Model 1911A1 are supposed to be all-parts-interchangeable and it's been my experience that it's nearly always true. Presumably, at some point in its long career, the original slide got dinged or damaged, so someone installed one by Remington-Rand and that was it.

To a knowledgeable eye, the basic pistol is obviously of M1911 breed, as its frame does not carry the crescent-shaped cuts on either side of the trigger that were part of the Model 1911A1 modification. What's more, its serial number — 268380 — indicates it was made by Colt in 1918, as given in various reference sources for such data. It is somewhat younger than the Ihli Colt, with its serial number of 242531, by about 25,849 units, assuming they didn't overlook a block or two of digits at the hard-pressed Colt works of that era; a *faux pas* that has been known to happen.

I had referred to the $25 Colt rather extensively in earlier books, calling it my Model 1911 Remington-Rand;

it got me some number of responses from keen-eyed readers, advising me that such an artifact was on a dead-level par, plausibilitywise, with 1962 Cords or 1987 Edsels, to cite but a pair of examples. Remington-Rand made a whole tall stack of pistols for use in WWII, all in Model 1911A1 pattern, but no pistols for WWI; none whatsoever. I've also referred to the same pistol as "Ol' Loudmouf," and continue to think of it by that monicker.

Diametrically unlike PFC Ihli's M1911, my M1911 has had nearly everything changed, except for the serial number. I am sure there are other M1911s that have been modified even more extensively than mine, but a great many have not been modified as much.

The Model 1911 became the Model 1911A1 after WWI had been attended to, sometime in the early Twenties. The new version incorporated a number of changes, some primarily cosmetic and others desperately needed.

The worst trait of the M1911 was its dogged penchant for biting the hand that fed — and fired it. As the rearward-moving slide came back to re-cock the hammer, it was

...as can be seen in this more recent photo of "Ol'Loudmouf," as I've come to call the faithful companion. This is how it looks after a trip to Kerrville, Texas for extensive accurizing by Ace Hindman, who plated the frame in electroless nickel and put a Colt MK IV/Series '70 slide in place of the somewhat worn Remington-Rand job, with a sleeker set of target sights. As a result of Hindman's ministrations, it groups quite gratifyingly.

By way of further contrast, this is a strictly as-issued Model 1911A1 of World War II vintge, as manufactured by Colt.

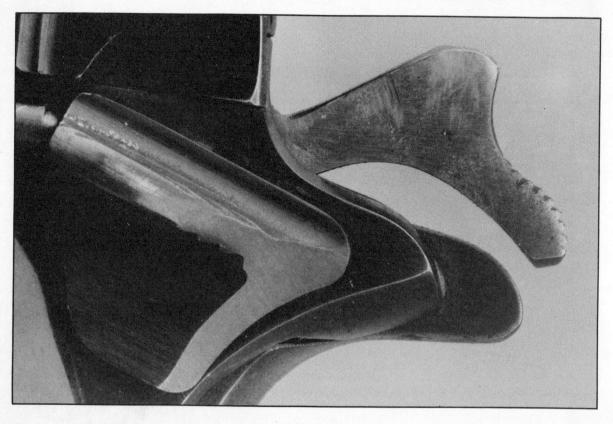

Top photo, facing page, shows the configuration of the grip safety spur and hammer spur on the original Model 1911, much prone to nip the back of the shooter's hand. The lower photo shows the same parts on the Model 1911A1 modification, which is pleasantly less ferocious. Merely changing the grip safety is not enough, as the hammer tang of the M1911 hits it, requiring replacement of the hammer with a 1911A1 type. Photo above shows the broader, nicely checkered hammer spur of the M1911 and its narrow-notched sight.

swept back a trifle farther than really necessary, moving up to be caught by the sear as the slide moved forward. In so doing, it was notoriously prone to nip a gobbet of flesh from the web between thumb and palm of the shooter's hand. Even if you were well aware of the hazard and placed the pistol in your hand with great care, it was quite apt to nip you anyway.

Curing that particular problem turned out to be largely a matter of lengthening the tang on the grip safety. The hammer spur was lengthened at the same time, but not so extravagantly as to allow a reprise of the same problem. The M1911 hammer spur was broader at the rear. The M1911A1 hammer spur was of the same width throughout.

If you happen to own an as-issued M1911 and essay to retrofit it to A1 credentials by the simple substitution of a Model 1911A1 grip safety, there are heavy odds that the spur of the M1911 hammer will not function properly and will collide with the new tang to hang up operations. That is rather a pity, as the broad-spurred hammer of the M1911 is a picturesque artifact in its own right. Making it all the same thickness must have saved some useful amount of production time.

The M1911A1 incorporated crescent-shaped relief cuts on either side of the frame, just to the rear of the trigger. I tend to regard this as the least significant of all the changes involved. Absence of the crescent cuts is a firm indication of the M1911 frame. A great many M1911s have been retrofitted to M1911A1 format, more or less, but I doubt that many, if any, have included the crescent cuts on the frame.

The sights on the slide came in for their share of attention. Both the front sight blade and the notch in the rear sight were widened to nearly twice the original width and that made for a faster acquisition of a comfortable and efficient sight picture.

The original M1911 trigger was a lengthy affair, soaking up a lot of space within the small confines of the trigger guard. In producing the Model 1911A1, they pared it back by the better part of a quarter of an inch to improve the fit and feel in the shooting hand by substantial amounts. The original M1911 trigger had a smoothly rounded face and most of the shortened triggers have vertical striations on the front surface.

In the original M1911 the mainspring housing at the lower rear of the grip had a straight profile. In the M1911A1,

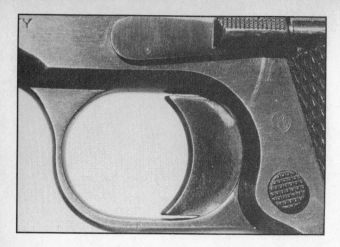 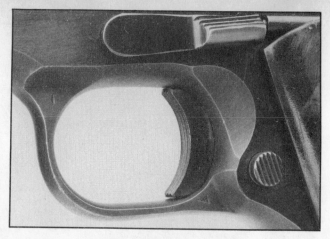

Left, the trigger surrounding area on the M1911 Colt, showing the original, longer trigger and the absence of milled cuts in the frame behind the trigger. The M1911A1 trigger area is as illustrated in the RH photo.

This is the straight mainspring housing of the Model 1911 design. Refer to top of facing page.

they changed that to what is termed an arched configuration. What that means is that the straight line has been bent into a sort of quasi-parabola, with the sharper curve at the bottom of the grip area.

Here, we have an area in which opinions vary sharply in both directions. I have encountered Government Model shooters who proclaimed themselves totally discontented, unless the pistol had the long trigger and straight mainspring housing of the original M1911 design. To date, I have yet to meet up with any who insisted upon a return to the short-tanged grip safety and original hammer spur contours. Nor have I encountered any who insist that the cres-

The arched mainspring housing of the Model 1911A1. This is on a commercial model, sans lanyard ring.

cent cuts behind the trigger be filled in with heli-arc welding and milled back to M1911 contours.

> *"...That lusty gun, that trusty gun,*
> *The Army Automatic...."*

The M1911 auto and its teeming progeny trace their roots back to what some used to term the Gay Nineties; the 1890s, that is. Although often termed automatics, it is more accurate to call them autoloaders or semi-automatics. A true automatic will continue to fire at some given cyclic rate so long as its trigger is held back.

At first thought, that might seem desirable. In actuality, full-auto fire is much more a liability than an asset, particularly in a firearm designed to be held and fired in one hand. When a handgun is fired, its muzzle tends to rise, due to the axis of the departing bullet and its resulting recoil being above the supporting area of the shooter's hand.

The shooter needs time to recover and re-align the sights with the intended target. A full-auto handgun makes no allowance for that. Mindful of all that, nearly all handguns are designed so that, after firing the given shot, the trigger is disconnected from the sear mechanism that will fire the next shot. It is necessary to relax pressure against the trigger and allow it to move forward under spring tension to connect back up with the sear for firing the next and following shots.

The late nineteenth century was, even by contemporary standards, a remarkable interlude in technology. Particularly in the instance of firearms, the traditional

An enlarged view of the rampant colt trade mark on the Model 1911 Colt; looks frisky, doesn't he?

boom-dust was being superseded by a newfangled compound chiefly composed of nitrocellulose, with admixtures of nitroglycerine, nitrolignin and other nitrated organic substances.

The significant difference between black powder and the various nitro powders — often called "smokeless" powders, because they tend to produce somewhat less smoke than the older type — lay in the fact that, in black powder, the oxygen to burn the fuel was nearby in a mechanical mixture. In the nitro powder, it was incorporated into the basic molecule of the nitrocellulose or whatever.

Black powder leaves a lot of residue in the process of burning to develop quantities of hot, high-pressure gas to drive the projectile down the barrel, out of the muzzle and off to make trouble for the target. The residue builds up inside the barrel and, after no more than a few shots, the shooter removed the accumulated deposits by manual cleaning.

The so-called smokeless powders build up some amount of residue and metal rubbing off of the departing projectiles, adds to the mess. Even so, it is possible to fire a great many rounds propelled by smokeless powders before the shooter has a serious problem.

Autoloading and automatic firearms had to await the arrival of smokeless powders before they could take their

*Above, details of the M1911 hammer, safety catch and grip safety, with hammer down.
Below, rollmarking on the slide of the M1911, giving a rundown of the patent dates.*

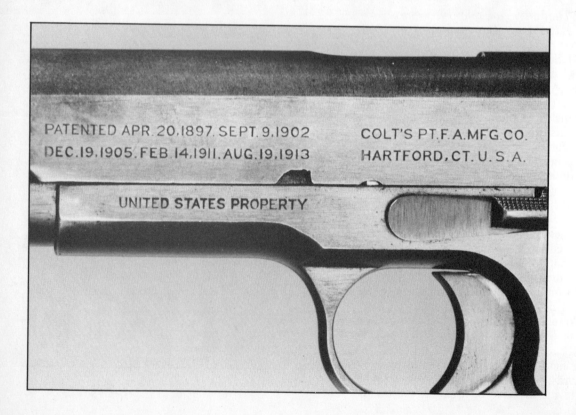

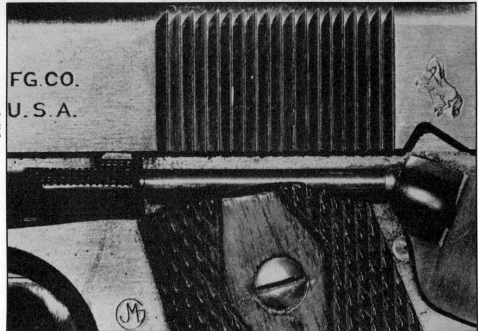

If you've ever wondered as to the number of cocking serrations milled into the rear of the Colt slide, there are nineteen.

place in the march of progress. That singular mechanism, the Gatling gun, had been able to function with black powder after a fashion due to its multi-barreled design, but other systems, trying to pour all their output through a single barrel — if you can forgive me for putting it this way — just couldn't gattle.

World War Ace marked the first time the U.S. serviceman encountered the mechanism of the autoloading pistol and there were occasional instances wherein they were somewhat short of compatible. You will have to quest and forage through stores specializing in old books to find any of the works of Leonard Hastings Nason, but you may find it worth the effort. Personally, I tend to regard Nason as the Bill Mauldin of WWI. I have sent one of his books to the Bill Mauldin of WWII and he professes himself unable to see the connection, but so it goes.

In Nason's book, *Chevrons,* copyright 1926 by George H. Doran Company, on pages 142-3, he narrates a truly poignant incident certain to bring a rueful smile to the face of anyone who has spent much time cohabiting with a Colt Model 1911 or 1911A1.

The book's protagonist, one Sergeant Eadie, had been gassed earlier in the book, was sent to the hospital and, in time, was pronounced fit for duty again. Whereupon, he had been issued a .45 auto pistol and sent back to the front. By page 142, the Germans were staging a counter-attack and I'd like to quote a few paragraphs:

"A counter attack! More shouting, more grenades! Eadie unbuttoned his holster and drew his pistol. How come? Was he hit? His hand came away from the butt wet and sticky. Blood? *Cosmolene!*

"Well, I'm damned!' said Eadie. Here he was in a shell hole in the midst of a red hot fight, a counter attack under way and his pistol still in the cosmolene in which it had been issued. Cosmolene is thick, heavy grease, the weapon was full of it, the barrel was packed with it, and even if he could get the firing mechanism to function, the gun would jam on the first shot if it did not burst. Well, he had his choice of cleaning it then and there with such materials as he had or of holding up his hands to the first boche that came along.

"The exterior grease he removed to a great extent by wiping the gun on his puttees. He tore a strip from his handkerchief and, taking a pencil from his musette, prepared to clean the barrel. His hands shook like leaves and his teeth rattled so that he several times bit his tongue. He dared not listen to see how the attack progressed. The machine gun fire still continued and made his labors all the more difficult, curled in a ball as he was at the bottom of the hole. The barrel of the automatic is removed by dismounting the slide. There is a little button just under the muzzle which is pressed and this allows a locking cam to be turned, so that the barrel and slide can be removed. Eadie pressed this button down and turned the cam. Now under the button is a strong spring that returns the slide to its normal positon after it has recoiled from the shock of the cartridge being fired, and in Eadie's nervous state he neglected to exert enough pressure on this spring, so that once the cam was turned and the button was free, the spring leaped under Eadie's astonished finger and went soaring out of the shell hole.

"Finish!" said Eadie. He hurled the rest of the pistol after the spring. Then followed a bitter moment for the sergeant. He had drawn that the gun in the replacement camp and had left it in cosmolene, because he had been too lazy to clean it. The night before the drive at Saint Mihiel he had no time and since then he had not given the weapon a thought. It was heavy, it was always banging his hip sore, and what time in camp it was not dangling from the spare pole of the fourgon, it was tucked away under a tarpaulin

Having salvaged the pistol from the abandoned rolling kitchen at Meuse-Argonne, the rescuer added his name.

on the caisson lid. And now, of course, just when he needed it badly, it was impossible to use it. A court-martial composed of twelve Sergeant Eadies trying Sergeant Eadie for neglect of duty at that minute would have given a sentence of death by slow torture. Fool! A non-commissioned officer and he didn't know enough to keep his pistol clean. And furthermore he didn't know how to clean it when he had the opportunity. He was a damned fool to carry an automatic that was full of springs and things. If he got out of this alive, a revolver for him. A revolver or a rifle (...)"

Ever since I first read that passage, quite a number of years ago, my vocabulary has been enriched by addition of a phrase: "Pulling an Eadie." Down the interim, I've pulled more than what I regard as my fair share of Eadies. Nason's nomenclature is a trifle confusing. It's the barrel bushing that you release and rotate to remove the parts and the recoil spring plug is the part that goes "*Sproingg!*" If inadvertently released, the recoil spring tends to remain in place. The heck of it is, the pistol will not function without the recoil spring plug.

I have been taking M1911A1 pistols apart and putting them back together for somewhat more than forty-four years and it would seem plausible that I've sort of caught the knack of it by now, right? Wrong! The ceiling above my desk at the office carries a clearly visible indentation to commemorate the time I was disassembling one of the early Randall versions of the basic Colt M1911A1.

After some amount of scrummaging about on my hands and knees, I succeeded in relocating the recoil spring plug from the Randall. Just a bit later, I was working with one of the AMT Long Slide Hardballer pistols, quite similar, but not identical to the M1911A1. On that occasion, I was working in my driveway at home. Despite decades of experience, I pulled a truly classic Eadie and the recoil spring plug went sizzling into the hedge fence that separates my neighbor's driveway from mine.

Unlike the hapless sergeant of artillery, I was not undergoing a Boche counter-attack, for which I was more than grateful. Nonetheless, I needed to restore that long-barreled pistol to functioning capability so as to meet editorial deadlines. I didn't hurl the rest of the pistol after the missing part, but I made a really dedicated effort to find the errant recoil spring plug, which is somewhat longer on the Hardballer than on typical M1911A1 pistols and thus not interchangeable.

A view of the right-hand side of the Model 1911 U. S. Army pistol.

The gadgetry available in the shop includes a powerful permanent magnet with about thirty square inches of working surface and I spent a lot of time passing that over all of the probable fallout areas, absolutely to no useful avail. In the dire extreme, I got on the phone to Arcadia Machine and Tool, requisitioning a replacement recoil spring plug from the factory; an expedient that was not available to Sergeant Eadie.

As to the insidious cosmolene preservative, I can relate to that on the personal level, also. In the days when I was assigned as an aerial gunnery instructor at the USAAF base near Tonopah, Nevada, I got an assignment dumped squarely onto my reluctant lap. The ground gunnery range had received a replacement shipment of caliber .50 air-cooled Brownings, some fifty or seventy-five of the burly brutes, each heavily coated in protective but adamant cosmolene. My assignment was to get all the guck off and out of the guns so they could be put into service.

By various means, I determined that the base motor pool had a live steam hose and managed to get the entire batch of caliber fifties portaged back to that point, with enough supporting personnel to aid in the project.

I got it down to hardly over five minutes to get most of the goop off any given gun, with supporting helpers fetching

The custom of branding the slide with all the details of copyright dates is practiced but rarely, these latter days.

them in, disassembling, reassembling and carting them off. The only casualty of the campaign was the pair of GI coveralls I was wearing at the time. The base laundry couldn't get the splatters of cosmolene out of them and I had to sign a statement of charges for a new suit. In retrospect, I viewed it as a bargain.

Sergeant Eadie should have had it so good....

CHAPTER 2

JOHN MOSES BROWNING (1855-1926): THE FATHER OF MODERN FIREARMS

Singular Circumstances Produced A Most Remarkable Individual!

Jonathan Browning (1805-1879) was the father of John M. Browning and a notable gunsmith and inventor in his own right. His repeating rifle is on the facing page.

John Moses Browning, at about age 18, bears no more than a token resemblance to the image of Browning in his later years, with which most of us are familiar.

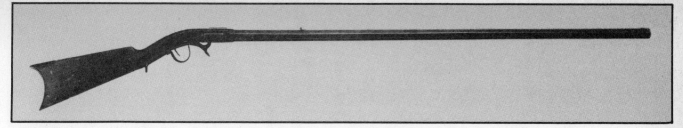

Jonathan Browning's repeating muzzleloading rifle used percussion caps in a block with three or four chambers that were moved into firing position by means of a thumb-actuated lever arrangement.

TO UNDERSTAND and appreciate the works and sheer genius of John M. Browning, it is necessary to examine his heredity and the special conditions of the pioneer culture in which he grew to maturity.

The Browning family came to this country in 1622 in the person of Captain John Browning, aboard the *Abigail*, going on to found one of the first families of Virginia. One such sibling was Edmund Browning, born on November 14, 1761, in Culpeper County, Virginia. After the close of the Revolutionary War, Edmund married and moved to Tennessee, establishing a farm near the village of Brushy Fork, in Sumner County, where the seven children of Edmund and Sarah Browning were born, including Jonathan Browning, on October 22, 1805.

At that time, there were scattered farms about the area, but no real community as such. Jonathan's early education was acquired primarily on a catch-as-catch-can basis. In his early teens, he performed a week's work on a neighbor's farm in exchange for an old flintlock rifle that no longer worked. He was to recall it in later years as the only enthusiastic farming he ever did.

There was a blacksmith shop about a mile from the Browning farm and Jonathan was fond of hanging about and watching the cheerful 'smith at his work, occasionally lending a hand. Using the shop facilities, Jonathan managed to get the ailing rifle repaired and sold it back to the original owner for four dollars in cash: a considerably more substantial clump of money at the time than it might sound like today.

Jonathan kept his easygoing father reasonably happy by doing his assigned chores early in the morning and late at

From left, Sam Browning, George Browning, John M. Browning, Matthew S. Browning, Ed Browning and Frank Rushton, taken about 1882 in Utah Territory.

A formidable live bird trap squad in Utah's early days, the "Four B" team consisted of, from left, G.L. Becker, John M. Browning, A.P. Bigelow and Matthew S. Browning. Becker has a Model 1887 Browning lever-action shotgun; the two Brownings have Model 1897 pump-action Brownings and Bigelow a side-by-side double-barrel of a make not readily identifiable. The Model 1887 lever was Browning's first shotgun invention.

night. During the days, he worked with the blacksmith in return for freedom of the shop, an occasional dollar or perhaps a sack of corn. He learned the details of the blacksmith trade; knowledge that was to prove invaluable in the years to come.

At age 19, Jonathan stood over six feet and was burly for his height. He considered himself a reasonably competent gunsmith, having repaired and reconditioned a great many guns, using tools of his own design and construction. He began to think of making guns, as well as repairing them. To that point, he had never encountered another gunsmith, but he came upon a rifle bearing the stamp of one Samuel Porter, in nearby Nashville.

A short time later, he borrowed one of Edmund's horses and jogged the thirty-odd miles to Nashville. He and Porter hit it off uncommonly well and Jonathan served his apprenticeship for three months. At first, he worked without wages for the sake of acquiring the vital know-how, but after a little while, Porter began paying him $2 per week, which was clear profit, as his meals were provided, along with a hayloft in which to bed down.

Heading back for Brushy Fork, Jonathan carried a

quantity of tools he had bought or been given, coming close to the carrying capacity of his horse. He had gone to Nashville as a gun tinkerer and he was returning as a gunmaker. The rifle he packed on the return trip carried a barrel made entirely by his own hands and it was stamped

Markings on an octagonal barrel in the Browning Museum. Note the U.T., for Utah Territory. All but nine of the photos in this chapter are by courtesy of Browning Arms.

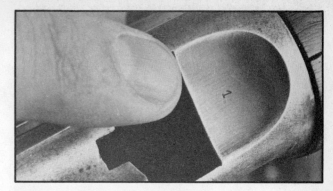

On display in the Browning Museum is the first Browning autoloading shotgun, as evidenced by the serial number 1 in the photo at right. Apart from its somewhat straighter trigger, it looks good for a prototype.

JONATHAN BROWNING 1824. In the years to come, a prodigious number of other guns would be stamped with that surname, but Jonathan's squirrel-scalper was the first of a noble line.

The early Nineteenth Century was time of yeasty unrest and growing pains for the young republic. A letter from a younger brother advised that Quincy, Illinois, seemed to offer a superb location for a gunshop. It was a move of about four hundred miles and it took a fair while to make the trip. As they passed through towns and villages along the way, Jonathan was prone to track down any sound of metal clanging against metal, so as to check out blacksmith shops, picking up a skill here, a knack there and perhaps another tool or two to pack aboard the wagon.

It was 1834, when Jonathan Browning arrived in Quincy with his family and creaking wagons. About the same time, a Scottish clergyman, one Alexander John Forsyth, had succeeded in adapting metallic fulminates for use as primers to set off charges of powder in firearms. The original discovery of the singular properties and characteristics of metallic fulminates had been made about 1662, but it took that long to devise a practical way to utilize them for a firearms ignition system.

Jonathan was fascinated by the percussion priming system, which was to obsolete the flintlock much as that had, in turn, obsoleted the earlier matchlock. Sam Colt had invented the revolver a few years earlier and various gunmakers had endeavored to adapt the principle to repeating rifles with no more than limited success. There is a natural tendency to grasp a rifle by the forend with the hand not engaged in pulling the trigger and that invites a blast of hot gas from the gap between cylinder and barrel.

Jonathan devised and built a few repeating rifles based upon Colt's revolver system, but the aforementioned gas leakage problems, coupled with the technical difficulties of machining the cylinder to the required precise tolerances made that approach somewhat impractical. What he wanted was a design for a repeating rifle that could be hammered out with minimal difficulty, sacrificing nothing in performance.

In time, Jonathan devised one of the simplest repeating rifles ever conceived. It had few parts and those were easy to make and assemble. It had a rectangular block with four or five chambers that could be loaded and inserted into the breech. After firing the first chamber, actuating a small lever with the thumb advanced the magazine to bring the next load into line with the barrel. The design was a minor sensation at the time and Browning had more orders for the new rifle than he was ever able to fill. Everything possible had been done to simplify the design for ease of manufacture and long-term reliability. For example, the hammer was moved from the top to the bottom of the rifle and the

A somewhat older John M. Browning holds one of his autoloading shotguns. Whether it's the same one in the photos at the top of the page is a darned good question.

Browning comtemplates a water-cooled version of his formidable caliber .50 machine gun on a tripod mount.

tempered trigger guard did double duty as the mainspring.

The year was 1840 and the Mormons were building their city of Nauvoo, some forty-three miles north of Quincy. One of their number brought a repair job to Jonathan's shop, along with the evangelical fervor typical of the group. In a rather short time, Jonathan was converted to the new belief. A dozen years later, it would lead him to load his wagons and follow the long and rutted trail across plains and mountains to the valley of the Great Salt Lake.

At that time, the church advocated polygamy and Jonathan followed the practice to the extent of taking two more wives. First married at the age of 21, he brought eleven children of that marriage with him. Two years after his arrival in Ogden, he married Elizabeth Clark, who became the mother of John, Matt and a daughter who died in infancy. Five years after his second marriage, he married Sarah Emmett, who bore him seven more children, for a total of twenty-two. The children of the first family were considerably older and developed little in the way of intimate ties with John and Matt.

That was far from the case with the four boys of the third family: Ed, Sam, Will and George. Jonathan built homes across the street from each other to house families two and three. Due to the nearness and similarity of age, the six boys grew up in close association. For their entire lives, their homes were no more than a block apart.

To a large extent, his father's gunshop served as John's school, a state of affairs with which he had no complaints. Ogden was thousands of creaking, weary miles from the

Inattentive students in gunnery school were sentenced to march around the company area with an air-cooled .50 Browning, packed rifle-fashion. J. Curtis Earl snapped this photo of author and eighty-pound beast.

I made the photo of Ed Baggett, my maternal grandfather, about 1948 and feel it resembles Browning, at right.

mines and mills of the Eastern seaboard and there was hardly any such thing as a useless metal item. There was a junk pile in the corner of the shop and the boys spent endless rapt hours pawing through it. It was from that midden-heap of parts and pieces that John became familiar with the components of firearms almost before he mastered the alphabet.

He was hardly 6 when he foraged up a box to serve as his work bench, set it up conveniently close to the shop junk pile and embarked upon his career. Even then, Jonathan was prone to ask John to retrieve some needed part from the junk pile and, if necessary, to remove the rust with file and buffer. Now and then, school interrupted the shop work, but not often, nor for long. The many nearby canals took a greater toll of time and attention with swimming and catching trout, suckers or chubs that strayed in from the rivers. Initially, the fish were caught with bent pins, but it was not long before John used the shop facilities to begin producing his own fish hooks, adding to his own knowledge and his supply of trade goods for bartering with his contemporaries.

John was 10 when he and brother Matt made their first gun out of parts salvaged from the junk pile. Harking back to the dawn of firearms, it bypassed the lack of lockwork and functioned as a matchlock. With powder and shot pilfered from the supposedly hidden hoard of Jonathan — who was gone for the day — they made a joint sortie that

bagged three prairie chickens with the single shot. That left the problem of accounting for the game on Jonathan's return. They enlisted Elizabeth's cheerful aid and Jonathan was halfway through breakfast before it occurred to him to ask about the birds.

John explained and was told to fetch the gun for examination. John brought it from the shop and his father's only response was, "John Mose, you're going on 11; can't you make a better gun than that?" Jonathan had made no mention of the powder and shot, nor of the sin of stealing. He had zeroed unerringly upon the lad's pride. It was a telling shot and it smarted.

Up here, trudging toward the end of the twentieth century, we tend to think of John Browning in his latter years; lean, eagle-eyed, with a toothbrush moustache and a brow reaching for the back of his head. That is how you may find him depicted on the receiver of a Browning Auto-5 shotgun, for example. A personal note: One of my own grandfathers looked quite a lot like John M. Browning — or, perhaps, vice versa. The other one bore a closer resemblance to Samuel Langhorne Clemens.

That's all very well, but it gives you little or no inkling of JMB as a lanky, gangling teenager: the youth destined to be the father to the man.

It is hardly a moment too soon to note that a vast amount of the information in this chapter has been derived from a remarkable book, titled *John M. Browning American*

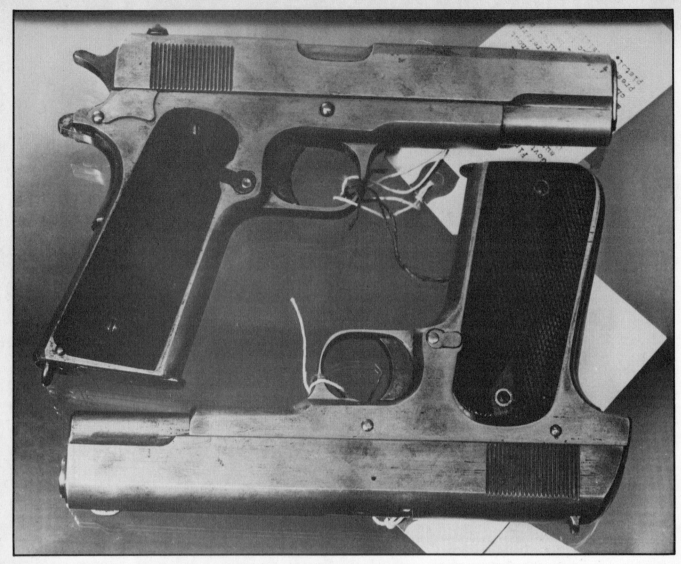

The board appointed to select a new pistol for the Army was undecided between an exposed hammer or a concealed hammer. Browning's solution to the problem was typical of the man; he built them one of each.

Gunmaker, by John Browning and Curt Gentry. It was published in 1964 by Doubleday & Company, Incorporated and copies can be obtained from Browning, Route 1, Morgan, Utah 84050. Inquire for current price. It is one of the most absorbing and informative biographies I have encountered to the present and I recommend it without reservation.

For but one thing, the book brings JMB's brother, Matt Browning, onto the stage as a most intriguing shadow-character about whom all too little is known. It was JMB who hatched the basic concepts and flashes of sheer genius, granted, but it was Matt Browning who translated them into ferrous flesh, as it were, by making the prototype patent models and lent a remarkably helpful hand to making all the good things happen.

After the incident of the crude matchlock rifle, stung and goaded by his father's contemptuous comment on it, John went on to build a right and proper shotgun. He and brother Matt collected quantities of game for the Browning table with it.

After reaching Ogden, Jonathan never built any more of his remarkable repeating percussion rifles, but John found one of the barrels that had been used in them and talked his father into letting him build up one of the rifles for brother Matt, who lost little time in becoming considerably skilled in its use.

Still youthful in appearance, John ran the family gun-shop while his father was busy with countless other affairs of the community. All too often customers entering the shop would ask John, "Where's the gunsmith, sonny?" John M. Browing found that intensely irritating.

Thus it came to pass that the driver of a freight wagon passing through Ogden stopped to have his rifle repaired and made the usual mistake of asking John as to the whereabouts of the gunsmith. Fuming inwardly, John had the man's rifle apart and fixed up, good as new, in less than half an hour.

John charged him a dollar for the service and the teamster protested the charge was too high. John responded that another gunsmith might have taken two hours and

As it worked out, the model with the exposed hammer was the one selected and this is the original working model. A few changes were made, including the addition of the thumb safety lever and plunger tube but the prototype bears a strong resemblance to all the later production guns, even to the lanyard ring. (Photographer: E.A. Metzger, Rock Island Arsenal.)

charged a dollar and a half for the work. Somewhat grudgingly, the man agreed, whereupon Browning complimented him on the excellence of his rifle. The owner agreed and voiced conceited opinions of his own skill at firing it.

That was precisely the response John had been trying to get from him. He bet the man the dollar just received, against a sack of salt from his wagon that his younger brother could outshoot the teamster and his highly touted rifle.

The teamster shot first, whereupon Matt came up to the line, fired and earned his sack of salt. The driver, a good sport, roared with laughter and wanted a repetition of the contest. John pointed out that the sack of salt was worth considerably more than a dollar — closer to five — and generously offered to bet the sack of salt against a dollar, so as to even the odds a bit.

The bet was made and Matt repeated his feat of marksmanship. The teamster gave them their salt and climbed aboard his wagon, promising to pass the word about the good gunsmithing firm in Ogden, meanwhile warning his listeners not to engage in shooting matches with the gunsmith's kid brother.

The Browning boys watched the wagon on its way out of town. Matt made some remark to the gist that he was sad to

see the man go, as that was the first dollar he'd ever earned.

John, staring after the departing wagon, commented, "Matt, that fellow could shoot a damn sight better than I expected."

John's first outright invention came along in 1878 at the age of 23. It was a single-shot, breechloading rifle and he sold the patent rights on it to Winchester for $8000. He was to recall that in later years as a salient high point of his career, despite the fact that he was to sell a great many patents in the years ahead, virtually all of them for much larger sums. For one thing, it freed him of the need to worry about money and, for another, it proved that he could work up inventions and sell them for good prices.

Once the ice was broken, the young inventor began to turn out new guns in a steady spate. There were lever-action rifles, machine guns, an autoloading shotgun and any number of autoloading pistols. Only one man in the history of firearms invention is known to have produced more than five original and profitable firearms in a lifetime and the intials of that man are — as you may have guessed — JMB.

Although several of his early auto pistols were commercial designs, Browning had a firm conviction the military sidearm of the future was to be the autoloading pistol. As

Here's another view of the concealed-hammer version, bearing an understandable resemblance to the Model 1903 Colt pocket model pistols chambered for the .32 and .380 ACP cartridges; safety catch, but no lanyard and you'll note its trigger is somewhat shorter than those of the classic Model 1911s. (E.A. Metzger photo.)

early as 1902, Colt brought out one of his designs as the Military Model. It fired a caliber .38 cartridge dimensionally identical to the contemporary .38 Super round, but loaded to somewhat lower peak pressures. The design was in line with the military thinking of that era and comparable in power to the .38 revolver cartridge then in use by the U.S. armed forces.

The Colt Military Model attracted some amount of interest and John was consulted several times by the board appointed to select a replacement for the .38 revolver. There was unanimous agreement that the new cartridge would have to be larger, more powerful than the Army .38. It had proved woefully inadequate against Moro insurrectionists in the Philippines who demonstrated many times they could take two or three body shots from the revolver without being slowed down appreciably.

It was agreed early on that the new handgun did not need high velocity or long range accuracy. The envisioned use would be at short distances and the prime prerequisite was stopping power as close to instantaneous as could be accomplished.

It became apparent the board was interested in a cartridge with a bullet of about .45-inch diameter, so John designed a cartridge in that diameter for use in his initial experiments.

The board was divided in opinion as to whether it wanted a pistol with an exposed hammer or a hammerless model. By way of aiding them in reaching a decision, John designed and built one of each type. It seemed to him a simpler approach than trying to argue with one faction or the other. He had more urgent work that needed doing and it was a matter of taking the easy way out to obtain time to get the needful projects completed.

The .45 pistol was a personal favorite among the many arms Browning designed. During the time from the initial development of the gun to its final acceptance, when John happened to be in Ogden, it was his usual custom to leave the shop about four in the evening, with a pistol and a couple hundred cartridges and roam the foothills, disturbing the placid welkin. As a great many of us have discovered in the decades since, that is a most diverting way to dispose of any given amount of free time.

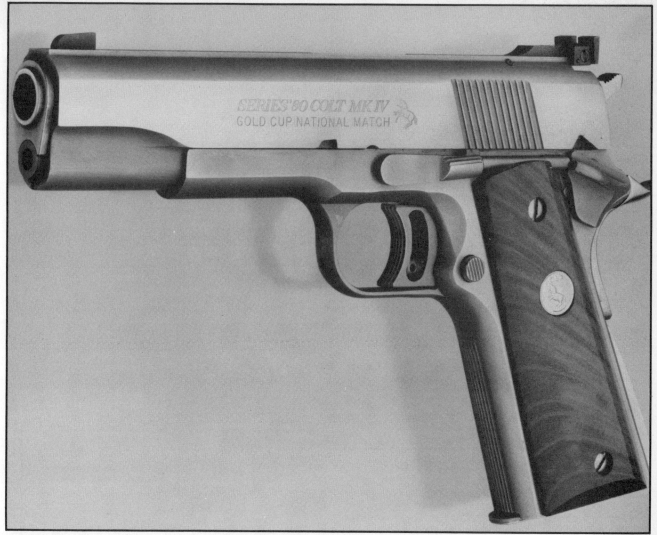

By way of contrast to all the prototypes and early military versions shown up to this point, here is an example of a contemporary, state-of-the art Colt. In this instance, it's their Gold Cup National Match version, done up in stainless steel, with homemade stocks of Osage orange wood and the arched mainspring housing added.

With the date set and the time for the acceptance trials approaching, John went to Hartford to assist in production of the model that would be submitted to the board. Earlier, in working with Colt on some of his machine gun designs, he had encountered a young Colt employee named Fred Moore, who had impressed him most favorably. Gradually and tactfully, John had Fred advanced and he ended up as production manager of the entire factory, holding that position for the rest of his life.

Browning and Moore worked in close cooperation on the test .45, part by part, with infinite pains and attention to assuring that every piece would be just so; incapable of being made better.

Competitive trials for the .45 were begun on March 3, 1911. Requirements were that each pistol fire 6000 rounds. One hundred shots would be fired and the pistol would be allowed to cool for five minutes. After every 1000 rounds, the pistol would be cleaned and oiled. After firing 6000 rounds of standard ammunition, the pistol would be tested with deformed cartridges — some with bullets seated too deeply, not seated deep enough or with

dented cases. In conclusion, competing pistols would be rusted with acid and tested, then re-tested after dust had been sprinkled into the working parts.

Colt's managing president, Colonel C. L. F. Robinson, and Fred Moore accompanied John to the trials. Two of the foreign entries had been withdrawn after publication of the requirements. The only competing design was one that did not worry them particularly; an assessment that proved to be correct.

Browning was quick to quash any hopes on the part of his companions that the tests would be a walkover. He pointed out they were going up against the weight and tradition of the revolver, backed by the army's entrenched love of the *status quo*. A revolver, for example, might break a mainspring or a sear and the test panel's response would be that such things happen. An autoloading pistol, on the other hand, would not enjoy any such easy-going and tolerant attitude. Going up against tradition, Browning reminded his friends, was tantamount to contesting one hundred percent.

Moore was deeply jittered by the fact that key generals

It's said that Browning got the basic idea for the design when he noticed grass blowing about from the muzzle blast of a shotgun and decided to try harnessing that force to operate the action. In the photo at right, I'm pulling the operating lever down. In action, powder gas from a port beneath the barrel does the same thing.

were late in arriving for the tests. John strolled idly about, hands in pockets, or took his serene ease on a handy bench, calm as any cucumber ever pickled.

After a time, with his cool severely frayed, Moore accosted Browning and wanted to know, "John, haven't you got a nerve in your body?"

"Fred," John replied, as Fred later told it, "I've got lots of nerves in my body, and they are all standing on end, like this." He held up both hands, with fingers writhing furiously. "But not a damned soul except you and me is ever going to know about it."

After endless delays, the tests began. A number of men had been trained in the simple procedures of firing the seven cartridges in a magazine, dropping the empty and snapping a fresh one into place. Other men were refilling the magazines, staying well ahead of the actual shooters. The magazines were emptied as quickly as a trained shooter could work the trigger and switch magazines.

Everything went with crisp precision, so it hardly seemed like more than a slight hesitation between magazines: On and on, with a rhythmic booming and, if the gun became too hot to hold, it was doused in a handy bucket of water for the necessary few seconds.

The torture-test lasted for two days. Browning had served as an advisor in its preparation, but reverted to a role as a spectator when the shooting commenced. Later, he conceded it was not an easy time for him. He found it rather a strain to count off each seven-round magazine, with no time for a faint sigh of relief before the next one started blasting.

As the count grew, the strain increased in something close to a geometrical progression. At length, there came an end to the yammering, hammering, stammering and Browning was far from certain whether it marked the end of the trial or the long-dreaded malfunction. There was a long, loud silence, broken at last by a stentorian bellow

Like many another notable artist, Browning tended to sort of put his signature into the lines of his designs. A classic example is the Sport Model Colt Woodsman, my personal nominee for one of the prettiest pistols ever made and one of the few designs perfectly proportioned for the .22 long rifle cartridge. Much the same applies to the Model 24 Remington autoloading rifle, another Browning design, here at the bottom of the photo.

from one of the soldiers who had been busily stuffing cartridges into the magazines.

"She made it, by God!" he roared, in gleeful jubilation. There was a burst of laughter, quickly followed by three cheers for Browning and urgent demands for a speech from the successful inventor.

John climbed atop the bench at which he'd been seated, doffed his hat and waited for the uproar to subside.

"Gentlemen," he said, "the young man who spoke so eloquently a moment ago expressed my feelings precisely. There isn't a word I can add, except thank you all."

The test pistol went on to cope capably with the freak loads, the rust, the dust and the rest of the ordeal. Under painstaking examination, every part and component remained good as new, presumably ready to take on another 6000 rounds. It was the first autoloading arm to rack up a perfect score in a government test; a record not challenged until 1917, when Browning's recoil-operated machine gun fired 40,000 rounds without a stoppage. Neither record has since been equaled — or even closely approached.

Thus, it came to pass that the examining board submitted its report on March 20, 1911: "The board recommends that the Colt Caliber .45 Automatic Pistol of the design submitted to the Board for tests be adopted for use by foot and mounted troops in the military service in consequence of its marked superiority to the present service revolvers, and to any pistol, of its extreme reliability and endurance, of its ease of disassembly, or its accuracy and of its fulfillment of all essential requirements."

Orders from the Chief of Ordnance of the General Staff and Secretary of War dated March 29, 1911 made the adoption of the Model 1911 official. If you happen to own a cherished specimen of the Model 1911, as a great many of us do, and if you fancy making up a birthday cake to celebrate its anniversary, you have your choice between two suitable dates on any given year.

John Moses Browning was a unique and thoroughly improbable individual. If he hadn't happened to come along, as he did and when he did, our contemporary world would not have been the same as it is. There is a time-worn saying about a given person to the effect that, "when they made him, they broke the mould." In the instance of J. M. Browning, that certainly is true, in cards, spades and Big Casino.

I speak as the appreciative owner of a number of Model 1911 variants and dare to hope I speak to a goodly number of other owners of like mind. For my part, I'm damned grateful they didn't break the mould until *after* they'd made John Moses Browning. I tend to reflect upon that every time I press the trigger on one of the gorgeous artifacts.

CHAPTER 3

THE WEIRDEST .45

You Might Term It A Sort Of GI Zip-Gun, But It Did Yeoman Duty In Its Day!

The Liberator, also known as the Woolworth and, sometimes, as a flare pistol, was manufactured to be air-dropped behind enemy lines in WWII to arm resistance fighters in occupied territory. One million of the crude single-shots were produced and it is believed they accounted for more casualties among Axis forces than all the M1911A1 service pistols in the hands of members of the Allied armed forces.

Photo by Bob Olsen

SOME GUNS are exquisite examples of elegant design and meticulous workmanship; objects of art by any standard one might care to set. The topic of our present discussion stands solidly at the far, opposite end of that particular spectrum. Put bluntly, when it comes to innate charm and charisma, the Liberator pistol ranks right in there alongside a mud puppy with psoriasis.

It seems to have been known by various names and terms, of which Liberator is perhaps the most common. It has also been referred to as the Woolworth pistol, though it's far from clear whether someone of that name had a hand in its design or if it refers to the chain of five-and-dime stores and on its manifestly inexpensive ambience. Other sources referred to it as a flare pistol, presumably to cloak its true, intended purpose.

The Liberator — as we'll continue to call it, hoping it won't be confused with the Consolidated B-24 bomber that also saw service in WWII — was dreamed up and hatched fairly soon after the USA entered the conflict in December 1941.

The Axis Forces — Germany, Italy and Japan — were occupying territories in wholesale quantities at that particular time and a large percentage of the conquered natives

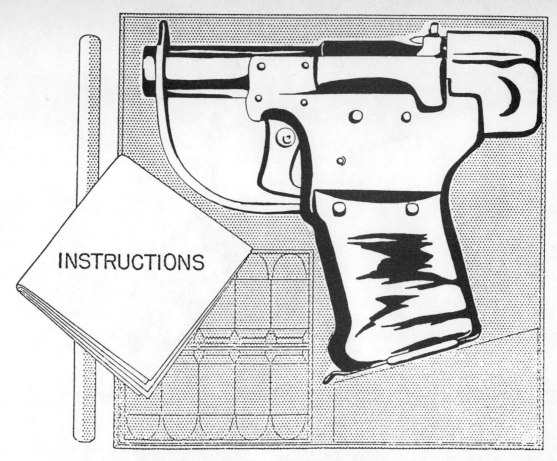

Each Liberator pistol was packed in a sturdy, waterproof carton with ten rounds of .45 ACP ammunition, a sheet of instructions and a wooden stick for poking the empty cases from the chamber. A sliding buttplate gave access to storage space for carrying the spare ammo.

felt considerably discontented with the state of affairs. Various terms were applied to such personnel: Resistance, Freedom Fighters, Underground, Guerillas, Patriots and so on. The Office of Strategic Services — or OSS — felt it would be helpfully advantageous if such friendly forces could be supplied with a tool for giving the overdogs their condign come-uppance and the Liberator pistol was the direct result of that philosophy.

The U.S. Ordnance Department drew up the preliminary plans and specifications for the Liberator and turned them over to the Inland Manufacturing Division of General Motors for preparation of the final drawings. The Guide Lamp Division of General Motors tooled up and produced one million of the pistols in the space of thirteen weeks, during the time span of June through August 1942.

Each gun was packed in a sturdy, waterproof carton together with ten rounds of .45 ACP ammunition and a sheet of instructions. These cartons were packed twenty to a case. Also included was a small wooden stick of appropriate dimensions to use for pushing the spent case from the firing chamber. A case of twenty Liberator kits weighed fifty pounds and took up one-half of a cubic foot in volume. Weight of each gun-pack, including ten rounds of ammunition, was one pound, seven ounces. A sliding gate in the butt of the pistol provided space to carry the ten rounds of rounds of ammunition initially supplied.

The instruction sheet was a masterpiece of subverbal communication. It transcended all barriers of language and literacy and, ostensibly, told any possessor of a Liberator kit exactly how it could be used to the desired effects.

In embarking upon this book, I felt the Liberator merited some coverage and, in all blithe innocence, commenced trying to locate someone who happened to have one. Hah! I incline to suspect there are more Antarctic igloos with window air-conditioners than surviving Liberator pistols in our contemporary culture; well, almost as many.

There are several reasons that may help to account for such a state of affairs. For one thing, the barrel of the Liberator is a piece of seamless steel tubing. The length is given in various reference sources as four inches/102mm or 3.97 inches/101mm. Whatever the length, the barrel carries no rifling. It's a smoothbore and contemporary restrictions are fairly tight on handguns with short, unrifled bores.

The Liberator was far from a masterpiece of structural integrity. As noted, the barrel was a length of seamless steel tubing, presumably opened at the rear to provide a slight ledge at the front of the chamber to support the cartridge against the blow of the firing pin. That, of course, weakened the tubing exactly at the point where a pistol barrel requires maximum strength and one might assume the service life of the gun would be rather limited. With that and the dubious legality of the Liberator in mind, it becomes

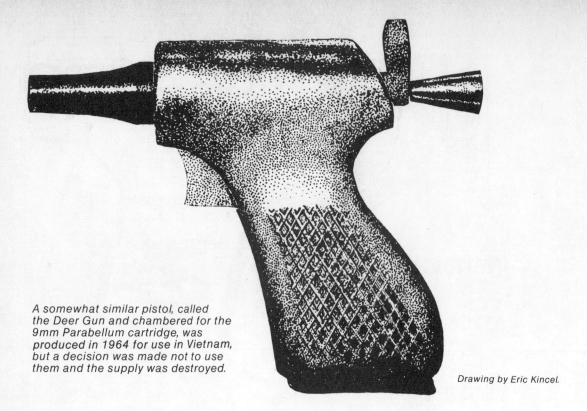

A somewhat similar pistol, called the Deer Gun and chambered for the 9mm Parabellum cartridge, was produced in 1964 for use in Vietnam, but a decision was made not to use them and the supply was destroyed.

Drawing by Eric Kincel.

less puzzling that so few of them survive to the present in private hands. Futhermore, considering the adamant ugliness of the gun, few would incline to own one.

The final cost to the OSS of Liberator pistols was just a trifle over $2 per unit and the entire construction was of non-strategic materials. Its purpose was at least two-fold: A would-be freedom fighter, armed with one, could stalk an isolated sentry to the requisite close range, dispose of him with a well delivered shot and take possession of the enemy's gun and ammunition supply, thus gearing up to go on to greater things. At the same time, awareness by Axis troops that their captives might have access to even such crude firearms tended to put a severe strain upon morale.

Reliable statistics upon the toll taken among enemy troops by the humble Liberator pistols is beyond all hope of obtaining. As well as could be ascertained after cessation of hostilities, it is believed Liberator pistols accounted for more enemy dead and wounded than did all of the .45 ACP service handguns in use by the U.S armed forces during WWII.

Despite the generally gratifying battle record of the Liberator, subsequent conflicts saw no further employment of that particular tactic. It almost came to pass, however. At the time of the Vietnam War, someone in the CIA retrieved the basic idea.

Thus came into existence something they called the Deer Gun. It was chambered for the 9mmP cartridge and the barrel was threaded into the receiver. To load or reload, the barrel was unscrewed and a stick was used to knock out any fired case. A cartridge was chambered, the barrel turned back into the receiver and the Deer Gun was ready for action.

Unlike the Liberator pistol, with its extravagant sheet metal trigger guard whose upper front tip served as the front sight, the Deer Gun had no trigger guard whatever and no sights, either. What it did have, in effect, was a sort of double-action trigger. Each time the exposed trigger was pulled, the striker came back and was released to drive forward at the end of the trigger stroke. Thus, if you happened to have a misfire on the first try, you had only to keep working the trigger in hopes a few more snaps would detonate the primer.

A considerable quantity of the Deer Guns actually were produced in 1964 and put up in foam plastic boxes, ready for parachuting. As before, they were packed with pictured directions for operation. The receiver appears to have a simple die-casting, complete with moulded-in checkering in the grip area, with storage space for spare cartridges in the butt.

As but one of the innumerable inexplicable facets of that most inexplicable conflict, about the time the Deer Guns were ready to be dropped, a political decree was handed down: Don't drop them; scrap them instead. No more than a few examples survive at present. Unit cost of the Deer Gun does not seem to be quoted in reference sources, but I'd risk a small wager it was substantially higher than that of the Liberator.

Some sources give the maximum effective range of the Liberator pistol as twenty to twenty-five yards; other shave that down to more like three to five yards and I regard the latter estimate as vastly more credible. I recall someone brought one of the little gizmos out to the ground gunnery range at Tonopah (Nevada) Army Air Force Base at a time when I was instructing on the pistol range and several of us clustered around to cant quizzical eyebrows at it.

I tried a few shots with it. Had I dreamed I'd want to

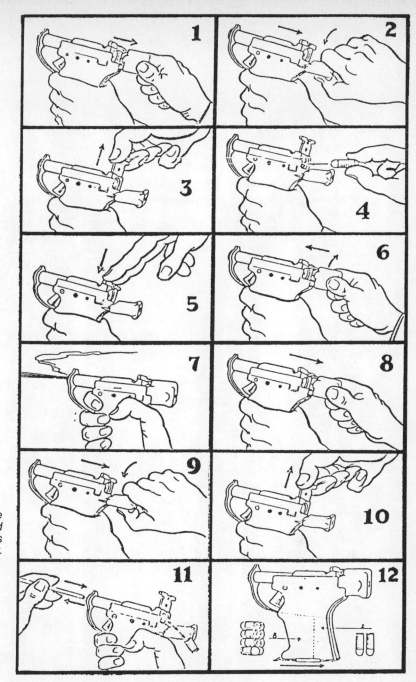

The instruction sheet packed with the Liberator was designed to transcend language and literacy barriers, so as to be understandable by any gun user.

write about it forty-five years or so into the future, I would have reviewed it more intently and thoughtfully, but how was I to know?

I recall the trigger pull fairly clearly. If you tried to haul a tomcat off a cedar shake roof by tugging on the end of his tail, the sensation would not be too different from dragging the Liberator trigger until it released the striker. Putting it another way: It was neither smooth nor crisp.

The Government Model pistol, caliber .45, Model 1911/1911A1, generates a substantial amount of recoil and muzzle blast, with its five-inch barrel and net weight of thirty-eight ounces or so, as many of us are well aware. Set off a round of GI hardball in a pistol weighing less than half that, out of a barrel an inch shorter — all this at a time when the helpful muff-type ear protectors were a decade or two

short of being invented — and the subjective effective was plumb, downright traumatic.

I think I fired two shots with it at the six-inch ten-ring of the six-foot by six-foot rapid-fire target at fifteen yards. The first shot hit something like twelve to eighteen inches wide of the aiming point and the second was off by about the same distance, more or less in the opposite direction. That was at a time when I'd gotten to the point where I could manipulate the M1911A1 with reasonably telling effect.

Candidly, I can't help feeling grateful my destiny didn't include having to take out an armed sentry in the dark with a Liberator pistol. Despite that, I'd have to concede it would have been a helluva lot more attractive alternative than having to do the same job barehanded.

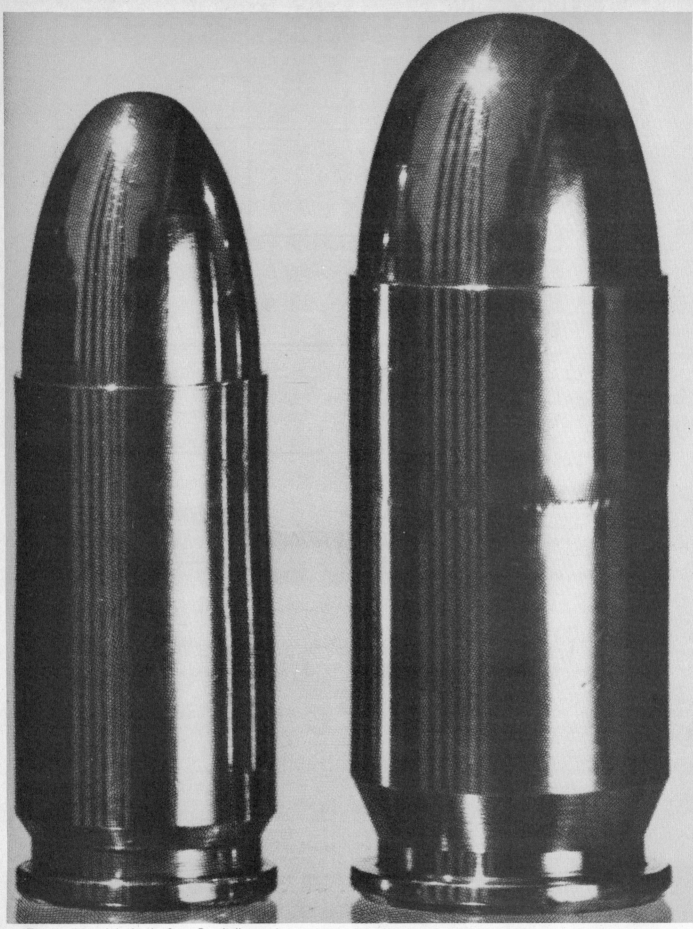

Two traditional rivals: the 9mm Parabellum or Luger and the .45 Automatic Colt Pistol or ACP.

THE GUN DIGEST BOOK OF THE .45

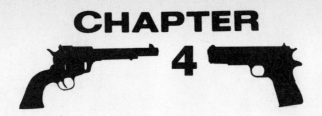

CHAPTER 4

.45 CARTRIDGES AND RELATED CALIBERS

Reviewing The Big-Bores, Along With Their More Significant Contemporaries

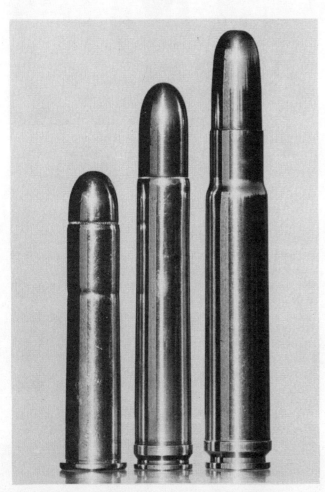

From left, the .45-70 Government, .458 Winchester magnum and .460 Weatherby magnum, as discussed.

I PROPOSE to discuss here the general category of cartridges that carry bullets between .45-inch and .46-inch in diameter, with side notes on certain other cartridges that have been used, or may be used in guns customarily made up for use of cartridges that take bullets of the aforementioned size. We'll cover most, if not all, of the cartridges for which the Colt M1911/1911A1-type pistols have been chamberd down the years, along with certain others.

I hope it won't upset anyone unduly, but I propose to cover cartridges up through and including the .45-70 Government, drawing the line just short of the .458 Winchester magnum, .460 Weatherby magnum and many a platoon of wildcat numbers that accept bullets of .458-inch diameter. My motive is somewhat subjective: On hand are at least one carbine and pistol in .45-70, but I sold my last .458 Win. mag. rifle several years ago. I see a clear line of demarcation at about that point.

It all gets back to the bedrock basic that you have to draw the line somewhere and, for this book, I'm scribing it just north of the doughty old .45-70 Government cartridge. My arbitrary yardstick lies in whether or not the cartridge has been used in handguns and shoulder guns. If it's strictly for handguns, it's included. If it is — or should be — strictly a rifle cartridge, it's not. Yes, I'm aware handguns have been made up in .458 Win. mag. I've seen them, but not fired them. My parents strove not to raise any dull children. We will be getting into the .460 Jurras cartridge, substantially more powerful than the .45-70, but it was born and bred as a handgun round and, as far as I know, never chambered in a shoulder gun.

Headstamp of an early military round of .45-70, made in June of 1882 and loaded with 70.0 grains of black powder. Diameter of the lead bullet was .458-inch.

Back in the leisurely pre-WWI days, they used to change the headstamp every month. This one came out of the Frankford Arsenal in January, 1914

Produced at some foreign arsenal, perhaps in February of 1957, this .45 ACP case has a Berdan-type primer and, for that reason, is impractical to reload.

By 1934, Frankford Arsenal no longer felt it worth the bother to stamp the month of manufacture.

.45 AUTOMATIC COLT PISTOL (ACP)

As was noted in Chapter 2, John M. Browning designed this cartridge at some point prior to 1911, to function in the auto pistols he worked up a bit prior to that date. It is doubtful whether he ever dreamed how well he wrought. A lot of decades have come and gone. The .45 ACP continues to rank among the great cartridges of all time, both as a target round and as ammunition for serious social shooting purposes.

Military loadings in .45 ACP usually carry a headstamp that identifies the armory of production and the last two digits of the year of manufacture. The information can be painfully pertinent, particularly as to the date. Prior to some point around 1952, the services clung steadfastly to their infatuation with the corrosive chlorate primers, finally shifting to the use of non-corrosive primers within a year or so of that time.

Early primers and percussion caps used metallic fulminates — usually mercuric fulminate — as the main ingredient of the priming mixture. That posed no appreciable problems with the old percussion guns and their muzzle loaded steel chambers. Mercuric residues from the black gunpowder, being highly corrosive, required prompt cleaning.

A portion of the residue left after mercuric fulminate does its furious thing consists of free mercury which can and will raise holy Ned with any copper-bearing alloy, definitely including brass cartridge cases. It causes the brass to crystallize and weakens it to the point where it's no longer of use for anything except, perhaps, contaminated salvage scrap.

The original solution to that problem was to substitute a priming mixture containing potassium chlorate, chemical formula $KClO_3$, along with suitable fuels to be oxidized. Potassium chlorate is a powerful oxidizer. With the application of a bit of heat and commotion, it disassociates from its three atoms of oxygen and becomes plain, garden-variety potassium chloride: KCl.

Like its close chemical relative, sodium chloride, $NaCl$, more familiarly known as common table salt, potassium chloride is powerfully hygroscopic. Even small residues suck moisture from the adjacent atmosphere and retain it. The resulting salt solution is capable of rusting iron alloys, including steels, quite rapidly.

Potassium chloride is soluble in water, but not in oils. Many modern bore cleaners are oil-based, rather than water-based and will not remove residue left from firing corrosive chlorate primers. Hoppe's No. 9 bore cleaner is water-based, having been developed in the days when corrosive primers still posed a major problem. Thus, Hoppe's No. 9 will remove the corrosive primer residues. It functions as a cleaner more than a preservative, so a suitable corrosion-resisting oil should be applied after cleaning with Hoppe's No. 9 bore cleaner.

Not included in the list on page 43, EC stood for the Evansville Chrysler Ordnance Plant, in Evansville, Indiana; another was ECS for Evansville Chrysler Sunbeam. All of their production carried corrosive chlorate primers, as discussed here at the left.

A quintet of elderly military .45 ACP cases: EC/42, ECS/43; WRA/51; WCC/53 and WCC 62/Match. In any given year, a maker is selected to produce the loads for the National Match and the cases are great for reloading.

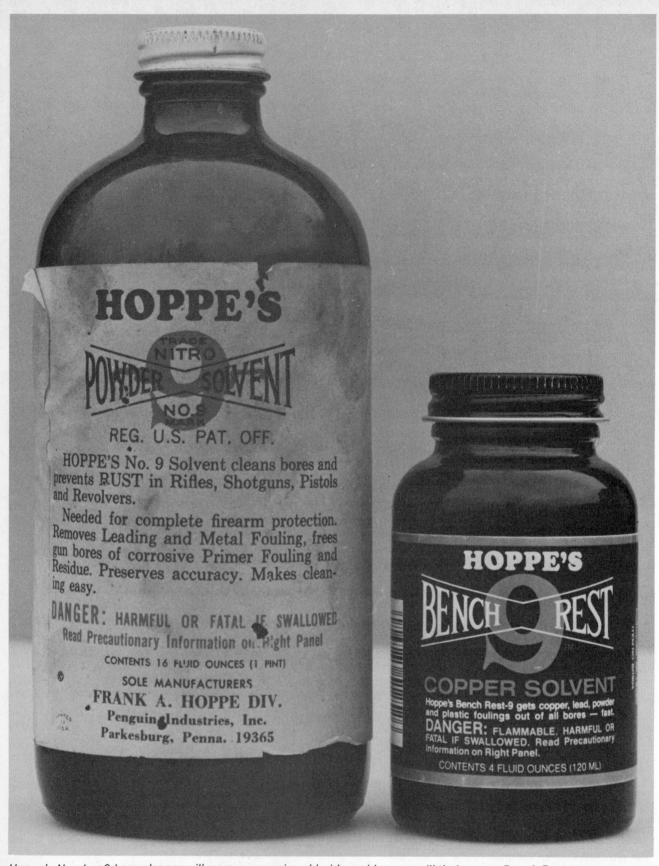

Hoppe's Number 9 bore cleaner will remove corrosive chloride residues, as will their newer Bench Rest type.

It has become the accepted custom to refer to certain alloys as stainless steels, most of which owe their corrosion-resisting properties to a percentage of chromium in their makeup. I beg leave to coin a new term and refer to the remaining steel alloys as *stainable* steels. As a matter of painful fact, even some of the so-called stainless alloys can show dismaying amounts of corrosion, if exposed to hostile compounds.

The point of the foregoing is that the chlorate-based primers will slaughter a stainable steel barrel in a matter of no more than scant hours, unless the bore is suitably cleaned and then protected by rust-inhibitors. Down the many years, a great many uninformed gun owners have found that out, to their considerable and costly regret.

Mercuric priming compounds went out of use about the time brass cartridge cases were adopted. They may have been used for a while in producing rimfire ammunition, where they presented no more than trifling problems, because rimfire cases are not reloaded. The highly corrosive chlorate primers were employed in most, if not all, military ammunition throughout WWII and on up through a major segment of the Korean War.

Commercial ammunition went over to non-mercuric, non-corrosive (NMNC) priming compounds at some point in the early Thirties, for which we all can and should feel suitable gratitude. A great many shooters find little or no enjoyment in cleaning their guns and, as a result, prefer to postpone the chore for some indefinite while. With NMNC priming compounds, that usually carries no overly severe penalty. With chlorate priming compounds, it puts you in the market for a new barrel; just that simple.

Commercial centerfire ammunition carries a headstamp that identifies the maker and the given caliber. Rimfires, having less area available for such purposes, carry some manner of identification of the maker.

The headstamps on military centerfire ammunition specify the caliber no more than rarely, if ever. It all gets down to the basic difference between ammo that's purchased by someone who wants to shoot it and ammo that's issued to someone who's been ordered to shoot it. This is all in line with the authoritarian attitude of the military. Corrosive primers posed no great problem because Privates Smith, Jones, et al., could be ordered to clean their weapons after firing. If they failed to do so, they could be hit with kitchen

Steel .45 ACP cases were produced as late as 1955 by Twin Cities Ordnance, headstamped TW over 5 and one of the few examples of a single-digit date. This one has been necked down to make a .38-45 Clerke case.

You can't tell in the black and white photo, but the tips of these bullets are lacquered red to indicate tracers.

police or statements of charges until they got the word and meekly followed orders.

Typical military ammunition carries a headstamp consisting of a few letters that identify the maker, plus a few numerals that specify the date of production. In the leisurely days prior ot WWI, they used to headstamp .45 ACP ammunition with numbers denoting not only the year but also the month. Somewhere about the place, I have some expended cases with a headstamp that reads FA over 1 14, meaning it was produced at Frankford Arsenal in January of 1914. That small nicety quickly went by the boards under the pressure of wartime production in WWI.

Frankford Arsenal .45 ACP cases, by the way, can present a unique problem to the reloader. For some given

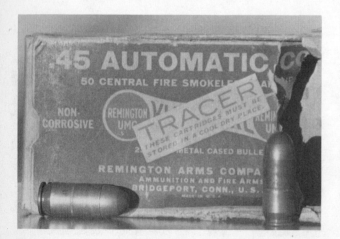
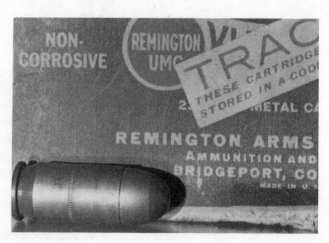

Two more looks at the Remington tracer loads and their picturesque old carton. Refer to photo on next page.

Tracer bullets are quite capable of starting serious fires and should not be fired for that reason.

while, they used a proprietary primer that was slightly smaller than the standard diameter of .210-inch, almost universally employed in large pistol primers. As I recall, the FA primers were about .206-inch in diameter, with primer pockets to match. Attempts to seat a new .210-inch primer in such cases were pretty hopeless. As the years slog doggedly onward, the odds that you'll encounter one of those old FA cases with the chintzy primer pockets continue to diminish. If you come upon one, I suggest you consign it to a suitable container for unlikely artifacts. I believe every reloading bench should have one of those.

It would be nice, at this point, to present a compilation of each and every single producer that ever turned out .45 ACP ammunition for use by the military, specifying the headstamp abbreviation they used. Regrettably, it is difficult to do so with unshakable conviction. During the course of two global conflicts, uncommon efforts were expended and a lot of organizations did what they needed to do, what they had to do, with somewhat less than the meticulous record-keeping that might seem desirable.

If you're willing to accept those conditions, the following is a list of headstamp abbreviations and makers, supplied by friend and associate Chuck Karwan. It's as complete as he could get it, but there could be exceptions:

MAKER	HEADSTAMP
Frankford Arsenal	FA
Federal Cartridge Corp.	FCC or FC
Lake City Ordnance Plant (?)	LC
Maxim Munitions Corp.	MAXIM USA
Maxim Munitions Corp. (?)	MMC
Maxim Munitions Corp. (?)	MAXIM
Peters Cartridge Co.	P.C. CO
Remington Arms	RA
St. Louis Ordnance Plant (?)	SL
Remington-Union Metallic Cartridge	REM-UMC
Twin Cities Ordnance Plant	TW
Union Metallic Cartridge	UMC
U.S. Cartridge Co.	U.S.C. CO
Winchester	W
Western Cartridge Co.	WCC
Western Cartridge Co.	WESTERN
Winchester Repeating Arms	WRA

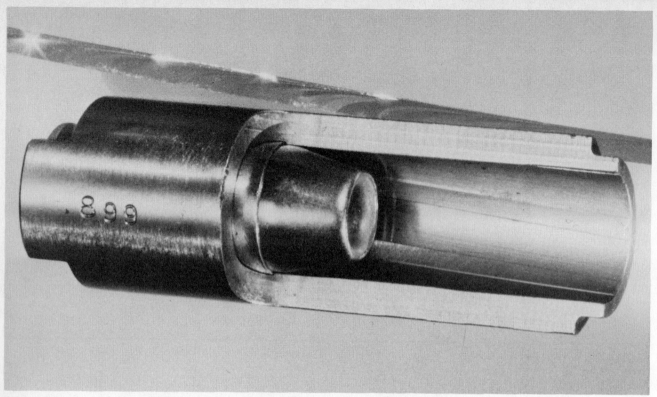

At one time, Bar-Sto Precision used to make these handy little chambering gauges from barrels rejected in production. They discontinued the practice, sad to say. These are handy for checking dimensions of reloads.

C-H Tool & Die Corporation can supply forming dies to make .45 ACP blanks. A dab of paint seals the nose.

Be it noted that inclusion of the LC and SL headstamps are on a sort of just-in-case basis. Both arsenals produced a lot of .30/06 ammo in their day and *may have* turned out some .45 ACP, along the way. If they did so, it's probable it was headstamped as indicated.

Do you mind if I enter a sheepish admission into the records? Endlessly, down the years, I've encountered .30/06 ammo with the SL headstamp and have looked at the letters and thought, "Aha, Salt Lake." In transcribing the foregoing, I went through an abrupt re-learning process.

With the firm stipulation that neither I nor the publisher will buy you a new barrel, if you lose the use of one, due to terminal corrosion, I will now enter the particulars as to when the various arsenals are believed to have shifted over to non-corrosive primers. The information is supplied by Chuck Karwan and he asks me to advise you that he also will not contribute to the cost of replacement barrels, should they be needed. This is a clear case of *caveat lector;* a nifty Latin phrase meaning, "let the reader beware."

Above, Speer's totally metal jacketed (TMJ) bullets have their jackets deposited by electroplating. Right, the usual full metal jacket (FMJ) .45 bullet has the lead at its base exposed, but that poses no special problems.

**INITIAL PRODUCTION OF .45 ACP
NON-CORROSIVE AMMUNITION**
(All subsequent lots were non-corrosive.)

INITIAL N-C PRIMER PRODUCTION

HEAD STAMP	MANUFACTURER	AMMO TYPE	LOT NUMBER	ACCEPTANCE DATE
FA	Frankford Arsenal	M1911 Ball	1542	July, 1954
FA	Frankford Arsenal	M26 Tracer	41	Mar., 1953
RA	Remington Arms	M1911 Ball	5544	Sep., 1952
WCC	Western Ctge. Co.	M1911 Ball	6375	Nov., 1952
TW	Twin Cities Ord.	M1911 Ball	18000	Aug., 1953
TW	Twin Cities Ord.	M26 Tracer	18000	Oct., 1953
FCC	Federal Ctge. Co.	M26 Tracer	1801	Nov., 1953
WRA	Winchester	M1911 BAll	22198	Nov., 1951
WRA	Win. Repeating Arms	M1911 Ball (Steel Case	S-22000 thru S-22007	Nov., 1951

The .455 Webley Revolver, Mark II cartridge, here at left with a .45 ACP, carried a 265-grain bullet and typical muzzle velocity was on the order of 600 fps.

A cast bullet for the .45 ACP, to which I'm rather partial, is the Hensley & Gibbs No. 938. Its conical point has an included angle of 70 degrees and it weighs between 175 and 180 grains depending upon the alloy.

All U.S. military .45 ACP ammunition made prior to 1954, other than those noted above, should be considered to be loaded with corrosive primers.

Caution: Repeating for emphasis, if you have any doubts as to the corrosive characteristics of a given lot or round of ammunition, it is much the wiser course to clean and lubricate the bore, as previously discussed!

Chuck Karwan also supplied the following listing of the standard types of U.S. military .45 ACP ammunition:

.45 Ball M1911
.45 Ball M1911, Steel Case
.45 Ball M1911, Match Grade
.45 Test, High Pressure, M1: Proof load, *not for service use.*
.45 Blank M9 (Pre-adoption designation, T31)
.45 Blank Steel Case
.45 Tracer, M26 (Pre-adoption designation, T30)
.45 Tracer, M26, Steel Case
.45 Dummy M1921
.45 Dummy M1921, Steel Case
.45 Shot M12 (Pre-adoption designation, T23)
.45 Shot M15 (Pre-adoption designation, T29)
.45 Blank M1918 (Can only be used with special barrel.)
.45 Dummy M1918
.45 Tracer M1

A few notes and comments on the foregoing: Karwan advises me he does not feel the listing of headstamps is one hundred percent complete and exhaustive, but it covers most of the domestic producers.

STEEL CASES

During interludes of acute material shortage, .45 ACP cases have been made of steel. With no more than unlikely exceptions, the steel-case ammo with corrosive primers carried the seed of its own undoing and the deposited salts caused the cases to rust into hopeless ruin.

Twin Cities Ordnance Plant made a substantial run of steel-case loads in 1955 and, departing from usual custom, headstamped it TW over 5. As that was after the transition to non-corrosive primers, the spent cases remain in good condition and they can be reloaded. What remains somewhat dubious is whether they *should* be reloaded. I'm referring to the M1911 Ball load, often termed G.I. Hardball. At the time of initial loading, some manner of coating was applied to the outside of the steel cases and they did not seem to pose any major problems at the first firing.

Driven to a little over 1300 fps out of the 10-inch T/C Contender barrel, the H&G 938 bullet nearly made it through this strip of 3/16-inch mild steel. Generally, the 938 delivers somewhat better-than-average accuracy.

An unusual bullet design, termed the FMJ SWC, this high-velocity Uzi match load is designed to feed reliably, meanwhile leaving a hole in the target paper that is somewhat larger than the diameter left by round-noses.

Ranch Products calls their two-round holders "Third Moon Clips." Three of them make up a full load.

In the course of reloading the steel cases, however, the original anti-grab case coating may come off, causing them to cling tenaciously to the chamber walls at the instant of firing and, quite possibly, put enough strain upon the extractor to break it. At least, I've heard reports of such problems. Personally, I can't recall having ever broken an extractor on a M1911-type pistol under any circumstances. I mention this mainly as a cautionary note to any reader with a large quantity of steel cases who contemplates using them for reloads. It might be prudent to put a spare extractor into stock.

TRACERS

The usual custom is to apply a bit of red lacquer to the tip of the bullet on tracer loads, regardless of the caliber and .45 ACP ammo is no exception. If you come into possession of a cartridge with the end of the bullet painted red, you'd be wise to regard it as a tracer and treat it accordingly.

A tracer bullet has a pellet of highly flammable compound in its base and the stuff is ignited by the hot blast of the burning powder. As the bullet goes out the muzzle, its

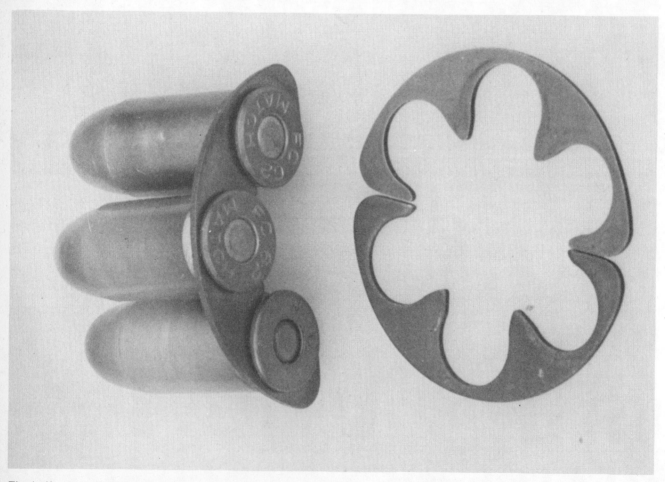

The half moon clips, developed for use in WWI, permit ready extraction of the rimless fired cases.

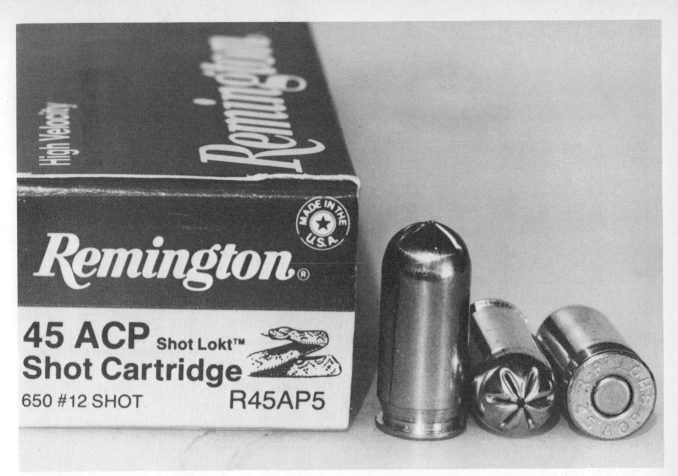

Remington currently produces this shot load in .45 ACP. The pellets are No. 12 size and spread rapidly.

fiery tail can be seen by the shooter with a degree of clarity, depending upon the light conditions and other factors. Tracer ammo dates back at least as far as WWI, possibly further.

The intent was to provide a visible indication of the bullet path to the operator of full-auto weaponry, to serve as a guide for bringing the cone of fire into optimum effectiveness. Whether or not it ever did so is a damned moot

CCI's .45 ACP shot load delivers a tighter pattern and carry No. 9 pellets at a brisk velocity. They are not recommended for use in revolvers, as recoil may open the nose seal, but they function the action of an auto, as do the Remington shot loads in the upper photo.

Strictly a collector item, Peters used to make these shot loads with a heavy paper capsule for use in a special version of the Thompson submachine gun.

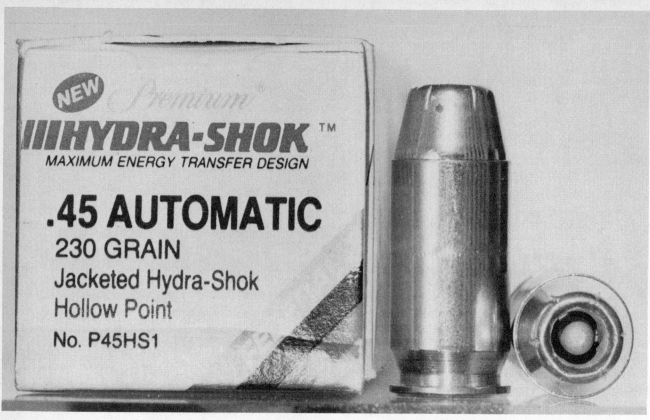

Federal now manufactures a .45 ACP load with the Hydra-Shok JHP bullet that has a central lead post within the cavity, as visible in the cartridge at the right here. It's intended to enhance penetration.

point, in my opinion. The usual procedure is to load a tracer for every fifth round, with standard ball or armor-piercing for the other four.

The tracer bullet is lighter in weight than its four companions and it loses weight as it goes along. Thus, it does not necessarily track with the rest of the pack in terms of elevation and wind dispersion. It may have served a useful purpose in some situations; a point I incline to view with polite skepticism.

Tracer ammunition in .45 ACP was produced and issued primarily for use in submachine guns. It served little or no strategic purpose in pistols and was fired in them no more than rarely, if ever.

Should you come into possession of .45 ACP ammo carrying red-tipped bullets, give thoughtful consideration before setting any of it off. If the bullet encounters flammable material before the tracer compound burns out, it is highly probable that it will start a fire, with attendant serious consequences. For much of the year, locally, the ground cover approaches the flammability of Hercules Bullseye pistol powder and they have prominent signs at the local ranges forbidding the firing of tracer ammo. If you operate in the rain forests of the Matto Grosso, let your conscience be your guide.

.45 ACP BLANKS

In a long and lengthening association with the M1911A1 pistol and its assorted ammo, I have yet to encounter a single G.I. round of .45 ACP blank. I recall concocting my own, rather laboriously, during an interlude at Tonopah when I was doing the initial familiarization lecture on the .45 auto in classrooms. It would have been ever so nice if I could have requisitioned G.I. blanks to save the bother of building them.

My improvised podium for such lectures consisted of a fairly common desk with a shallow drawer in the center and others running down both sides. I would stand behind the desk, doing my level damndest to command the attention of sixty or so assorted crew-member trainees, hardly any of whom gave a freckle-faced doggone to listen to me. I was but one more boring thing they had to endure, as best they could manage.

I tended to put quite a bit of emphasis on safety, covering such points as making sure the gun was empty and, even then, being extemely careful where its muzzle was pointed. I would lock the slide back, magazine in place and insert the tip of my little finger through the ejection port and into the chamber, noting that was one way to make sure it was *empty*. Then I'd ease the slide forward, leaving the ham-

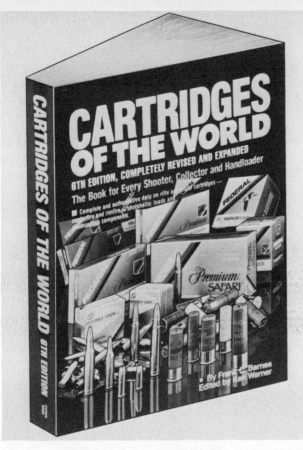 

Left, the sixth edition of Frank C. Barnes' Cartridges of the World *is the definitive reference book for information on any and all cartridges. Right, the curious cartridge at the right is a .38 AMU, for Army Marksmanship Unit. Shown next to a .38 Special, the .38 AMU was developed as a target load in auto pistols that had been converted to handle it, using the extractor groove on the semi-rimmed head to extract.*

mer cocked and lay it in the partially open drawer of the desk, meanwhile, keeping up a running line of further admonitions.

After a few minutes, I'd pick up the pistol from the desk drawer, bearing down on the bit about always being careful where the muzzle pointed, because you can never be really, *really* certain it's empty..."BAM!"

What I'd done, of course, was to plant the pistol loaded with the blank in the desk drawer before the students filed in. The ruse could be relied upon to get the full attention of the entire class for ten, maybe as much as fifteen seconds.

.45 ACP PERFORMANCE

Typically, down the nearly eight decades of its career to date, the .45 ACP has carried bullets weighing 230 grains: the traditional military hardball load. In line with military custom, the bullets are of full metal jacket (FMJ) design, with round noses (FMJ/RN).

According to specifications set forth by the Sporting Arms and Ammunition Manufacturers Institute (SAAMI), the maximum working pressure of the .45 ACP is 19,900 copper units of pressure (CUP). Staying within that limitation produces typical velocities on the order of 800 to 900 feet per second (fps), or 800/326 to 900/413, as I usually quote such data, the second number denoting the energy figure.

Bullets of .451-inch diameter have a frontal area of .159-square inch, compared to .098-square inch for the .355-inch diameter of the 9mm Parabellum. That's to say the .45 brings roughly sixty-two percent more area into collision with the given target medium.

For military applications, the FMJ bullet has long been what might be wryly termed a fact of life. Many believe the restrictions against expanding bullets were agreed upon the Geneva Convention but that is incorrect. Actually, it was the Hague Agreement of 1914 that forbade the use of what are sometimes termed *dumdum* bullets: thus named for the arsenal at Dumdum, India, where some of the first examples were made.

If you're restricted to non-expanding bullets, those of larger diameter transfer energy more rapidly to the target medium. In non-military situations, such as police work and home defense, there are no restrictions against jacketed hollow point (JHP) or jacketed soft point (JSP) bullets and they have come into quite extensive use.

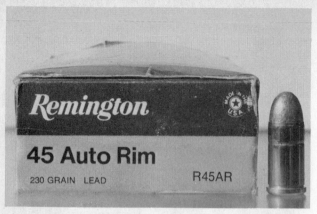

At present, only Remington produces the .45 Auto Rim, designed for added convenience in revolvers that also accept the .45 ACP. The load with the 230-grain lead bullet is the only one they make, but it's quite accurate.

.45 AUTO RIM

At the time the U.S. entered WWI, the newly adopted Model 1911 .45 auto pistol had not been produced in anything approaching the quantities that were urgently needed. By way of filling the gap, heavy-frame double-action revolvers chambered to fire the .45 ACP cartridge were produced by both Colt and Smith & Wesson, both makes being termed the Model 1917 or '17.

The .45 ACP, having no rim, presented a problem for use in revolvers when it came to ejecting the spent cases after firing. That was solved by introduction of the half-moon clips, holding three cartridges apiece. It made an effective system whereby the revolvers could be reloaded nearly as quickly as the autos.

After the war Peters introduced the .45 Auto Rim (AR) cartridge, with a rim thick enough to take up the space that had been occupied by the half-moon clip and the amount of .45 ACP rim that projected behind it. That gave users of the Model '17 revolvers the option of a rimmed cartridge that loaded and ejected in the usual manner.

SAAMI specifies a maximum pressure of 19,900 CUP

At one time, Peters Cartridge Company, Kings Mills, Ohio, made the .45 Auto Rim with the old balloon-head construction shown in this cross-sectioned case. Modern .45 AR cases are of stronger web-head design.

for the .45 ACP cartridge, but rates the .45 AR at no more than 16,900 CUP. Initially, the .45 AR cases were produced in the old balloon-head configuration, later changed to the web-head design. The difference is readily apparent if you look into the mouth of the empty case. The balloon-head cases have a distinctive circular depression around the flash hole. It is rather unlikely you'll encounter balloon-head cases unless you obtain some really old loads or brass and, if met with, they are best culled out and set aside.

Remington has marketed the .45 AR under both the Remington and Peters brand names, though the latter has been phased out in recent years. Winchester once produced .45 Auto Rim, but discontinued it.

In the era between WWI and WWII, Colt chambered their New Service revolver in both .45 AR and .45 Colt for commercial distribution, in barrel lengths of 4, 4½, 5, 5½, 6 and 7½ inches. There is a report — how accurate, I can't say — that the tooling for the New Service line was unceremoniously hauled out into a parking lot to make room for production of the Model 1911 during the emergency conditions of WWII and left to the dubious mercy of the elements for the duration. Be that as it may, Colt never resumed production of the New Service model after WWII.

Smith & Wesson also produced commercial versions of their .45 Hand Ejector Model of 1917 — as it's formally termed — in the interlude between wars. The quantity was quite small and they are rarely seen today. They were distinguished by checkered walnut stocks, rather than the smooth walnut of the military version as well as a brighter blued finish.

Sales of the S&W Model '17 were rather slow during most of the Twenties and Thirties, but in 1937 S&W accepted an order for 25,000 of them from Brazil, delivering them in the interval between February and October of 1938. Serial numbering of the S&W Model '17 commenced at 1 and reached 209,791 with the completion of the Brazilian order.

Production of the Model '17 was resumed by Smith & Wesson on May 14, 1946, eventually running the serial numbers to 210,782. On hand at that time were 10,868 frames that had been made up and serial-numbered during

Left, here's how the old balloon-head Peters .45 Auto Rim loads looked from the outside. Note the hyphen in the Auto-Rim headstamp. Such cases should be set aside and not reloaded for reasons of safety. Right, from left, a .45 Colt or Long Colt; .454 Casull and the .45 Winchester magnum, for size comparison.

The .454 Casull, despite the designation, takes bullets .451 to .452 inches in diameter. Its case is longer to prevent use in .45 Colt revolvers. It is loaded to high pressure for use in the five-shot single-action revolver made by Freedom Arms, in Freedom, Wyoming.

Left, the .357-45 Grizzly Winchester magnum, developed for use in the L.A.R. Grizzly pistol. Cartridge at right is the .357 Auto Mag Pistol (AMP), developed as an alternative round for the .44 Auto Mag, now discontinued.

the Thirties and those were assembled and sold as late as 1949, when Smith & Wesson officially dropped the Model 1917 from production, according to Roy G. Jinks' *History of Smith & Wesson.*

The same source notes that S&W dropped the Model 1917 in order to develop revolvers of greater appeal to civilian target shooters. The first was the Model 1950, also made in .45 Colt and .44 S&W Special. It featured the underlug barrel shrouding the ejector rod, first seen on the Hand Ejector First Model, originally introduced in 1908, as well as an integral barrel rib, square-backed Patridge type front sight and fully adjustable rear sight.

Sales of the Model 1950 fell well short of Smith & Wesson's hopeful expectations. In speaking with target shooters, there was a consensus that it needed a heavier barrel, target stocks and the broader trigger and hammer spur that S&W terms target-type.

All of these desired features were incorporated into the Model of 1955, introduced in that year. In 1957, Smith & Wesson adopted the new system of model designation, still in use. Suffix numbers served to distinguish various improvements and variations of the basic models. For example, late in 1959, there was a change to left-hand threads on the ejector rod of the Model 24 and it was designated the Model 24-1. In 1961, a change to a cylinder stop, eliminating the screw in front of the trigger guard produced the Model 24-2

While the Model 24s had been produced in at least three calibers — .44 S&W Special, .45 ACP/AR and .45 Colt — the Model 25 initially appeared in .45 ACP/AR, designated as the Model 25-2, with a later introduction of the Model 25-5 in .45 Colt. Early in 1989, S&W announced a limited run of the Model 625-2, in .45 ACP/AR, with a five-inch barrel and made of matte-finished stainless steel. Further details on that model will be given later.

Dick Casull, inventor of the .454 Casull revolver and cartridge, blasts a one-gallon paint can filled with water. The hydrostatic shock was sufficient to shatter a concrete block on which the can had been resting!

.45 COLT/.45 LONG COLT

This is a rather elderly cartridge, introduced in 1873 for the Colt Single Action Army revolver to serve as the U.S. service handgun cartridge for the next seventeen years or so.

Having been designed initally for use in single-action revolvers, which eject empty cases one at a time, the .45 LC has a somewhat vestigial rim that is not overly well adapted for used in double-action revolvers with swing-out cylinders. Some DA revolvers handle it quite nicely, while others may present occasional problems.

Designed in an era when black powder was the only propellant to be had, the .45 LC was dimensioned to hold about 40 grains of the stuff and, as a direct result, it has more powder capacity than it really needs for most of the modern nitro or "smokeless" powders.

It is possible to encounter .45 LC cases with the old balloon-head construction, though none too likely. As with the .45 AR, these are readily indentified by visual examination down the neck of the fired case. You are not apt to find such relics unless someone makes you a present of some really old fired cases, as factory loads have used the stronger web-head construction for the past many years. Any balloon-head cases encountered should be segregated to one side and not be used for reloading.

Many reloading authorities have proclaimed the .45 LC case to be weak and unsuited for high-pressure loading. That is not necessarily true. It is true that a great many guns chambered for the .45 Colt are rather weak and incapable of coping with hot loads. That is particularly true of the old Colt Single Action Army revolvers manufactured in the black powder era and, to some extent, those made down to recent times.

Several contemporary manuals and handbooks of load data include two separate sections for the .45 LC; one batch suitable for use with the old Colt SAA revolvers and the like, a second for use in the Ruger or Thompson/Center Contender.

If you happen to own and operate a Colt SAA and a Ruger or T/CC, it is an excellent idea to make distinctive identification of loads made up for use in the stronger actions, so as to prevent inadvertant use in the weaker guns. Daub the heads of the hot loads with red felt marking pens or use some similar approach.

There are many who believe the correct bullet diameter for the .45 LC is .454-inch. That is true only of revolvers produced prior to WWII. With resumption of production after 1945, all guns chambered for .45 Colt have had bore dimensions that do their best work with lead bullets of .452-inch diameter or jacketed bullets measuring .451-inch.

From left, a .45 ACP, .451 Detonics magnum and .45 Winchester magnum. Note the narrower, shallower extractor grooves in the latter two, as compared to the .45 ACP. Smaller grooves strengthen the head.

Left, many shell holders that accept the .45 ACP case will not take the .451 D-mag or .45 Win. mag. The RCBS No. 11 shell holder will work nicely with all three. Right, current loading of the .45 Win. mag.

.454 CASULL

This is a cartridge developed by Dick Casull, initially based upon the .45 Colt cartridge, later somewhat modified by substitution of a primer pocket to take the smaller, .175-inch diameter primers, and elongated to prevent its firing in chambers dimensioned for the .45 Colt cartridge.

The only gun in which the .454 Casull cartridge should be fired is the revolver with a five-shot, unfluted cylinder manufactured by Freedom Arms. Other makers have produced arms ostensibly capable of firing the .454 Casull and at least one owner of such a revolver has sent me some cases fired in it that I view as downright alarming.

The .454 Casull is, at least arguably, the most powerful repeating handgun in current production. There are single-action revolvers chambered for .45-70 and one might assume them capable of out-punching the Casull. I'd incline to doubt it. The Casull, though a smaller cartridge, is capable of operating at some truly berserk peak pressures and that makes the difference. How berserk? With no more than rare exceptions, most rifle cartridges limit out at around 55,000 CUP. For his own experimental load development, Casull works into about the 65,000 CUP bracket and gets away with it because the Freedom Arms single-action revolver is designed, engineered and manufactured

Kaswer Custom, Incorporated, 13 Surrey Drive, Brookfield Center, Connecticut 06805, produces the novel "Pin Grabber" bullets and loads, designed to dig into maple bowling pins.

Originally, the .45 Winchester magnum, along with the 9mm Winchester magnum, were designed for use in the gas-operated Wildey autoloading pistol. In quite recent times, Wildey has refinanced and gone back into production, from Box 475, Brookfield, Connecticut 06804. The empty case I've just fired is their wildcat .475 Wildey, based upon the .284 Winchester case, with .475-inch diameter JSP bullets made by Barnes.

in a manner calculated to make a bank vault door seem downright flimsy by comparison.

You will note the cartridge is called the .454 Casull, not the .454 Casull magnum. The magnum designation has become a rather empty buzz-word in recent times and the .32 Harrington & Richardson "magnum" may have delivered the *coup de grace*, challenging the gun world to maintain a straight face at the concept of a so-called magnum round operating in the low 20,000 CUP brackets.

Despite the numerical designation, the .454 Casull takes jacketed bullets of .451-inch diameter and .452-inch in cast, in weights well up into the 300-grain range. Freedom Arms makes and markets jacketed "soft" point bullets at weights of 260 and 300 grains, using a fairly hard alloy for the cores, which is why I put soft in quote-marks back there. It needs a fairly sturdy bullet to withstand the stresses of being fired at that kind of pressure.

What kind of performance can the .454 Casull shooter

expect? I plan to cover load data at a later point in the book, but I've put 31.8 grains of Winchester 296 powder behind the 300-grain Freedom Arms JSP bullet, using a Winchester No. 120M primer, fired it in my scoped 7.5-inch Freedom Arms revolver and velocities went from a low of 1564 to a high of 1606, averaging 1593 fps for 1691 average fpe. Center-to-center spread for a five-shot group off sandbags on the bench at twenty-five yards was just 1.422 inches.

There have been recorded instances of the .454 Casull putting bears down for the eternity count at practically halitosis range. I would not count upon it to do that every time, but it's probably the gun and cartridge combination most apt to do the job.

.45 WINCHESTER MAGNUM

The .45 Winchester magnum, together with the 9mm Winchester magnum, were developed in the late Seventies for use in a gas-operated auto pistol called the Wildey that never got into extensive production. For a time, Thompson/Center offered barrels in .45 Win. mag. for their single-shot Contender pistol, initially in the ten-inch length and later in the fourteen-inch size. The 9mm Win. mag. was not given serious consideration as a cartridge for the Contender because they already had barrels for rounds such as the .35 Remington, capable of considerably more robust performance.

We've all seen "stretch limos," usually with near-opaque glass windows to provide privacy for their affluent passengers. The L.A.R. Grizzly pistol could, with reasonable justification, be termed a stretch version of the basic Colt Model 1911, in that its handle area was elongated to make room for a magazine capable of accommodating cartridges such as the .45 Win. mag. For a brief time, the Grizzly was made in 9mm Win. mag. and I had a loaner in that caliber long enough to pin down a few particulars on what certainly must be one of the most little-known cartridges of all time.

Winchester offers but one factory load in .45 Win. mag., carrying a 230-grain FMJ/RN bullet and it goes about 1339/916 out of a six-inch barrel. The L.A.R. Grizzly also is available with a longer slide and a ten-inch barrel. The added tube length boosts the Winchester load to more like 1467/1099.

For various good and sufficient reasons, L.A.R. dropped the 9mm Win. mag. rather early-on and replaced it with a wildcat number of their own devising. We'll devote a separate heading to that one.

.357 GWM

This cartridge comes awfully close to duplicating that lost lamb, the .357 Auto Mag Pistol (AMP), developed as a smaller-bore variant for the .44 Auto Mag. They are not quite identical but they are, as noted, quite close in general dimensions. The .357 GWM is not a necked-down version of the .45 Win. mag. being somewhat longer in case length.

This is the control ring on the Wildey pistol. When turned clockwise, more force is delivered to the action and less if turned counter-clockwise. Thus, the amount of energy for cycling can be custom tailored.

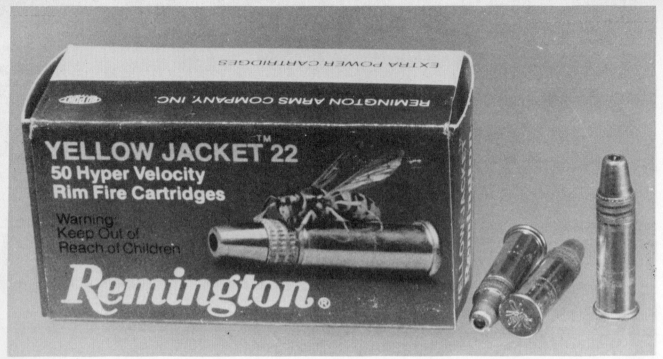

Colt Government Model pistols have been produced in .22 Long Rifle, as discussed here in the text. The Remington Yellow Jacket is one of the current hyper-velocity .22 LR loads and it's a real hummer!

It can be produced from the 7mm Bench Rest Remington case. It offers vigorous ballistics and exceptional accuracy, particularly in the long-slide version of the Grizzly.

.22 LONG RIFLE

The standard model of the Colt Ace first was marketed in 1931 and, in my opinion, was/still is an eminently desirable handgun to own and shoot. I've never owned one and hardly expect I ever will. Back in the early Fifties, I was a member of a gun club in Wisconsin and a fellow member of the club had a Colt Ace. He would bring it to the Thursday

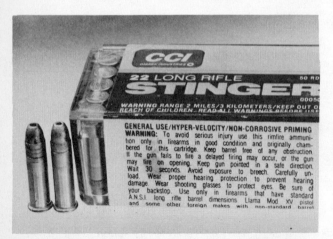

CCI's Stinger load is another hyper-velocity .22 LR load and its case is slightly longer, causing problems if it's fired in certain guns having non-standard chambers.

evening range sessions and, being a kindly soul, would allow me to fire it, now and again.

In a hasty glance at the exterior, one might mistake it for the usual Model 1911A1, but the distinction became quite apparent if you pulled the slide back, as its recoil spring was considerably weaker. The magazine held ten rounds of .22 LR and, firing it with reasonable care, in the offhand position from a distance of fifty feet, I could dot in some groups that came close to making me glow in the dark.

Accompanying photos illustrate a Colt Ace, vintage of *circa* 1931, owned by George DiLeo, proprietor of The Gunsight, in Fullerton, California. I have not fired DiLeo's pistol, but I'd not be surprised a bit if it came up to the performance of that other one, so long ago.

Six years later, in 1937, Colt introduced what they called the Service Ace, incorporating a floating chamber designed by David M. "Carbine" Williams. The special feature of that one was that it was supposed to offer a fairly accurate facsimile of the recoil of the regular Model 1911A1 in .45 ACP, meanwhile consuming the inexpensive .22 LR cartridge.

Like the standard Ace, the Service Ace was dropped from production at the start of WWII and, unlike the standard Ace, the Service Ace was put back into production early in 1978, gussied up with a Gold Cup slide. The trigger pull on the '78 version was bit hard; typically over five pounds, out of the box. Sales must have proved disappointing, as it was dropped from production after a year or so.

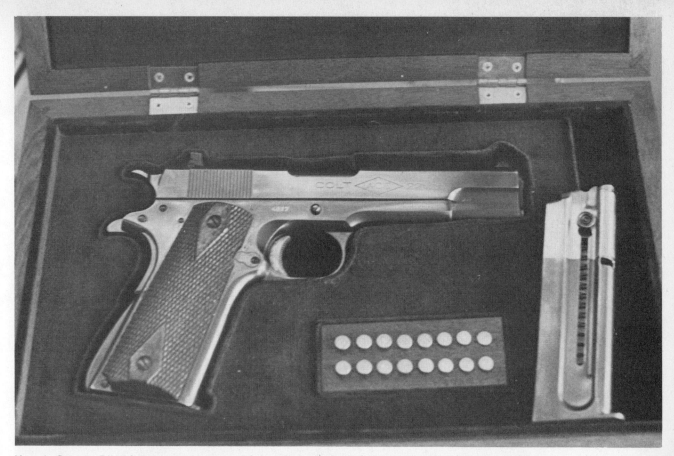

Here is George DiLeo's pride and joy, one of the original .22 LR Colt Ace pistols, produced in the early Thirties. This one had the one-piece barrel, without the floating chamber. Most such pistols shot accurately. Below, another view of DiLeo's Ace, with the slide locked back. The bluing brings a lump to the throat!

In 1978, Colt reintroduced the .22 LR Service Model Ace, giving it the Gold Cup slide with target sights and the serrations at the rear of the slide raked forward. I added a set of homemade stocks in Australian sandalwood and the resulting pistol is about as handsome as such things ever get. Perhaps because of the floating chamber, the accuracy leaves a little bit to be desired. Colt discontinued the Ace after a few years.

I've never been able to convince my right wrist that the recoil from the Service Ace is all that comparable to the bite-back from typical loads in .45 ACP, but then I tend to compound some fairly resolute combinations in the larger caliber. Be that as it may, I've never been able to coax

groups out of the Service Ace anywhere nearly as clannish as I used to get out of that standard Colt Ace long ago. I take such consolation as I can manage to extract from the fact that I have a Sport Model Colt Woodsman that punches .22 LR ammo into pleasantly tight clusters and another auto pistol or two that do ever better.

In this view from the right, you can see the juncture of the floating chamber and the rest of the barrel. Buildup of powder residue can be removed by use of Break-Free.

9mm LUGER/9mm PARABELLUM

This cartridge dates from about the turn of the present century and is in wide use throughout the world. SAAMI specifies a maximum pressure of 35,700 CUP — substantially higher than the 19,900 CUP ceiling they put on the .45 ACP — and, as a result, the two cartridges are matched fairly evenly as to delivered muzzle energy in fpe.

The standard military load for the 9mmP carries a FMJ/RN bullet of about 124 grains, compared to the 230-grain FMJ/RN bullet for the military .45 ACP load. In a typical target medium, penetration is close to the same for the two cartridges.

Cross-sectional area for a bullet of .355-inch diameter is .098-square inch, compared to .159-square inch for a

Shown rather larger than life-sized, this is an example of the classic 9mm Parabellum/Luger load with a long, round-nosed FMJ bullet jutting out of the case mouth.

From left, .380 ACP, 9x18 Ultra, 9mmP and .38 Colt Super, all taking .355-inch diameter bullets.

Uzi produces this special 9mmP load for use in carbines and submachine guns, with a warning on the box not to use the load in pistols. Such warnings should be heeded!

Winchester headstamps their cases as 9mm Luger, no doubt because Parabellum would take up more space.

bullet of .451-inch diameter, giving the larger bullet about 1.62 times the frontal area: an advantage not to be dismissed lightly, particularly in the instance where no further expansion is apt to occur upon impact.

At one time, Colt produced the Government Model in 9mmP, rollmarking it as the 9mm Luger on the left side of the slide and, conceivably, they might put it back into production again. I have one of the 9mm Colts and it is a truly superb shooter, reliable and accurate as anyone might wish. It is, perhaps, a purely personal failing but I have never been able to nurture a really hot infatuation for the 9mmP cartridge.

As noted in the text, current labeling of the .38 Super varies between that designation and .38 Automatic +P.

In my opinion, the best .38 Super ammo ever loaded came from the original Shelbyville, Indiana, Super Vel plant.

The classic .38 Super load carries the round-nosed FMJ bullet of 130 grains; it won't expand, but it feeds great!

.38 COLT SUPER

This is a beefed-up version of the earlier .38 ACP cartridge and it was introduced back in the Twenties as a chambering for the Government Model Colt. Like the 9mmP, it's specified by SAAMI for pressures up to 35,700 CUP and it takes the same .355-inch bullet diameter. Current trends among ammo makers are to term it the .38 ACP +P, rather than .38 Super.

Contemporary factory loads in .38 Super tend to be a bit disappointing in performance. Firing both cartridges from five-inch barrels, the warmer 9mmP loads can give the .38 Super a tough run for its money. Reloaders who know what they're about can coax better performance from the .38 Super and it has become quite popular with competitive shooters in those events where the given gun and load must develop a minimum velocity for the bullet weight, known as major power.

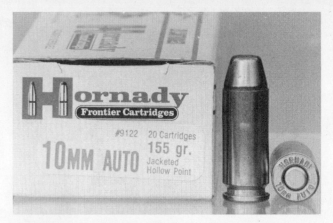

Hornady offers 10mm (.400-inch) bullets in various designs and weights and their Frontier Cartridge division loads them into top-performing ammunition.

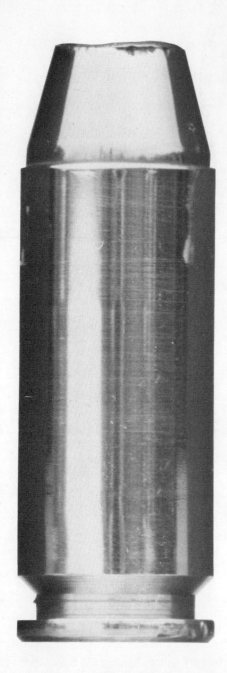

The 10mm Auto cartridge originally was developed for use in the Bren Ten pistol and seems to have survived the discontinuation of the gun. At present, bullets and loaded ammunition are produced by several makers.

10mm AUTO/BREN TEN

Ten millimeters is, of course, one centimeter, equivalent to .3937-inch, but a jacketed bullet the right size for use in the 10mm Auto cartridge is .400-inch in diameter; .401-inch for cast bullets after being sized and lubricated and that is exactly equal to 10.2mm. Calling a new cartridge the 1 cm Auto must have been viewed as lacking in sales appeal, hence the final choice of name which, as so often happens, is no more than an approximation of Real World bullet diameter.

Despite the fact that bullets of .410-inch have been around since the dawn of the .41 magnum, early in 1964, the developers of the 10mm insisted upon the .400-inch size. How much difference does that represent? A typical three-by-five-inch file card measures about .008-inch in thickness — I just went out into the shop and put a micrometer to one — so it's only a trifle more than the thickness of a file card.

The two sizes are close enough that the respective cross-sectional areas are .125- and .132-square inch.

Be all that as it may, for reasons none too readily scrutable, the formulators of the 10mm opted for the .400-inch approach, actually 10.16002mm and not all that nicely rounded a number. It couldn't've been dubbed the caliber .40, but metric is considered ultra-in, these latter days when it comes to cartridge designations.

Three auto pistols in 10mm Auto: From left, the L.A.R. Grizzly, original Bren Ten and Colt Delta Elite. In addition, Springfield Armory offers their Omega auto and T/C now has 10mm barrels for the Contender.

Petty quibbling aside, the 10mm Auto is a pleasantly impressive cartridge, viewed in the company of its peers. In typical factory loadings, it shoves a 200-grain bullet out of a five-inch barrel at about 1150 fps, good for an attention-getting 587 fpe.

The Bren Ten pistol, for which the 10mm Auto was engineered, was a remarkably engaging handgun and many of us regard it as a damned shame it did not get off the ground. It had double-action for the first shot and a staggered-column magazine holding ten of the capable cartridges.

Contemporarily, Colt offers their Delta Elite in 10mm, Springfield Armory has their Omega, L.A.R. chambers their Grizzly for it, Thompson/Center has Contender barrels for it and I've heard American Derringer also chambers for it. Other makers are reported to be examining it attentively and I'd not be surprised if further offerings are in the offing.

.41 ACTION EXPRESS

This rather interesting cartridge concept was dreamed up by Evan Whildin, vice president of Action Arms. The case has what is termed a rebated head: smaller in diameter than the rest of the case. The head dimensions are identical to those of the 9mmP, but the case accepts bullets of .410-inch diameter. Case length is 22mm, compared to the nominal 19.15mm of the 9mmP case and the designation on the ammo box end flaps is .41x22mm making it — to the best of my knowledge — one of the few if not the only cartridge split-nomenclated in both inches and metric.

The obvious advantage of the .41 AE is that it offers a simple conversion, by means of a barrel and magazine change in guns originally chambered for the 9mmP. Ballistics of the .41 AE are considerably better than those of the 9mmP, operating within comparable levels of peak pressures. The .41 AE has a tough, durable case head con-

The 9mm Action Express at left started backing out of the Uzi carbine chamber, ironing out the neck. Other two were fired in a converted Colt .38 Super pistol.

From left, .41 Express, 9mm Action Express, .38 Super and .38-45 Clerke; latter three work on bullets of .355-inch (9mm) diameter; .41 AE takes .410-inch.

The 9mm Action Express was a direct spinoff of the .41 Action Express, necked back down to .355-inch bullet diameter. Hotter than .38 Super, it's still a wildcat.

The .41 Action Express, on the other hand, is in full factory production at Israel Military Industries and is available in the U.S. by way of Action Arms.

Bar-Sto Precision can furnish barrels in 9mm Action Express for installation in 9mmP or .38 Super Colt pistols, perhaps for other suitable autoloading pistols, as well. In addition, Bar-Sto has .41 AE barrels.

struction and it runs fairly well neck and neck with the 10mm Auto, offering the owner of an existing 9mmP or .38 Super Colt the option of an upgrade at about the cost of the new barrel, rather than that of the complete pistol.

As for magazines, the .41 AE feeds quite nicely out of *some* .45 ACP magazines and, perhaps best of all, from Colt magazines for the 10mm Auto Delta Elite.

Colt's magazine for the 10mm Auto also functions to perfection with .41 or 9mm Action Express cartridges.

9mm ACTION EXPRESS

Not content with inventing the .41 AE, Evan Whildin put his thinking cap back on and conjured up the 9mm AE which is, in my opinion, a real wowser of a handgun cartridge. It is, quite simply, the basic .41 AE case, necked back down to accept a .355-inch diameter bullet. Case forming is an easy cinch: All you do is lube a .41 AE case lightly and pass it up into the full-length resizing die for the 9mm AE. Die sets are available from the RCBS Custom Shop, attention of Bill Keyes.

I'm not certain of the exact status of the 9mm AE at date of writing. Factory ammo for the .41x22mm or .41 AE is abundantly available, but I've seen no factory loads for the 9mm AE, to date. I hope it hangs in there and carves a niche for itself because it can deliver performance no one is

Headstamp of the .451 Detonics magnum case, produced for them by Winchester and now no longer available.

apt to wring from the .38 Super, let alone from the 9mmP.

Bar-Sto Precision can supply barrels in 9mm AE for the Colt autos in 9mmP or .38 Super, perhaps for other 9mmP auto pistols, as well. Sanctioned load data remains in damned tight supply, so far. I've obtained some remarkable results; so remarkable, in fact, I'm highly reluctant to confide them to others.

.451 DETONICS MAGNUM

As noted earlier, the .45 Winchester magnum case was produced with a head construction that was thicker and stronger than that of the .45 ACP, in all the important places. As a result, the portion of the case head hanging unsupported over the feed ramp could cope with peak pressures well into the low or middle 30,000 CUP brackets and, in so doing, produce substantially more interesting and gratifying ballistics.

Detonics took note of that and had a quarter-million cases made up by Winchester, at a case length of .945-.947-inch, with ostensibly the same head construction as that of the Win. Mag. with its nominal length of 1.198

Nominal case length of the .45 ACP, left, is .898-inch. The .451 Detonics magnum, center, has a .945-inch case and the .45 Winchester magnum, right, has a case length of 1.198 inches. All use .451-inch bullets.

inches. Nominal length of the .45 ACP case is .898-inch, so loads for the .451 Detonics magnum could not be used in guns chambered for the .45 ACP. The headstamps on the cases read: 451 DET over MAGNUM and the lettering was separated by a pair of triangles, points uppermost. The .451 D-mag cases were produced in the early Eighties, long before anyone at Colt came up with the Delta Elite, so the symbolism can be regarded as purely fortuitous and coincidental.

I'm not at all certain anyone ever came up with load data that took the .451 D-mag to the outer limits of its interesting potential. I did about as much work on it as time permitted and got the 178-grain Hensley & Gibbs No. 938 conical-point cast bullet up to 1603/1016 out of the six-inch barrel in my Detonics *Scoremaster*, but the pressure indications were such that I'd not care to give details on the load for use by others.

The .451 D-mag cases are costly little rascals, going for about thirty-seven cents apiece at last report, and I have the word the original quarter-million is fairly well exhausted. Whether there will be a restocking is an excellent question. Meanwhile, .451 D-mag brass can be produced by putting .45 Win. mag. brass through a properly adjusted case trimmer and the cost per case currently runs somewhat lower.

The .38-45 Clerke cartridge was invented by John A. "Bo" Clerke as a subcaliber target load for .45 pistols.

.38-45 CLERKE

This interesting wildcat cartridge for use in the Government Model Colt was worked up several years ago by John A. "Bo" Clerke, whose last name is pronounced Clark. It is, quite simply, the .45 ACP case, necked down to accept bullets of 9mm (.355-inch) diameter.

Clerke's original intention was to work up a smallbore cartridge that could be used in .45 ACP pistols for practice

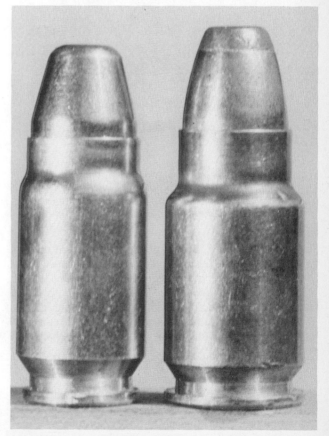

Left, a .45 Auto Rim case, put through .38-45 forming dies. It's an interesting looking round, but no gun for it exists. Above at left, the 9mm AE with a .38-45 Clerke.

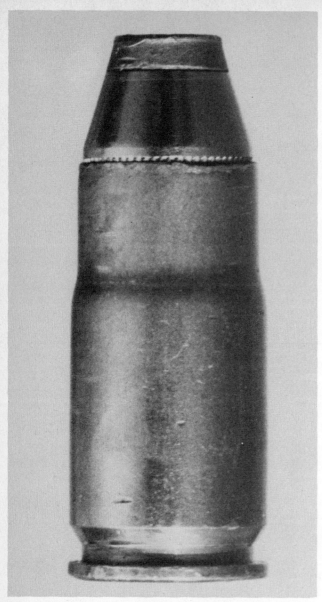

The .41 Avenger was a wildcat developed by J.D. Jones of SSK Industries as a conversion for .45 ACP pistols. It was made by necking the .45 ACP or .451 D-mag case to take a .410-inch diameter bullet; now discontinued.

years, any number of people have knocked out barrels and loading dies for use with the cartridge. The dimensional vagaries between this one and that one over there fairly well boggle one's belief.

I have two barrels in .38-45 Clerke, both ostensibly for use in Government Model Colt autos and the headspacing dimensions, from case head to a reference point on the shoulder of the case, vary by a full .020-inch; by no manner of means a trifling discrepancy. I also have a third one, a ten-inch bull barrel, scoped, for the Thompson/Center Contender single-shot pistol, in .38-45 Clerke, believed to be about fifty percent of the world's supply of such things. Old friend Warren Center made it up, at my wistful request, and went on to knock out a second for his own trove of unlikely Contender barrels.

You may have gotten the — entirely correct — impression that I've had problems with the .38-45 Clerke cartridge, down to the present. The primal bugaboo has been that, being formed from the parent .45 ACP case, it can be assumed that it retains the 19,900 CUP pressure limitation and, if one stays within that pressure level, it becomes tryingly difficult to concoct a load that will make the action function and put the hole in the target paper reasonably close to the point of aim. The next entry in the listing represents a fairly close approach to a shortcut around that particular dilemma.

Please take a thoughtful look at this rather gruesome example of why one should not put up overly warm loads in the standard .45 ACP case. The area of missing brass is an exact duplication of the portion of the case head that hangs unsupported over the feed ramp.

and target work. By means of a simple substitution of barrels, the basic .45 could be converted to take the wildcat cartridge, which fed quite nicely out of the standard .45 ACP magazines. He tended to wax rather rueful over the fact that fellow handgunners showed an alarming inclination to regard his brainchild as a vehicle for intrepid hotrodding, rather than the inoffensive target round he had in mind, initially.

Down the past several years, since some point in 1967, I've wrestled grimly with the challenge of getting the .38-45 Clerke cartridge to perform somewhere close to the levels I hopefully had in mind. I banged head-on into several factors that didn't make it a bit simpler.

First of all, the .38-45 Clerke is a wildcat and that means it is a chambering and cartridge that has never been standardized, nor marketed as a factory loading. Down the

.38-45 HARD HEAD

That was my private term for a .38-45 Clerke load, made up on a case originally headstamped .451 D-mag. With permissible pressures elevated to some point up in the 30,000+ CUP levels, it seemed likely the cartridge might be able to work its way out of the limitations that shackled it so painfully and, for at least once, it worked out as hopefully planned. After some decades of strife and travail, I finally was able to coax performance out the .38-45 Clerke cartridge that were fairly close to what I had in mind, all along.

.41 AVENGER

This was a wildcat dreamed up by old friend J. D. Jones. It was the .45 ACP case, necked down to take bullets of .410-inch diameter. By the time he came up with the concept, the .451 D-mag was on the scene and he dimensioned the chamber and dies so that cases could be made from .451 D-mag brass, if desired, with no need to trim off the excess case length.

The .41 Avenger seemed like a pretty good idea, but it never exactly took the gun world by storm and savaged it by its collective throats. As I get the word, J. D. Jones no longer traffics in stuff for the .41 Avenger and, speaking personally, I tend to regard that as sort of a pity.

A luxurious convenience when you need to do a lot of case trimming, Forster makes this power trimmer kit for installation in a drill press. Here, a .451 D-mag case is being trimmed back to create a .45 Super case.

.45 SUPER

This was a sort of logical spinoff from the .38-45 Hard Head idea. If the .451 D-mag case could be used to remove the hampering limitations from the .38-45 Clerke, why couldn't the same approach be applied to the painfully handicapped .45 ACP cartridge?

For years and years, we've been told the .45 ACP cartridge headspaces with the case mouth on a ledge up at the front of the chamber. The .45 ACP has a nominal case length of .898-inch and you can mike your way through a bushel of empty cases without ever encountering a single one that is quite that lengthy. Typical case lengths will run from .892- to perhaps as much as .896-inch, but .898-inch cases will be encountered but rarely, if ever.

The cold, flat truth of the matter appears to be that the .45 ACP cartridge is supported in its chamber by the extractor, holding it firm to take the slam of the inertial firing pin for light-off.

In the initial exploration of the concept, I had four auto pistols on hand, chambered for the .45 ACP, as well as a 1955 Model S&W and a ten-inch barrel for the T/C Contender in .45 ACP. By means of a bit of judicious trial and error, I determined that all four of the autos would lock up quite nicely on .451 D-mag cases that had been trimmed back to a length of .905-inch.

A wooden block goes under the drill press bed to hold a 3/8-16 bolt to secure the Forster collet holder in place. It takes some patient fiddling to get the length just right!

The S&W revolver needed a trim-length of .903-inch and the T/CC demanded a case length of no more than .901-inch.

After initial trimming, I found that the cases tended to shorten slightly upon subsequent reloading. Other gratifying discoveries included the fact that some of the guns could get down to dotting in groups that spanned just over .75-inch in center-spread when the cartridges actually did headspace on the case mouth.

Moreover, it became possible to obtain some highly gratifying ballistics, using cartridge cases not hobbled to 19,900 CUP pressure ceilings.

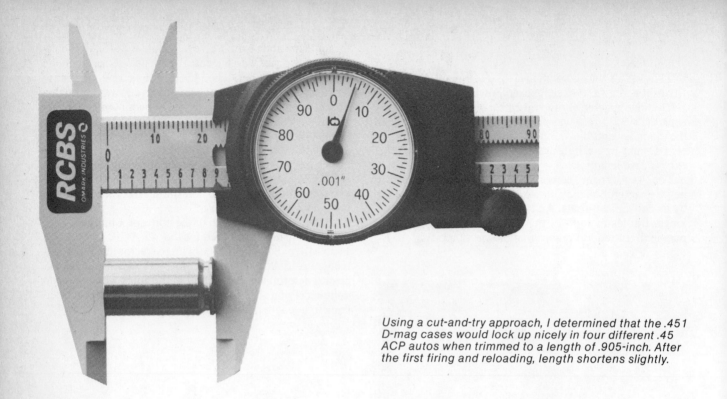

Using a cut-and-try approach, I determined that the .451 D-mag cases would lock up nicely in four different .45 ACP autos when trimmed to a length of .905-inch. After the first firing and reloading, length shortens slightly.

The case at right has had .040-inch trimmed off its neck in the process of being converted from the original .451 D-mag to the experimental .45 Super, intended to avoid disasters such as the blown head on page 72.

.45-70 GOVERNMENT

The latter portion of the nineteenth century saw the introduction of a great many rifle cartridges and the .45-70 is one of the few still being manufactured. Its designation indicates the original loading was 70.0 grains of black powder behind a .458-inch diameter bullet. The .45-70 was adopted as the service rifle cartridge in 1873, for use in the Springfield single-shot rifle widely known as the trapdoor. It remained in service until about 1898, when the .30-40 Krag was adopted.

SAAMI's maximum working pressure for the .45-70 is 28,000 CUP and factory loads stay at or below that level. Several manuals and handbooks carry two listings for the .45-70; one for trapdoors and a second set ranging up to 35,000 CUP or so, for use in stronger rifles such as the Browning, Ruger or bolt-action Model 98 Mauser.

While a few makers have produced revolvers in .45-70, predominant use of the cartridge in handguns has been in the single-shots, such as the Thompson/Center Contender or the MOA pistol. J. D. Jones' SSK Industries was among the first to offer custom .45-70 barrels for the Contender and T/C finally listed it as one of their factory chamberings for their Super-16 barrel, introduced in the No. 16 catalog for 1989.

For use in handguns, it is prudent not to reload beyond the listing of data that does not exceed the 28,000 CUP level.

.460 JURRAS

Lee Jurras produced a limited number of custom single-shot pistols on the T/C Contender action, calling his version The Howdah. There were five cartridges, all based upon the .500 Nitro Express case made by Brass Extrusion Laboratories Limited, termed the .375, .416, .460, .475 and .500 Jurras. The .460 Jurras worked with bullets of .458-inch diameter and topped out with a load that got the 500-grain Hornady bullet up to about 1195/1586. Setting off such a load in a handgun tends to rank among the more memorable experiences.

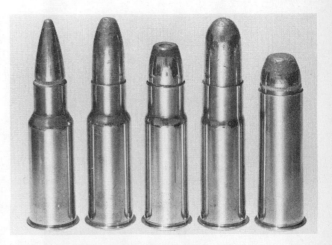

Left, a .45-70 Government load is to the left of the .460 Jurras, the latter having been formed from a .500 Nitro Express case made by Brass Extrusion Labs, Limited. At right, from left, the .375, .416, .460, .475 and .500 Jurras wildcat cartridges, made for use in the Jurras Howdah conversion of a T/C Contender.

CHAPTER 5

MAKING STOCKS FOR THE GOVERNMENT MODEL COLT

A Comparatively Simple Project That Lets You Make Use Of Any Material You Can Whittle!

My brother Ralph, who launched me into .45 stockmaking.

MANY PEOPLE refer to the handle slabs on a pistol as "grips" on the assumption a stock is something you put to your shoulder. That is not necessarily true. In the example of the pistol under discussion, the pair of wooden handle scales are termed a *stock set* by the factory that produces it/them. If the term is good enough for Colt, it's good enough for me.

For a considerable while, I was privileged to number the late Steve Herrett among my collection of friends. Steve was founder and president of Herrett's Stocks and, if you referred to such things as "grips" in his presence, his usually genial features would assume a truly pained expression and he would emit a throaty snarl: "I carry my clothes in a damned grip!"

My brother, Ralph, is a considerably more gifted and accomplished artisan than I'm ever apt to become. At some point back in the latter Fifties or early Sixties, he tried his hand at production of homemade stocks for the Colt .45 auto pistol and presented me with a set I used with much appreciation for a lot of years after that. For good measure, he gave me a spare pair of templates he'd made up from .050-inch stainless steel sheet stock to use in tracing the basic pattern onto blanks.

Some samples to give you an idea of the effects obtainable through choice of woods. This is quilted maple and ripples in the light when moved.

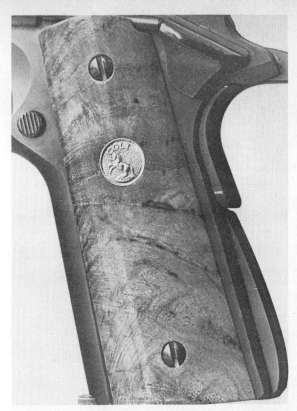

A set in nicely burled teak, fitted out with a Colt gold colored medallion on each side. Medallions are on a line between screws, one inch below the top screw.

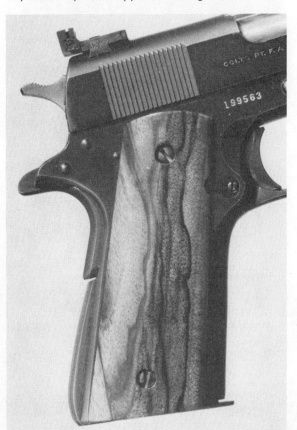

From a scrap piece of Bastogne walnut, this set is quite handsome, with colors ranging from a Naples yellow through burnt sienna: wish I had a cord of it!

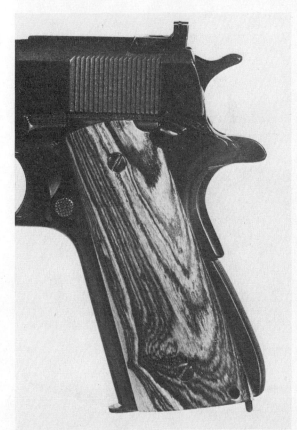

Then we have bocote, pronounced bow-coty, with its striking grain pattern, sharply contrasting from yellow ochre through deep burnt umber in coloration.

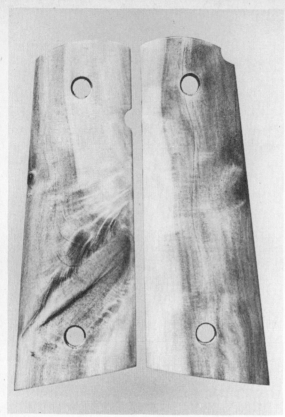

Australian sandalwood is a total delight. It has a fragrant smell when worked, spectacular color and grain and ripples in the light like moire silk.

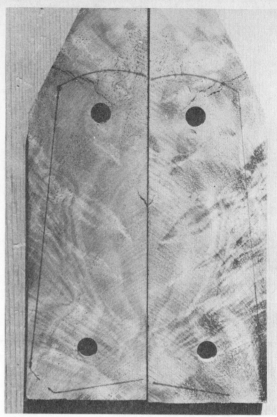

A set shaping up in genuine GOK wood. That stands for Gosh Only Knows, but it looks promising. The holes have been drilled and counterbored, so far.

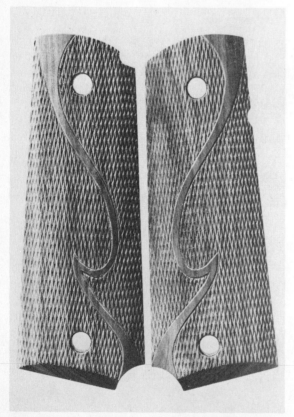

If you want to get fancy: A professional gunsmith checkered this set I made from pau ferro wood and ended up with stocks that would grace any gun.

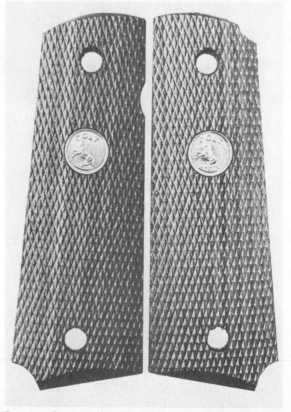

By way of comparison, here is a set of factory stocks from contemporary production. Note the alignment of medallions, from side to side.

Ralph's stocks were a trifle thicker than the usual .270-inch of the standard factory set. Although most of my personal dimensions are about average, I'm blessed with large hands, long fingers and unusually long thumbs — suggesting I was custom-designed for firing handguns or, perhaps, for hitch-hiking. I've long been grateful for such a happy state of affairs. The slightly fatter stocks felt just great on my pet .45 of the era, which I still have.

The singular virtue of the Government Model Colt as a recipient of homemade stocks is the delightful simplicity of their production. No complex inletting is required. Fairly common shop tools account for most of the needfuls. You'll want a table saw; a drill press; a belt sander; an accurate set of calipers, preferably dial-type; a Dremel Moto-Tool; a modicum of woodworking experience; and it will be quite helpful if you own or have access to a metal lathe.

At a point in the early Eighties, I decided to try my own hand at making M1911 stocks, motivated by assorted considerations. For one thing, at the time, there was a local firm that did custom woodworking in a really bewildering variety of fancy exotic woods. If they wound up with a piece of scrap not apt to be of further use, they tossed it on their remnant table for sale to any passing browser with the asking price.

I stopped in to check their scrap heap with fair frequency and made the acquaintance with a lot of fancy woods I'd never encountered before: putumuju, rosadillo, sandalwood, purpleheart, padouk, canarywood and a teeming host of others. There are over two hundred varieties of wood on the market, but most are encountered rarely.

You do not need all that large a piece of wood to make a pair of .45 stocks. If possible, I try to cut both sides from the same strip, as it gives a better match in color and grain. For that, you'll need a piece about nine inches long, 1.64 inches wide or so and at least .250-inch in thickness, preferably somewhat thicker, anywhere up to .4-inch or a bit more. If necessary, you can work with a pair of 4.5-inch pieces, with other dimensions about as mentioned.

There is one really crucial dimension involved in making a pair of .45 stocks and I'll give you that right now: 3.074 inches. That is the distance between centers of the holes you drill for the two stock screws that hold the stock slab to the stock screw bushings. If you get them spaced 3.073 inches or 3.075 inches between centers, you are not going to be all that happy with the way the stocks go on and come off, although it can be done if you employ a spot of force. I suppose you could go half a thousandth either way and live with it, but it's ever so much nicer if you can

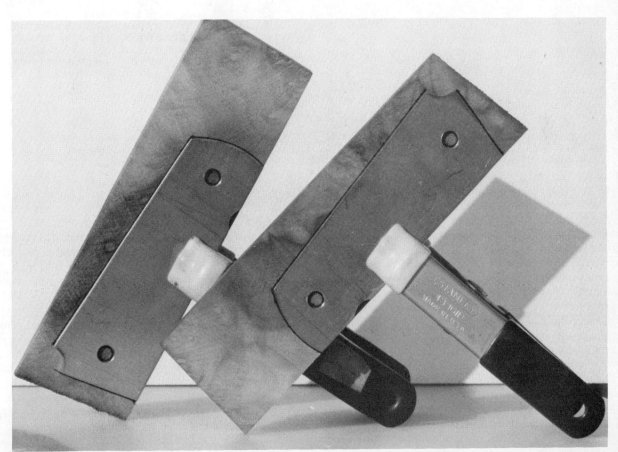

Having cut the wood to suitable size for stock blanks, the stainless steel templates are positioned and held in place with a pair of spring clamps. Then the outlines are traced with a fine-point pen, including screw holes.

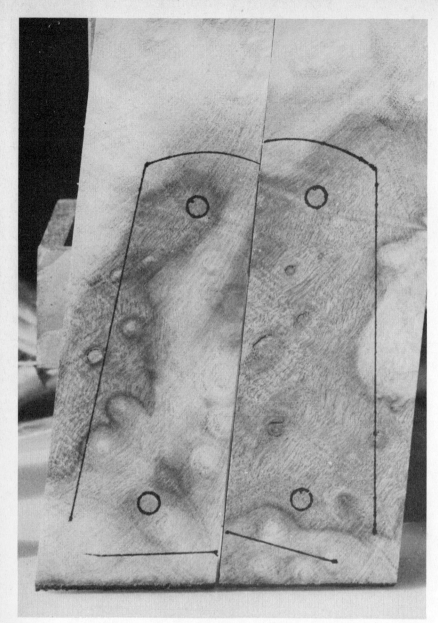

This could be some more GOK wood, but I think it's some kind of walnut; a wood that wears a million faces, but nearly all of them are nothing but great. The outlines have been traced and it remains to center a punch-mark in one screw hole, then come in with the trammel and center the second mark in the other hole at the precise 3.074 inches of separation. After that, you drill the holes with the brad-pointed letter B bit, go in from the top with the blue counterbore, in from the underside with the green one and go on from there: Simpler than it sounds!

accomplish what I tend to think of as a "plock-fit." By that, I mean you drop the drilled blank onto the bushings and it just sort of drifts down and goes *plock* against the side of the receiver by its own weight, but doesn't woggle back and forth much, if at all.

You can verify the center-spacing on any given pistol by measuring the distance between stock screw bushings, outside-to-outside, then going on to subtract the diameter of one bushing. Conceivably, it could vary, though I've never encountered any that did.

The stock screw bushing — part number 50173 — turns into the sides of the receiver with a .236-60NS thread and is threaded internally to accept the stock screw, which has a .150-50NS thread. Brownells, Incorporated, (210 South Mill, Montezuma, IA 50171) can supply taps in either thread size and they can prove handy enough to be worth a lot more than their modest cost now and again.

Once in place, the stock screw bushings have a base flange that is anywhere between .267- and .273-inch in diameter and pretty close to a thickness of .040-inch. The projecting portion that goes up to hold the stock slab in place can be anywhere from about .232- to .236-inch in diameter.

When you drill the two holes at the specified center-spacing, they need to be pretty close to .2380-inch in diameter. The nearest inch-size bit is the 15/64 inch, at .2344 inch: just a pesky trifle too small. Moving over to the letter-size series of bits, the letter B is .238-inch and the letter C is .242-inch. It's been my usual experience that most, if not all, drill bits tend to bore holes that are slightly larger than the nominally rated bit diameter.

Letter-size drill bits are not apt to be stocked by nearby hardware stores, but they are available from specialized suppliers such as the aforementioned Brownells or from B-

Stock screw bushings can be painfully fragile little artifacts and need to be handled with care. A .250-60NS tap can prove super-handy if the threads in the receiver get battered about a bit.

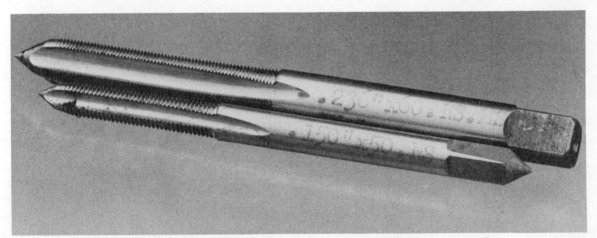

The necessary taps are available from Brownells and the one to match the threads on the stock screws is .150-5NS. You don't need them often but, at times, you need them badly.

Square Company, (Box 11281, Fort Worth, TX 76110-0281).

Over the duration of my stockmaking career, I've used the letter B drill bit for the basic holes at 3.074 inches between centers and it has worked out quite well. I suppose a letter C bit might offer slightly more charitable tolerances, but I have never tried that size.

If you're using an unmodified letter B bit, the preferable procedure is to lay out a pair of prick-punch marks with the trammel, divider, compass or similar instrument; enlarge the punch-marks slightly with an awl, then drill starting guide holes with a number 2 countersink centered on the punch-marks. Switch over to the letter B bit and C-clamp the blank in place, with a piece of scrap wood beneath it.

If you try to hold the workpiece in position with one hand while operating the drill press with the other, the workpiece is quite apt to climb up the drill, about the time the hole is

The drill bit at the right here is a standard letter B size, nominally rated at .238-inch diameter and just right for the holes through the stock blanks. The bit at left has been reground to a brad-point configuration by Ron Perry and it performs much better.

completed, fairly well ruining that particular blank. I can confide that this only happens to the blanks of the most expensive woods, with the most impressive grain pattern and exquisite coloring, in strict compliance to the laws of Murphy.

So what you do is buy a regular letter B drill bit and send it out to have it brad-pointed. I'm sure there are any number of gifted machinists who can do the job, but I only know the name and whereabouts of one such. His name is Ron Perry and he gets his mail at 471 Pittsford-Henrietta Town-line Road, Henrietta, New York 14467. Upon receipt of the customer's standard metal-boring drill bit in just about any reasonable diameter, he can turn it into a magnificent brad-point production and return it for a fee. Mindful of the ongoing inflationary spiral, I suggest you submit an inquiry, accompanied by a self-addressed stamped envelope for a

current price quote. I have some of his brad-pointed bits in several handy diameters and would not part with them for any price, if I couldn't get replacements.

One of the things that makes home production of M1911 stocks such a pleasantly simple project is the fact that the inside surface is flat, with no need to relieve or inlet the wood at any point apart from cutting away a little bit at the top of the left-hand stock to clear the plunger tube. That can be done on a typical table saw, given a bit of patient care.

Getting the holes 3.074 inches apart between centers is not all that simple a matter. Having a metal lathe in the shop — a truly sybaritic luxury, I think — I constructed a small adjustable trammel, its points tooled out of concrete nail stock and sculptured to shape with the cutting wheel of the Dremel Moto-Tool, while the workpiece was rotating

The clearance cut for the plunger tube can be made on a table saw, using scrap wood to make certain you have the dimensions just so. Customarily, this is done before the outer surface of the blank has been shaped on the belt sander, as in this example.

After rounding the outer surface to shape on the belt sander, the rear of the plunger tube clearance cut can be contoured to a more pleasing shape by a .225-inch Dremel burr. I prefer to put the burr in the drill press for this operation, for better control.

in the chuck of the drill press. One point is held in place by a 10-32 set screw, the other is secured in the movable/lockable portion by means of a dab of Stud N' Bearing-grad Loctite.

As a basic tool for measuring and layout, I find it handy about the shop. Once I finally managed to get it set acceptably close to 3.074 inches, I took the sensible precaution of making some punch marks in a small piece of hard white maple scrap and labeled it prominently, storing it in the same drawer with the trammel. As a result, if I've been using the trammel for some other application, it is a simple matter to use the piece of maple to get the points back to the 3.074-inch spacing.

Assuming you've gotten the letter B or C holes properly spaced, there remains the necessity of relieving them, top and bottom, to accommodate the head of the stock screw and the flange of the stock screw bushing. The good news is that, given access to a metal lathe and my faithful Dremel tool — which I tend to refer to as Mister Moto — I was able to cobble a reasonably effective double-ended cutter together. That's good news, because I regard myself as one of the more redundantly credentialed twelve-thumbed machinists the human race has produced.

That is to say, if I can do it, just about anyone should be able to do it, at least equally well. The cutter bit can be worked out of common, cheap, cold-rolled bar stock and

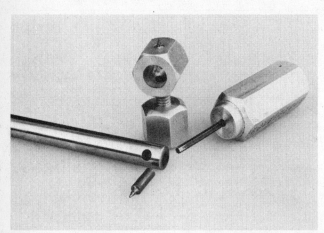

Details of the small homemade trammel: Points are made from hardened nails intended for use in concrete, cut to shape while rotating in the drill press chuck, using the abrasive cutting wheel on the mandrel from Dremel.

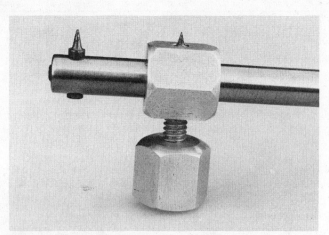

One pin is cemented into the movable collar with Loctite sealant and the other is held in place by a 10-32 hex-head set screw. The locking collar has a ¼-20 thread and the knob and collar are produced from hexagonal aluminum.

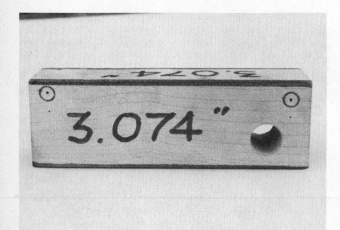

Once the critical dimension was established — no small feat! — punch marks were made on a scrap piece of hard maple and circled, with eye-catching identifications.

If the trammel has been used for some other purpose, as often happens, it can be re-set with the aid of the maple block, back to the original 3.074-inch spacing.

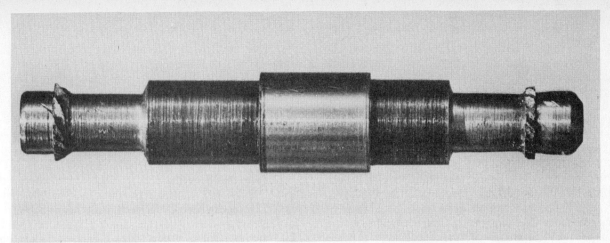

As discussed, the homemade counterbore was turned to the proper dimensions on the lathe, then the teeth were cut freehand, using the absolutely indispensible cutoff wheel in the Dremel Moto-Tool. The left end, here, is color-coded blue and the other end is green for easy identification of each.

Here, the blue end has gone from the top to do the upper counterbore. The pilot stub on the end serves to limit the depth, so as to leave a neat shoulder for the stock screw head to bear against, as noted.

Ron Perry tried his hand at producing a counterbore and did a vastly more workmanlike job of it. This is the "blue end" of his version, with the cutting surfaces exquisitely formed and ground, followed by final heat-treatment for long life and heavy duty. Really lovely, but my crude one works just as well!

can be used without further hardening or heat-treating in the production of a great many sets of stocks. I made mine as a double-ended affair for use in the drill press and I used a couple of felt-marking pens, blue and green, to identify the function of the two ends of the bit.

I've become partial to a simple mnemonic code to identify which end goes up and which end goes down. The blue sky is overhead and the green grass is underfoot. Accordingly, I color-code the end that goes in from the top blue, with the end that comes up from the bottom green. Before you break into coarse guffaws of raucous mirth, give it a try and you're apt to find it works quite well.

The end coded blue that goes in from the top has a stop nub at the lower end that arrests further relieving to provide a solid ledge of wood for the stock screw to bear against. The end that comes in from the bottom cannot be checked in the same manner, because thickness of stock blanks may vary from one to the other. It needs to create a relief cut that is about .273-inch in diameter to a depth of at least .040-inch. If it's a trifle larger or, if it goes a bit deeper, it's no big thing so long as the securing ledge is left at the top of the hole for the outer perimeter of the stock screw to bear against.

The two counterbore heads are turned to the basic dimensions and the teeth are cut by hand, using the little No. 409 cut-off wheels for the Dremel Moto-Tool.

The end that goes into the top of the screw holes — the "blue" end — has a cutter diameter of .275-inch to match the .273-inch diameter of the stock screw head and the projecting stub that arrests further counterboring extends for .203-inch below the cutting edges. Height of the installed stock screw bushing is about .175-inch, giving a respectably solid ledge of wood for the screw head to bear against.

Here and on the facing page are three close-up photos of a screw hole that has been cross-sectioned to give a clearer understanding of the way the two counterbores afford a precise and secure job of anchoring the stock slabs to the receiver. Here, you can see how the lower counterbore provides easy clearance around the flange at the base of the stock screw bushing and the small distance that the upper ledge ends up above the top of the bushing, giving the stock screw a surface to bear against.

Here's a view of the cross-sectioned hole, with the stock screw bushing on one side and the stock screw turned into it to about the final depth. In final finishing excess wood will be removed from top.

This is how the bushing and screw fit in the counterbored hole, with bushing removed from receiver.

The end that goes in from the lower surface — the "green" end — has a cutter diameter of .272-inch to match the .269-inch diameter of the flange at the bottom of the installed bushing. If you make the cutter about .040-inch thick, it will match the thickness of the flange and you need only relieve the opening until the upper surface of the cutter is flush with the surface of the wood. As was noted, you can't use a bottoming stub here, because the stock blanks are apt to vary in thickness.

At the peak of my stockmaking interlude back in the early Eighties, I tried to persuade my old friend, Bob Brownell, to offer a kit of the basic needfuls in the Brownells catalog. He looked into the possibilities and concluded that, at the cost involved, it would not move enough units to justify catalog space. I suspect he may have been entirely correct in his evaluation.

In fact, I do not estimate that much over a few dozen readers of this book are apt to be sufficiently fired with enthusiasm to tackle the business of tooling up for it. Accordingly, I'll offer to supply any reader with a piece of reasonably hard hardwood, with punch-marks 3.074 inches apart, free of charge, on request. You can use that for setting dividers, trammels or whatever and it will get you over one of the more challenging hurdles. Request from the address given on the inside front cover and, if you get no response in a reasonable time, request again. Sometimes, with the best of all possible intentions, I lose track of reader letters that I want to answer. A large part of the problem is that I was born without the soul of a filing clerk.

I will make tracings of the two templates that my brother, Ralph, made up so long ago, including them in the illustrations at exact life-size. You are free to trace them and make your own templates. Durable cardboard will work after a fashion, if you don't have any .050-inch stainless steel sheets handy. Fairly thick transparent plastic will work even better, because it will enable you to move the blank into position to take advantage of the choicest grain pattern of the given blank.

When I'm working with a nine-inch blank that will yield both stocks, my usual procedure is to attach the two templates to the wood, with the front edges of the templates flush with one edge of the blank, allowing about three sixteenth inch of space between the two upper edges for cutting them apart. The templates are held to the wood with a pair of spring clamps and I trace the outlines of the templates onto the wood with a fine-pointed pen, including the outlines of the two screw holes.

Making sure I have the adjustable trammel set for 3.074

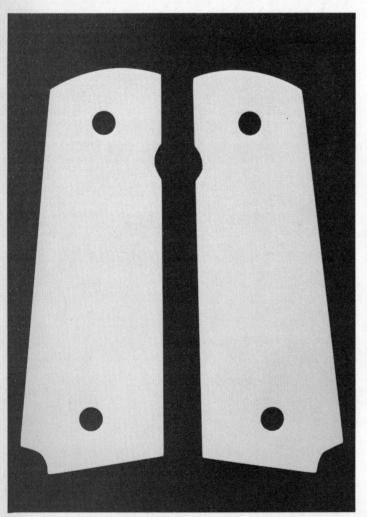

If all goes as planned, illustration at left shows the two templates at exact life-size, so they can be traced and reproduced. If in doubt, measure the hole spacing.

Two handy production jigs, with flanges to fit the grooves in the table saw. The one at left is for the relief cut to clear the plunger tube in the LH blank and the other makes the cuts at the back and bottom.

Blanks are laid out with the front surface flush with the template. Steel pins are located in the jigs to hold the blanks in correct position to trim off excess wood from the bottom, as about to be done here.

Excess wood from the bottom of a LH blank has just been cut away and we've switched to a carbide-tipped saw blade.

Here, the excess wood from the rear surface of a LH blank has been whisked off. Beware of unguarded blade!

inches between centers, I center one point in one of the traced circles, then come down on the other in the center of the second circle, repeating the operation on the other blank.

I install the brad-pointed letter B bit in the drill press and put a piece of scrap wood beneath the blank, bringing the pointed tip of the bit down to locate in one of the punch marks left by the trammel, turning on the motor to drill the hole and repeat the procedure for the other three.

I install the counterbore — blue end down — and place a small piece of scrap bar stock beneath the blank to avoid marring the bed of the drill press. The projection that arrests further counterboring at the correct point also serves as a pilot to make certain the holes are aligned and centered.

I reverse the counterbore and relieve for the flanges of the stock screw bushings. Attending to the holes is one of the first steps, because they are needed as the process continues.

The .225-inch Dremel burr, installed in a drill press, makes it simple to do a neat job of relieving front edge of RH stock to clear magazine release tip. Mark location and move the blank against the side of the rotating burr. Below, a "blind" clearance cut is a further possibility.

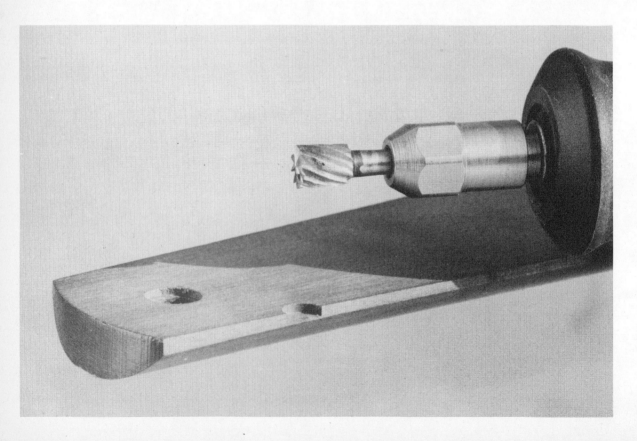

I've made up a small jig that rides on strips of wood that mate to the channels in the bed of the table saw. The holes in the stock go onto steel pins that locate the blanks for cutting the lower edge and rear edge.

The right hand stock needs a clearance cut on the front edge to allow the magazine release to operate. Sometimes, I mark the location and just put a .225-inch rotary burr from the Dremel kit into the chuck of the drill press and come down to a depth of .050-inch or so, checking to make sure the magazine catch will drop the magazine freely. Note that is best done before rounding the outer surface of the stock. I've become rather partial to such "blind" relief cuts. If the tips of the mainspring housing pin portrude from the sides of the frame at the lower rear corner, the same Dremel burr can be used to make shallow relief holes to clear them, as well.

The clearance cut for the plunger tube at the top of the left-hand stock is made on the table saw, using a finished stock to set the miter gauge to the correct angle and some scrap wood to check the depth of the cut, which wants to be about .142-inch. This is another operation best done before rounding the outer surfaces. After rounding, the plunger tube relief cut will show a sharp corner, but the same .225-inch Dremel burr can be used to round it to a graceful and pleasing contour.

If you want the lower edges of the stocks to be dead flush with the frame, they can be put in place on the bushings so a fine line can be scribed on the inner surface against the frame. The miter gauge can be angled to cut them to the precise hairline in a series of patient passes; again, do this before rounding the outside.

You'll be doing a lot of trying and fitting as you go along and will find it handy to have an M1911-type pistol with the stocks removed to serve as a gauge for getting things just so.

Although I usually leave the lower rear corners solid, removing the stocks to disassemble the receiver, this set of bocote stocks has a pair of clearance holes to permit driving the housing pin out with a drift punch.

The housing pin is .155-inch in diameter, so a number 23 drill bit, .154-inch in diameter, can be used to drill down through the receiver into a blank positioned against the screw bushings, first one, then the other.

Here, the assembly has been C-clamped to the bed of the drill press, against a piece of scrap wood and is ready for drilling the clearance hole. Use great care!

If you prefer a more conventional clearance cut, the radius is supposed to be .344-inch, but ⅜-inch is close enough and that can be produced by a ¾-inch router bit. Here, stop strips are clamped to the router plate and the stock is fed — with the greatest of care — against the whirring cutter to remove the right amount.

On standard Colt factory stocks, about a quarter-circle is relieved at both lower rear corners to permit driving out the mainspring housing pin when disassembling the receiver unit. The cut has a radius of about .344 inch, plus or minus .010 inch. That is reasonably close to 11/32 inch and it

Here's a close look at the area around the housing pin. Lower edge of this set has been beveled to 45 degrees.

will not look all that grotesque if you go to three eighths inch. I note that, because a Forstner drill bit can nip out the material quite neatly. This is especially true if you construct a small set of jigs to C-clamp to the drill press bed for positioning both right and left-hand blanks.

My usual, admittedly maverick approach is to omit the lower rear clearance cut entirely. In normal routines, I don't remove the mainspring housings from my pistols all that often and, if I do, I just remove the stocks to get at the securing pin. On a few sets, I've drilled a hole of the proper diameter in the right place so the pin can be driven out without removing the stocks. These are among the things that you, as the maker, can decide for yourself.

In the same manner, standard factory stocks have the lower edge beveled at an angle of forty-five degrees. I've made a few sets with that feature, but my usual approach is to cut the lower edge at ninety degrees.

Design specifications call for the stocks on both sides to be rounded to a radius of 1.031 inches. I've sometimes thought it would be nice to get a belt-sander and rig a fixture into which the stock blank could be secured to sand the outer surface into perfect specification contour, all in one easy pass.

For the present, I have made up a stock blank holder, with a pair of steel pins set into the upper edge at a spacing of — you guessed it — 3.074 inches between centers. With the workpiece blanked out to all the critical dimensions, I slap it into the pins and get ready for the final contouring.

I have a Black & Decker belt-sander that I clamp, inverted, into a B&D Bench-Mate that has been secured to the top of a small work bench. It takes a 3x24-inch sanding belt and I usually use one of 80-grit for the initial shaping.

Any number of hardwoods produce sawdust and sanding dust that are more or less toxic and harmful to the human system. Some, in fact, can puff you up or break you out at least as effectively as poison oak, sumac or ivy. Make it a routine practice to wear a breathing mask. Position a fan to blow sanding dust away from you. Wash your hands and arms carefully with strong soap and hot water as soon as you finish working on the project at hand.

Some woods are quite innocuous in that respect, but the nasty ones include the various varieties of rosewood, padouk, zebrawood, cocobolo, pau ferro and purpleheart; quite possibly others, as well.

Until or unless you engineer a setup that produces an outer contour with a precise radius of 1.031 inches all in one easy pass, the rounding off has to be done by feel and eyeball. That is not as formidable as it might sound. Just take it down by slow, easy stages, leaving about .062-inch of right-angled edge, front and back; plus or minus .010-inch.

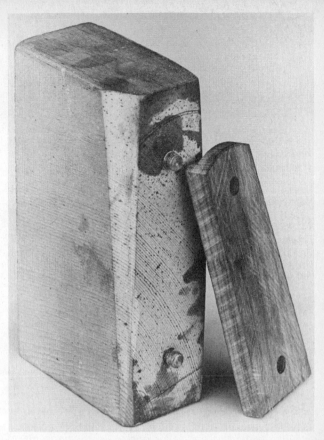

The block for holding the blanks while rounding them on the belt sander was informally fashioned from a piece of shop scrap, with the two steel holding pins spaced at the requisite 3.074 inches between centers. Below, the sander has been inverted and fastened in the Black & Decker Bench-Mate for rounding blanks as shown.

(Above) Here, one medallion has been press-fitted into the RH stock of a set in kingwood and a second one lies near it, along with the primitive looking but surprisingly effective homemade bit for making the relief openings.
(Below) This is a closer look at the business end of the bit, with its guiding pilot and a brad-pointed No. 12 drill bit.

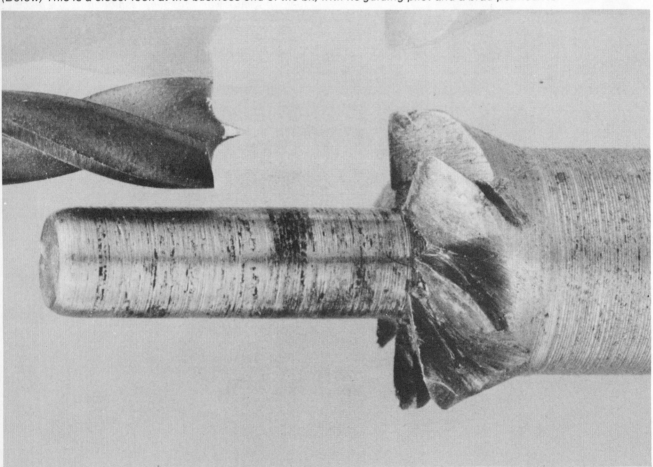

Another view of the medallion bit and medallion. When friend Tom Ferguson learned I'd acquired capability of installing such things, nothing would do but I had to put a set in his prized genuine ivory stocks. I'll confess I sweated ice cubes at the prospect of having to return a collection of fragments, but it worked fine.!

This is a marking gauge, with steel pins to match stock holes and a point to locate the point to drill for the medallion, which must be on a direct line between the holes, with its center 1" below center of top hole.

Stock sets can be checkered, if you regard that as desirable. Personally, I prefer smooth stocks and do not checker my output. My usual finish is spray can Varathane and I prefer the glossy over the satin. I've made a pair of small stands from scrap wood to hold the stocks while they're being sprayed and I put a No. 6x½ sheet metal screw in each of the holes to keep the finish from building up at that point. The holding blocks have matching holes to accept the projecting ends of the sheet metal screws.

It's much better to apply several light, uniform coats, allowing the finish to dry for several hours between coats, rather than trying to do it all with one pass. Excess finish will bead up and look messy.

I have a small supply of the gold-colored Colt medallions and sometimes install them in a set that's destined to go on a Colt pistol. The medallion shank is about .197-inch in diameter and the medallion diameter is .515-inch, with a rim thickness of .055-inch.

The medallion goes on a center-line between the two screw holes, one inch on center below the center of the upper screw hole. I've made a small marking jig, with steel pins that go into the two screw holes, with a sharpened steel pin in the right place to mark the hole for drilling. I use a No. 12 drill bit, .189-inch diameter, also brad-pointed by Perry.

The cutter to open the recess for the medallion is another

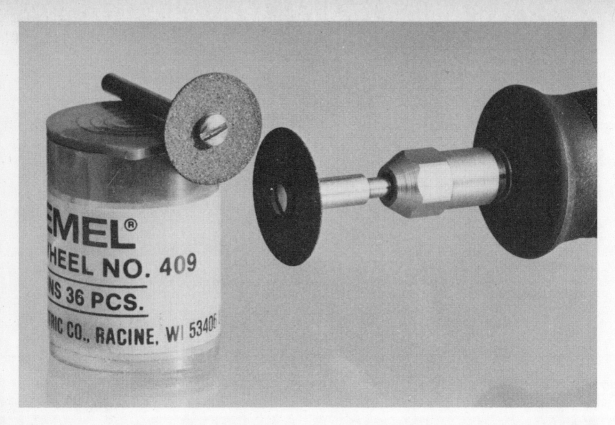

Above, the one Dremel accessory I use much more than all the rest together is their No. 409 cutoff wheel and I have the cordless Dremel Freewheeler that goes anywhere.

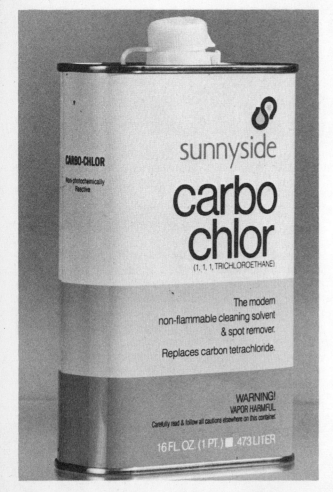

homemade affair, .502-inch in diameter and a steel pilot pin, .188-inch in diameter, was installed in the center after the teeth of the cutter were formed.

With the medallion holes drilled and relieved, the medallion is lightly started, rotated to the correct alignment, then pressed into place with the end of a short piece of seven sixteenths-inch hardwood dowel in the chuck of the drill press. At the factory, the medallions are expanded at the lower end of the shaft, riveting them in place. With the press-fit I use, I've yet to have one come loose or fall out. Note that medallions are installed after the stocks have been given their coats of finish.

The same holding block used in rounding the outer surfaces on the belt sander can be used in the bench vise for final sanding, going through progressively finer grits. It might serve equally well if you decide to try your hand at checkering.

The friendly firm of custom woodworkers closed down their shop a long time ago, but I still have a considerable quantity of exotic woods on hand and doubt if I'll ever have

Left, with spray can Varathane finish applied and dry, a paper towel with a bit of Carbo Chlor can be used as a buff to create what I call a solvent polish. People have looked at stocks thus finished and asked, "Is that plastic?" I choose to regard that as a compliment, though I wince.

Black & Decker sander, powered by a ⅜" electric drill, makes a handy rig for small shaping chores.

to fall back on boxelder and similar humble materials. Among the varieties I've tried with a high degree of satisfaction are Osage orange, Hawaiian koa, pau ferro, bocote, kingwood, padouk, quilted maple, birdseye maple, mesquite, Australian sandalwood, rosewood, teak, persimmon, cherry and walnut.

I got into making .45 stocks because I thought it would be fun and it certainly was. At one time, I hoped it might develop into some manner of cottage industry, pulling in a bit of added income. In that respect, it was rather a fizzle. There are any number of highly automated makers who can turn out stock sets that retail down in the $10-20 brackets. As a result, it's not easy to move sets for much higher figures. It is remarkably easy to channel twenty bucks worth of time and effort into a single set, with nothing left for profit.

You can, however, produce sets for your own use to your own personal specifications and tastes. Or you can turn out occasional sets to bestow upon special friends. They seem to appreciate such things sufficiently to offset all the expense, fuss and bother, with some to spare.

Lower edge can be scribed against receiver with a sharp knife. After that, excess wood can be ground off to provide an exquisitely precise wood-to-metal fit.

CHAPTER 6

THE CONTENDER IN .45-70 GOVERNMENT

Joe Wright,
President Of The Thompson/Center Association,
Recounts His Experiences

Joe Wright, president of the Thompson Contender Association (Box 792, Northboro, Massachusetts 01532), is tall, bulky and built for shooting .45-70 Contenders!

THE CONTENDER from Thompson/Center Arms of Rochester, New Hampshire, has established the reputation of being a flexible and fun type shooting system. Those of us who are members of the Thompson/Center Association tend to refer to the Contender as the ultimate handgun.

When polling members for information regarding their favorite chamberings for both the Contender and Thompson/Center TCR rifle, the .45-70 was one of the top two calibers mentioned. With T/C's decision to offer both the Contender and TCR in a variety of configurations chambered for the .45-70, the firm satisfied the pent-up desires of many T/C fans.

The .45-70 is an enigma, but an interesting one. Adopted by the U.S. military in 1873 for use in the single-shot "trapdoor" Springfield rifle, it was replaced after nineteen years of service by the .30-40 Krag cartridge. The latter was the country's first venture into a smokeless powder cartridge for military rifles and its career was even shorter than that of the .45-70. The .30-40 Krag was replaced by the .30/06 Springfield cartridge; that one survived two global wars and a lot of decades, being by no means defunct to the present.

With all of the foregoing in mind, it may seem more than slightly mystifying that the .45-70, after roughly 117 years, retains a considerable degree of popularity. Various explanations can be offered for that.

Although the .30-40 Krag replaced the .45-70 in 1892

The Thompson/Center Contender shown here has a 16½-inch .45-70 barrel by SSK Industries, with a 3x T/C Recoil Proof scope in SSK's T'SOB mounting system. It has nine recoil control ports on each side of the muzzle, helping to tone down the lusty backlash of the cartridge, illustrated here in profile and headstamp. With a barrel of that length, you have the option of using a pistol grip or putting the Contender carbine stock in place to fire it from the shoulder.Thus far, this one — owned by Grennell — only has been used as a pistol.

for active service, many state militia units continued to train with the .45-70 well into the early Twentieth Century. In fact, some states continued to use the trapdoors as their standard drill weapon up into the Thirties.

In my opinion, the primary reason for the .45-70's ongoing survival lies in the innate capabilities of the cartridge. It is accurate within its effective range. It is capable of throwing a heavy slug of generous diameter, and it is remarkably versatile and flexible in that it can be down-loaded to run the gamut from informal plinking up through serious hunting or competitive shooting. More, when fired within its effective range, with careful bullet placement, it is capable of taking just about any game animal on the face of the earth.

Stacked against the many cartridges currently offered as factory loads, there are few that can match the specialized credentials of the .45-70 Government. That offers an insight as to why Federal, Remington and Winchester continue to market it as factory loads.

As with several other cartridges, such as the .44 Special and .45 Colt, factory loads are held to fairly moderate peak pressures out of deference to all the fragile relics capable of setting the cartridges off. Ostensibly, factory .45-70 loads won't harm a Springfield trapdoor in good condition. In point of practical usage, the diet of the old trapdoors should be restricted to black powder loads or, better yet, the rifle or carbine should be hung on the wall and never fired at all.

Ancient .45-70 cartridge cases should be viewed with the same skeptical regard. They needed a lot of case capacity — 70.0 grains of Fg black was about a capacity load — so they had the old *balloon-head* case construction that was much weaker than contemporary web-head designs. More, they may have been fired with mercuric primers that crystallized and weakened the cases critically or black powder residues may have gotten in their dirty work. When loading and firing the .45-70, *always* use modern cartridge cases!

To repeat, the .45-70 was launched as a black powder cartridge and it has more case capacity than it really needs

One of the problems in reloading the .45-70 is that the brass in the case neck is thin and prone to snag when the bullet is seated. One helpful trick is to install a tapered punch in the drill press and adjust the press table to put a slight flare in the mouth before going on to seat the bullets, crimping as usual.

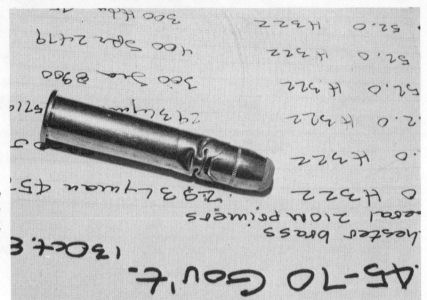

If you neglect the approach outlined above, you are quite apt to end up with a grotesquely unsuitable/unshootable specimen such as the one pictured here!

for most, if not all, of the modern smokeless powders that deliver today's best performance.

The second black powder legacy of the .45-70 is its case design and construction. It needed a substantial volume to hold 70.0 grains of black powder. Current smokeless powders do not need all of the available volume the case provides. The case walls, particularly at the neck, had to be rather thin to assure reliable sealing of the system at the moderate gas pressures generated by black powder.

At the same time, the chamber dimensions of the many thousands of firearms chambered for the .45-70 and the .458-inch bullet diameter of the chambering dictate that the ammunition companies have little latitude in establishing case wall thickness. As an inflexible result, the reloader of the .45-70 must maintain a cautiously conservative attitude in load development.

Since Thompson/Center Arms began production of the Contender in 1967, barrels have been available in over forty different factory chamberings. While T/C has done an excellent job of satisfying the demands for different chamberings, they have never been able to accommodate all of the specialized desires of the legion of Contender aficionados. The problem is that T/C must maintain some specified minimum level of sales volume in order to justify keeping barrels of a given caliber in the catalog.

That particular hard fact of life has fostered the appearance of a small number of custom pistolsmiths who can, and happily do, provide the barrels in exotic chamberings that T/C does not regard as practical. The group includes: Lee E. Jurras, Box 680, Washington, IN 47501; SSK Industries, J.D. Jones, 721 Woodvue Lane, Wintersville, OH 43952; Bullberry Barrel Works, Ltd., Fred Smith,

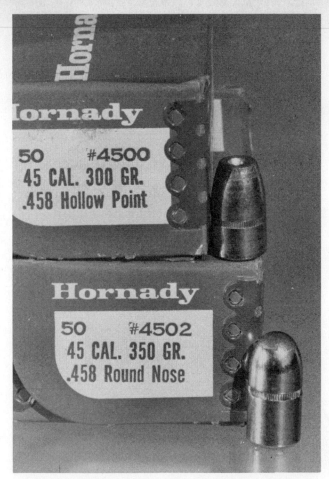

These two bullets from Hornady are well suited to use in reloading the .45-70 Government cartridge. Hornady also has 500-grain FMJ and JSP bullets available.

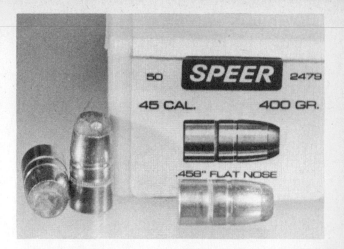

Speer's 400-grain JSP bullet, above, has two crimping grooves to accommodate two different seating depths. Sierra's 300-grain JHP, below, is exceptionally well suited for use in .45-70 handguns, offering a combination of moderate recoil and excellent expansion capability.

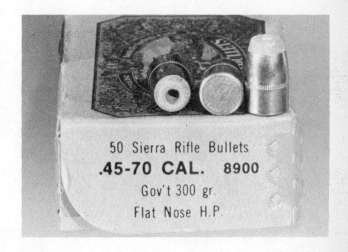

2430 W 350 N 67-5, Hurricane, UT 84737; The Gun Shop, David Van Horn, 1302 East Rawhide, Gilbert, AZ 85234; and Thompson/Center Custom Shop, 400 N. Main Street, Box 1700, Rochester, NH 03867.

It was from custom gunsmiths such as these, the .45-70 first became available, along with a number of other exotic numbers, several of them quite lusty in performance. I believe Lee Jurras was the first custom maker to offer .45-70 Contender barrels on a limited basis.

After Jurras moved away from the more conventional cartridges to develop his line of Howdah cartridges — based upon shortened .500 Nitro Express cases — for use in highly modified Contender frames, several others moved in to fill the void.

J.D. Jones, the well-known advocate of handgun hunting, established SSK Industries in the late Seventies to produce custom Contender barrels, along with complete handgun hunting rigs. Contender barrels in .45-70 Government were among the first SSK offerings.

Quality barrels, along with reloading guideline informa-tion, contributed toward making the .45-70 among the top three Contender offerings amid the eighty-odd cham-berings currently offered by SSK.

Other custom makers currently offering .45-70 Conten-der pistol or carbine barrels include the aforementioned Fred Smith of Bullberry Barrel Works, Ltd., and David Van Horn of the Gun Shop. While owning a variety of barrels in different calibers from all three of these sup-pliers, I added a .45-70 Contender barrel from SSK to my working battery several years ago. Its performance has been so gratifying I jumped at Dean Grennell's invitation to contribute this chapter.

The .45-70 remained a custom-only chambering in the Contender for a little over the first decade of its career. The situation changed in 1988. At that time, Thompson/Center Arms made an uncataloged run of their Super 14 Contender barrels in .45-70 for one of their distributors.

One of the ongoing policies of the Thompson/Center Association has been the offering of such uncataloged items to association members and we were able to include

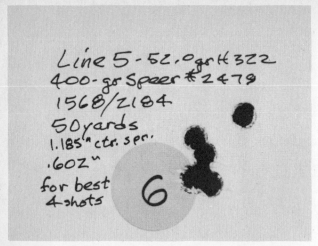

Here are three fifty-yard targets fired by Grennell at the 1¼-inch aiming pasters. The best four hits on this one represent a center-spread of 1.14 minutes of angle. The pistol used was the one illustrated on page 99.

Accurate Arms 5744 was a tubular powder, no longer available from them. 30.0 grains was a maximum load for 400-grain bullets with this double-base powder.

Like the load with Hodgdon's H322 at upper left, this load with Hodgdon H4895 powder got the 400-grain Speer bullet nicely over the one foot-ton energy level.

the .45-70 Super 14s as one such offering. Based upon my experience with the cartridge, it came as no surprise at all when the .45-70 barrels were snapped up eagerly by a great many members.

About that time, Thompson/Center Arms opened Fox Ridge Outfitters as the sole source of the output of their Custom Shop. It was an event long and eagerly awaited, largely delayed by the difficulty in finding qualified personnel in the nearby area.

Fox Ridge offers the .45-70 in a wide variety of Contender pistol and carbine barrel lengths, as listed in the catalog that is free on request at the address given. They also have several accessory barrels for the TCR single-shot rifle.

Personnel at Fox Ridge say all varieties of the .45-70 barrels for T/C products are selling like the proverbial hotcakes. The 1989 catalog from Thompson/Center Arms saw the introduction of the new Super-16 barrel; a concept suggested by Dean Grennell, a dedicated Contender buff

in his own right.

The Super-16 Contender barrels actually measure 16.25 inches in length, making them legal for use with the Contender carbine stocks — provided the overall length of the assembled gun is 26.5 inches or more — and likewise usable as pistol barrels, with the original Contender stocks installed. There's little doubt in my mind that the .45-70 Contender is here to stay and I ordered a .45-70 Contender carbine barrel from Fox Ridge to round out my battery.

It is by no means uncommon for people to ask me, "What good is such a monster?" First of all, the .45-70 Contender isn't all that terribly monstrous. Yes, it is possible to configure the Contender and load cartridges for it that attenuate the recoil rather markedly. It is also possible to work up loads that will generate considerable trauma for the novice big-bore handgunner. Both effects can be controlled — and *should* be.

My experience indicated the .45-70 Contender can be

Even though you may be firing the reloads in a pistol, the .45-70 Government case is designed to accept large rifle primers and those are the type that should be used.

IMR 4198 powder, formerly supplied by Du Pont and now marketed by IMR Powder Company, works well in the .45-70, as does Hodgdon's H4198 that's quite similar.

notably accurate with the right loads, hence capable of rewarding target shooting or some extremely potent plinking.

In that respect, I recall Grennell relating how, years ago, noted silversmith Sid Bell of Tully, New York, quizzed him as to his favorite trophy animal, saying he wanted to make up a bolo tie for him. Grennell identified the given trophy and Bell shrugged and said, "Well, I guess I can handle that."

The result was a remarkably distinctive bolo, sporting a tin can that had been riddled by a fusillade of bullets. After some number of years, Bell added it to his regular line, making it available to any interested purchaser.

The .45-70 Contender is a can-roller, *par excellence,* with the minor problem that any reasonably square hit rolls the can a long distance. That tends to make subsequent hits considerably more challenging. It tends to help quite a bit if you replace the tin can with a five-gallon paint pail.

Probably one of the most logical employments of the .45-70 Contender is for hunting big game. With the bullets about to be discussed, the .45-70 Government — given judicious bullet placement, of course — is thoroughly capable of humane, one-shot kills of anything on the North American continent. That includes targets inclined to or capable of chewing up the shooter and, in such confrontations, it's always a highly pertinent consideration as to which adversary ends up sinking teeth into the other's ham.

Apart from potentially dangerous game, the .45-70 offers the hunter of such species as elk or moose a large-bore, heavy-bullet capability with excellent potential for deep penetration and decisive anchoring.

What's more, it makes an outstanding rig for whitetail deer. There, it may represent somewhat more capability than the quarry absolutely requires. The popular term for that is *overkill.*

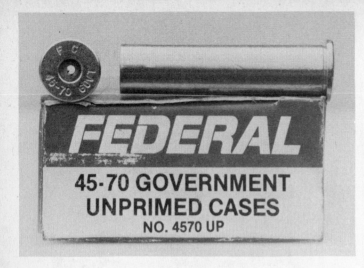

Half the secret of success in reloading the .45-70 lies in starting out with a good case in good condition and the unprimed cases from Federal are hard to beat. Right, Hercules Reloder 7 and 12 both are well suited for use in the .45-70 cartridge, either for handguns or rifles.

My response to that objection is that I'd rather overkill than overwound and leave a cripple to a painful and lingering death and a windfall to predators. Rest assured, the .45-70 will leave a goodly amount of unmutilated venison to take up just about all the available space in your freezer.

There are those with greater experience at such pursuits who regard the .45-70 Contender as amply qualified for taking African, Asian or Australian buffalo; arguably, elephants, as well.

Evaluating the .45-70 Contender objectively, it makes a lot of difference as to which particular knothole in the board fence you select for viewing it. If you judge it as a handgun, which it certainly is in the Contender, the .45-70 musters pretty respectable velocities and delivers a notably heavy-weight bullet of generous diameter. True, there are other handgun/cartridge combinations capable of higher velocities, but they launch bullets a lot lighter and more svelte as to profile.

If, on the other hand, you rank the .45-70 as a rifle cartridge, the knee-jerk term will come back, automatically: rainbow trajectory!

Yes, it's all too true. In a contemporary world that views effective rifle velocities in the brackets of high-3000 to low-4000 fps, the .45-70 comes on as a knock-kneed also-ran. The obvious response to that might be, "Where the hell was the .22 CHeetah in 1873, when we really *needed* it?"

Up in Canada, there are intrepid shooters who use .45-70 rifles in competition at distances out to six hundred and a thousand yards and some of the groups they fire might impress you. Yes, it has a rainbow trajectory, but the pertinent point is it has a remarkably *consistent* rainbow trajectory.

In noting that, I do not mean to advocate the .45-70 Contender as the ultimate long-range varmint-vaporizer. Given a challenging target at 337 yards, or 737 yards, the chances are you could get respectably close, given a sufficient number of sighting shots and sight-correcting adjustments. It must be conceded, however, the .45-70 is not ideally qualified for making effective hits on distant targets of opportunity, with the distance no more than roughly estimated.

As if the rainbow trajectory syndrome weren't sufficient handicap, the .45-70 Contender has at least one more: It kicks! Mathematical formulas are fairly well established and available for rating such things. How serious is the situation? Well, if you're firing a 400-grain bullet or one weighing 500 grains — the equation puts a lot of emphasis upon projectile weight — the .45-70 Contender can generate backlash equal to five times what you get from a .30/06 rifle, three times that of a .44 magnum revolver firing a 240-grain bullet at 1400 fps — or somewhat more!

In a worst-possible scenario situation, a .45-70 Contender can come barreling rearward and bonk you atop the boko. It is a contretemps worth going to a lot of attention and effort to avoid and prevent.

For one thing, you don't start out with SM loads. The abbreviation does not stand for sado-masochism. What it does stand for is "suicide-maximum." The basic concept was invented, several years ago, by a veteran experimental ballistician, seeking to establish a *status quo* to avoid at any possible cost. It can be regarded as the ultimate *bete noire* of all reloads everywhere. *Bete noire,* if the term is unfamiliar, means black beast: something well worth going to a lot of effort to avoid encountering.

In brief, you start small and timorous. Then you work up by modest increments, firing the output as you go along,

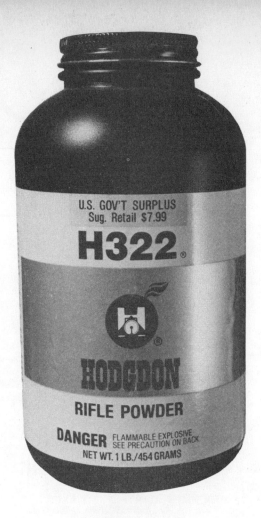
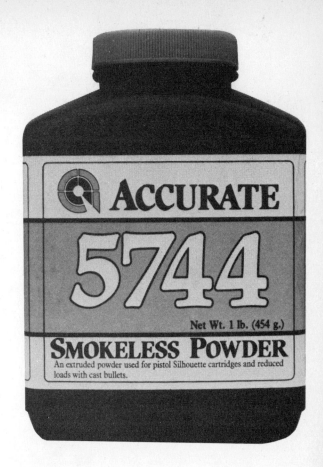

As noted on the label, Hodgdon H322 now is available as a surplus powder again, at a favorable price. The current booklet of load data from Accurate Arms continues to list 5744 loads, for the sake of supplies on hand.

always keenly mindful that unpleasant surprises are among the worst kind.

Any and all load data listed in this chapter should be regarded with caution and healthy skepticism. Each and every individual firearm is a unique law unto itself; no two are quite identical. A load that performs magnificently in one can and quite possibly will cause destructive and dangerous damage in another gun, nominally identical.

While the Contender is a fine, strong action, the head diameter of the cartridge has a considerable effect upon the strain the action must withsand. The .608-inch head diameter of the .45-70 is one of the largest apt to be encountered in the Contender, making it necessary to work up loads for it with all possible care and prudence. Good reloading practice dictates that you start at the lowest loads listed, working up by small increments to determine the optimum accuracy and acceptability in your pistol.

As a usual rule, the Contender will show indications the pressures are excessive. The symptoms include such things as a greater amount of effort being required to open the

action and, once the action is opened, resistance to extracting the fired case. Such things can be useful when working with cartridges of smaller head diameter such as the .223 Remington; they serve as a signal to reduce the powder charge, bullet weight or both.

Be keenly mindful, however, when working with cartriges of large head diameter, signs of excessive pressure such as those just described are a clear indication you've already gone too far.

If you've done most of your "Contenderizing" with cartridges of smaller head diameters, *do not* follow an approach of "increase the charge weight until things get sticky." Down that path, disaster lurks.

Most of the more resolute .45-70 loads will let you know you're unleashing something pretty significant via another route. I'm referring to the felt recoil, muzzle flip or both.

Various approaches work to mute the kick. You can increase the weight of the gun, decrease the weight of the projectile, reduce bullet velocity and/or add recoil-control ports, muzzle brakes or similar devices. Arriving at the

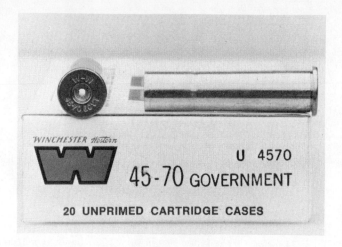

In addition to the 300-grain load above, Remington makes another with a 405-grain bullet and Wright used that in his preliminary tests, as well as the 300-grain Federal load, right above. Right, Winchester as well as Remington offers unprimed cases in .45-70 Government.

best possible solution to the problem involves a number of compromises and trade-offs, as so often seems to be the case.

My own .45-70 Contender pistol has been fitted with a Pachmayr rubber forend and Gripper stocks, both of which add useful amounts of weight. The extra five or six ounces in the forend is out there where it helps to soak up muzzle-flip and the Gripper stocks ease the sharpest bites of recoil in the early stages. I've also installed a scope sight which, with its mount and rings, adds another ten or eleven ounces. As presently set up, the Contender scales about 4½ pounds.

Probably the most effective component of the recoil reduction system is the four-port Mag-na-port muzzle venting. Two ports vent to the side and two more bleed off powder gas in an upward direction. I avoided additional ports on the underside of the muzzle so as to avoid having powder gas blast ground debris in my face when taking shots from a prone position. I regard Mag-na-porting as mandatory for the .45-70 Contender.

In the instance of the .45-70 Contender carbine, Fox Ridge Outfitters offers several different barrel lengths and profiles. I chose to go with the heaviest one available and got the twenty-one-inch bull barrel. After assembling the package, with a scope, shoulder stock, forend and so on, I ended up with a handy little carbine that weighs just one ounce over six pounds. Even with the bull barrel configuration, there just is not a lot of metal left after you put a .458-inch rifled bore in a Contender barrel.

I decided to find out how it felt to fire the combination without any form of recoil-reducer. After touching off a few rounds of Federal's 300-grain factory loads, I decided to add a PAST recoil pad to the shoulder of my shirt. That seemed to do the trick, allowing me to chronograph a few hundred shots through the carbine at each sitting. No, I do not have a high threshold of pain. In fact, I'm quite amazed at how effective the PAST recoil pads really are.

Both my SSK pistol and T/CC carbine carry scope sights. As both are envisioned for use in short-range hunting situations, I chose scopes with low magnifications. The pistol has a 1.5x Thompson/Center Recoil-Proof scope in SSK Industries' three-ring T'SOB mount. Its base is attached to the barrel by six screws, rather than the usual four, to avoid being sheared off by recoil and it uses three rings to hold the scope rather than the usual two. The additional ring serves to minimize the forces trying to bend the scope tube during recoil by supporting the scope body over a greater length. As the tube flex is limited, the optical components and adjustment turret hardware are not so apt to pop loose under recoil.

The T/CC carbine carries a Nikon 1.5-4.5x variable scope in a conventional two-ring mount and base from

Lyman's No. 457191 mould produces a nice plain-base bullet with a flat tip or meplat on the nose. Weight was 293 grains in the batch of casting alloy used.

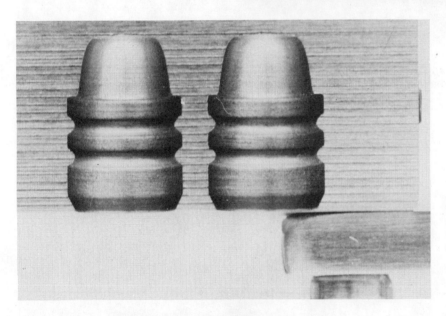

Though not specifically listed in the Hensley & Gibbs catalog, this is their No. 78BBS at about 215 grains and it's capable of being resized to .458-inch. It makes an excellent lightweight for casual plinking in the .45-70 cartridge.

Thompson/Center Arms. Due to the greater weight and reduced recoil, the carbine enables this combination to survive and keep on performing quite nicely.

I'll admit to being heavily in favor of six-screw bases and three-ring mounts for scopes on heavy-recoiling numbers such as the .45-70 Contender. You've hardly sampled real adventure until you've had a scope shear off the top of a gun and home in upon your noggin. Even if it misses your head — sparing you the tab for a hasty visit to the emergency ward — damage to the scope is going to cost more than you saved by not getting the SSK T'SOB base and three-ring mount in the first place.

At first glance, the .45-70 looks like a typical straight-walled case. On closer examination, it turns out to have a fair amount of body taper, from .505-inch just in front of the head, to .480-inch at the case neck. This presents no real problem in reloading other than making it highly impractical to produce a tungsten carbide resizing die for the .45-70 cartridge. Actually, that amount of taper was necessary to assure reliable extraction in guns such as the old trapdoor Springfield, in the era of copious fouling from black powder.

Reloading dies in .45-70 are available from all of the major makers of reloading equipment. I've used dies from Hornady, RCBS and Redding with a high degree of satisfaction.

As a routine procedure, I remove burrs from the case mouth by chamfering the inside and outside lightly. Remember, you're only getting rid of the burrs, not making it for use as a cookie-cutter. Not all makes of inside/outside

RCBS. INCORPORATED, OROVILLE, CA 95965

The expanding die of the RCBS set for .45-70, taken apart in the photo above, to show the area that puts a gentle flare in the case neck for ease of seating the bullet. Photo at right shows the punch head stamping.

deburring tools are large enough to cope with outside-deburring the .45-70 neck, but the handy little tool from Lee Precision accepts diameters up to .510-inch or so and the one from Forster Products works equally well. The unique design of the Lee tool does a lot to simplify outside deburring.

The next significant area is the crimping operation. Working with cast bullets and relatively fast powders, taper-crimping did a fine job for me. I fired a ten-shot group at sixty yards in the carbine, using 405-grain cast bullets and Hercules Unique powder and it measured less than five-eighths-inch in spread.

The same approach, with jacketed bullets and slower-burning powders, resulted in targets resembling shotgun patterns. Returning to a conventional roll-crimp brought groups down to acceptable sizes. I attribute this to two interlocking factors: ignition characteristics of the given powders and the .458-inch diameter of the jacketed bullets against the .460-inch diameter of the cast jobs.

I've come to favor a roll-crimp for all jacketed bullets and a taper-crimp for cast bullets, when using powders such as Unique or 2400 with the latter. I have not completed my investigations into rifle-speed powders with cast bullets, so I'm reserving decisions in that area.

Then there is the matter of available case volume in which the .45-70 offers an embarrassment of riches. Loads

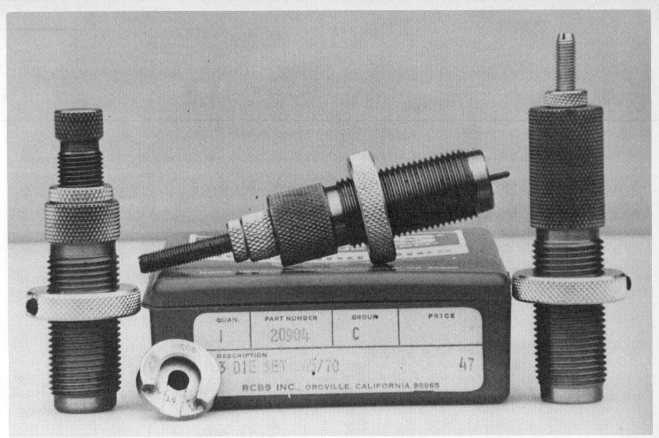

Here's the complete set of .45-70 reloading dies, with the No. 14 shell holder that fits .45-70 cases. This is an old but well preserved set, dating from before the takeover of RCBS by Omark Industries; see photo below.

that put a lot of air space behind the bullet are apt to be erratic in ignition, often leaving a large quantity of unburned powder in the bore and breech area. Some favor approaches such as using tufts of a lightweight material such as kapok to keep the powder charge back next to the primer. Others favor a bulk filler such as Super Grex polyethylene powder to take up the vacant space. In this regard, I have yet to find a solution with which I'm satisfied.

Rather, I prefer to use those powders where recommended load data as to charge weight leaves little or no empty air space behind the bullet. That works well with jacketed bullets, but leaves unanswered questions in regard to the lighter cast bullets and powder charges suitable for casual plinking. As for such loads, using inert filler materials, I plan to avoid them until a lot more solid information has been established as to what works and what does not.

In the area of jacketed bullets readily available from the major makers, there is quite a good variety from which to choose. Hornady has a 300-grain JHP/FN, No. 4500; a 350-grain JSP/RN, No. 4502 InterLock; a 500-grain JSP/RN, No. 4504 InterLock; and a 500-grain FMJ/RN, No. 4507. Remington has a 300-grain JHP/FN and a 405-grain JSP/FN. Sierra has a 300-grain JHP/FN, No. 8900. Speer has a 400-grain JSP/FN, No. 2479.

The smaller custom makers can provide a greater variety, though at a higher cost in most, if not all instances. Examples include:

Alaska Bullet Works, (Box 54, Douglas, Alaska 99824), flat-nose and round-nose in weights of 400 grains.

Barnes Bullets, (Box 215, American Fork, Utah 84003),

A close look at the stamping on the top of the seating dies shows the set was produced by RCBS in 1974.

Here you have a closeup view of the No. 14 shell holder and therein lies a small story. Fred Huntington, who founded RCBS, saw no need for the milled relief cut leading up to the central opening, visible here around the stamped number 14. If a primer was left protruding from the head of the fired case, you encountered difficulty in getting the case head into the shell holder. After a lot of complaints, Huntington finally okayed the addition of the milled relief cut in RCBS shell holders, but he hated having to do it and always voiced bitter resentment.

300-grain in flat-nose and semi-spitzer and 400-grain in the same configurations.

Cor-Bon Bullets, Incorporated, (Box 132, Fruita, Colorado 81521), a 300-grain round-nose and Trophy Bonded Bullets, (Box 262348, Houston, Texas 7727), 350-grain bullets in both round-nose and semi-spitzer.

Due to the somewhat painful cost of these custom bullets, the results reported here were obtained by using bullets from three of the major manufacturers listed earlier. Upon request, the custom makers may be willing to furnish suggested reloading data.

In the area of suitable powders, as with the bullets, there are a number of choices. I tried to stay with rifle powders, as I prefer to avoid using nominal pistol powders in rifle cases of large capacity. The traditional powders for the .45-70 are IMR-4198 and IMR-3031. Both are extruded "stick" powders, giving minor problems in rotary powder measures.

Other extruded powders, somewhat shorter in granule length and thus easier to crank through rotary measures, include Hodgdon H4895, Hercules Reloder-7 and Reloder-12 and Hodgdon H322.

Though some recommend hot magnum-type primers, all of the powders I used are relatively easy to ignite, so I settled upon the Federal 210M match large rifle primer for all of my test loads.

Federal, Remington and Winchester offer both loaded ammunition and empty brass in .45-70. I settled on Federal by reason of their metallurgy and case-wall thickness. I hold both Remington and Winchester in the most cordial regard, but my long-term experience with Federal brass leads me to select it in nearly every instance. Apart from that, I've long felt Phil Sharpe had a good point when he noted he usually matched up both cases and primers from the same maker.

Before testing any of my reloads, I decided to check performance of a couple factory loads in both pistol and rifle. I chose Federal's 300-grain JHP/FN and Remington's 405-grain JSP/FN as representative, testing both for accuracy as well as velocity.

Due to the limited magnification of the pistol scope, I checked its accuracy at fifty yards, finding the Federal load grouped about one inch in spread. In view of the hefty recoil of that load, I was more than pleased with its group size. Out of the Contender carbine, the same load grouped right at 1.25 inches at a hundred yards.

The Remington load did fine work in both the pistol and carbine out to fifty yards. Beyond that, gravity exacted its grim toll and there was a fair amount of vertical dispersion at one hundred yards. Quoting the velocity in feet per second, together with the muzzle energy in foot-pounds for each load in both guns, my averages ran:

Tom Hayden — not the politician, a different Tom Hayden — is clocking some .45-70 loads through Grennell's usual test setup here. The chronograph is an Oehler 35P that prints out two readings for each shot by way of a double-check. Hayden shoots left-handed, so the top of the portable shooting bench has been reversed.

LOAD	WEIGHT	14″ PISTOL	21″ CARBINE
Federal No. 4570A	300-grain	1515/1529	1658/1832
Remington No. R4570G	405-grain	1060/1011	1163/1217

As we move on into reporting performance of reloads, I feel a need to lay down a few explicit stipulations. These were experimental tests and all appeared safe in both of my test guns. That by no means implies nor guarantees they will be equally safe and trouble-free in any and all other firearms chambered for the .45-70 Government cartridge.

Should you decide to try these loads, it is imperative that you start at the lowest listed charge and, at your own risk and discretion, work up from that point by gradual charge weight increases should you see fit to do so. Repeating an earlier warning, for necessary emphasis, you can be in bad trouble with this gun/cartridge combination, long before encountering any of the customary symptoms of excessive pressures, as indicated when firing cartridges of smaller head diameters in the Contender action.

As neither the present writer, the author of the book, nor its publisher have any control over the equipment, components and techniques used in reloading by others, nor over the condition and fitness or mechanical integrity of firearms in which such reloads may be fired, they cannot and do not assume any liability, either expressed or implied, for injury, damage or death caused by, or alleged to have been caused by use of reloading data quoted here. Any use of such data is clearly and specifically at the risk and discretion of the reloader who uses it and/or the shooter who fires such reloads and/or such bystanders who may be in the immediate vicinity of such firings.

At the bottom line, consider the probable long-term effects of such firings on the given gun. While it may withstand one round of a load, or a dozen, or a hundred, it is for you to decide whether or not routine and continuous use of the given load may impose an unacceptable amount of wear and tear upon the action and component parts.

With all of that clearly stipulated and accepted by the reader, average test results are shown on page 112 with the listed bullets and charge weights, all loads having been made up with Federal .45-70 cases and Federal No. 210M match primers, as was noted!

300-GRAIN SIERRA NO. 8900 JHP/FN BULLET
Cartridge overall length: 2.550″

POWDER CHARGE, GRAINS	14″ PISTOL	21″ CARBINE
36.0 IMR 4198	1430/1363	1407/1319
39.0 IMR 4198	1594/1693	1519/1537
42.0 IMR 4198	1661/1838	1793/2142
43.0 Reloder 7	1743/2024	1767/2080
46.0 Reloder 7	1770/2087	1847/2273
49.0 H4895	1162/900	1318/1157
52.0 H4895	1220/992	1470/1440
48.0 H322	1113/825	1386/1280

350-GRAIN HORNADY JSP/RN, NO. 4502
Cartridge Overall Length: 2.565″

	14″ PISTOL	21″ CARBINE
35.0 IMR 4198	1360/1438	1442/1616
38.0 IMR 4198	not tested	1620/2040
41.0 IMR 4198	1626/2055	1768/2430
36.0 Reloder 7	1198/1116	1388/1498
39.0 Reloder 7	1327/1369	1536/1834
42.0 Reloder 7	1394/1511	1669/2165
45.0 Reloder 7	1542/1848	1800/2519
52.0 Reloder 12	1217/1151	1474/1689
55.0 Reloder 12	1349/1415	1577/1933
58.0 Reloder 12	1506/1763	1721/2302
45.0 H322	1232/1180	1504/1758
48.0 H322	1445/1623	1653/2124

400-GRAIN SPEER JSP/FN No. 2479
Cartridge Overall Length: 2.540″

	14″ PISTOL	21″ CARBINE
34.0 IMR 4198	1327/1564	1321/1550
37.0 IMR 4198	1446/1858	1464/1904
40.0 IMR 4198	1546/2123	1682/2513
37.0 Reloder 7	1331/1574	1343/1602
40.0 Reloder 7	1491/1975	1530/2080
48.0 Reloder 12	1164/1204	1330/1572
51.0 Reloder 12	1318/1543	1487/1964
54.0 Reloder 12	1529/2077	1641/2392
39.0 H322	951/803	1113/1101
42.0 H322	1105/1085	1243/1373
45.0 H322	1179/1235	1344/1605

Another view of Joe Wright, on the right — fittingly enough — with Ken French of the Thompson/Center Arms Co.

NOTES ON RELOAD TABLES:

These are *not* recommended loads. The data is quoted solely for the sake of showing performance possibilities.

All of the foregoing tests were conducted at ambient temperatures ranging between forty and fifty degrees, Fahrenheit. If the same loads are made up and fired at higher ambient temperatures, higher velocities are apt to result, along with correspondingly higher peak pressures.

All reloads were assembled in Federal cases, using Federal No. 210M benchrest primers. Substitution of cases and/or primers is apt to cause substantial variation in peak pressures and overall performance.

I am not reporting the group sizes fired with the listed loads, because I've found that accuracy varies markedly from gun to gun. I can say that Hercules Reloder 7 and Reloder 12 have come to be my particular favorites, with IMR 4198 a strong third choice. Results with H4895 were sufficiently discouraging that I've dropped it from my roster for further exploration in this cartridge. I still like it in several other calibers and will continue to use it in those.

Tests with Hodgdon H322 brought a number of surprises. My original starting loads were below those listed. Ignition, when sustained, was quite erratic with the lighter charges. In both the pistol and carbine, I had lighter charges of H322 leave bullets lodged in the bore, needing to be driven out with a rod and mallet. To me, that suggests the urgent need to become thoroughly familiar with the given load and its probable performance before taking it afield against dangerous game species.

It well may be that H322 requires a hotter primer such as the Federal No. 215 large rifle magnum. My own inclination is to abandon further research into it, in favor of those powders that are more interesting and there appears to be a fair number of those.

Summarizing, both Reloder 7 and IMR 4198 showed reliable ignition and performance with the lighter bullets tested. With the 300-grain Sierra bullet, IMR 4198 showed a moderate edge over other powders. With both the 350- and 400-grain bullets, Reloder 12 really stood out. It fills the big case nicely and I'm sure that contributes heavily to its efficiency. This was my first encounter with Reloder 12. It certainly will not be my last!

You may have noted a few instances in which the pistol generated more velocity than the carbine with identical loads. Such results tended to occur at the lowest charge weights for the given bullet/powder combination and various factors could account for the apparent anomaly.

Perhaps the shape and dimensions vary between the two bores and contribute toward the effect. Layne Simpson, who has done some outstanding work with the Contender, refers to this as "fast" or "slow" barrels. I can't think of a better way to put it.

Another possibility is that the comparatively small charge had burned completely by the time the bullet had traveled fourteen inches up the barrel and the longer rifle barrel only served to slow it back down through frictional resistance.

I've found the .45-70 Government cartridge well suited to the Thompson/Center Contender. It is an interesting combination, capable of fine accuracy and well suited for many hunting situations. If you share enthusiasm for this firearm system, you're invited to join the Thompson/Center Association, Box 792, Northboro, MA 01532, details on request.

CHAPTER 7

THE MODEL 1917 REVOLVERS AND OTHER NON-AUTO .45S

The year was 1955 or perhaps 1956 and I had this rather nice old Model 1917 Colt in as-issued condition. I no longer recall exactly what I did with that one; probably swapped it for another gun.

Above, the "Full Moon" clip from Ranch Products holds all six rounds of .45 ACP for use in the Model '17s. Below, from same source, the "Third Moon" clips hold two apiece and you need three per load.

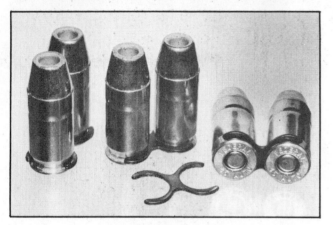

Above, the traditional half-moon clip, developd in 1917 to use .45 ACP ammo in the Model '17 revolvers. Below, some .45 Auto Rim as well as .45 ACP in clips.

Manual Operation Can Simplfy Things To A Useful Extent!

THE GOVERNMENT Model Colt auto pistol had been adopted by the armed services only a few years before the outbreak of WWI and, when the U.S. entered that conflict, there were nowhere nearly enough service handguns available to fill the suddenly expanding need.

Tooling and production facilities were in place, however, to turn out revolvers capable of handling the .45 ACP cartridge at both the Colt and Smith & Wesson plants. With emergency circumstances exerting severe pressures, orders were placed for as many units of either make that could be delivered and, together with production of the Model 1911 auto pistol, a sufficient number of handguns were delivered to see the Allies through to victory, as of November 11, 1918.

The .45 ACP cartridge is a rimless number, leaving nothing for the extractor star of a revolver to push against. If you happen to have sturdy fingernails, it is possible to just stuff the cartridges into the chamber, fire them and pluck the empties forth by main force. Or if you can just worry an empty case free, you can use that to pry the other spent cases from the chambers. Either way you look at it,

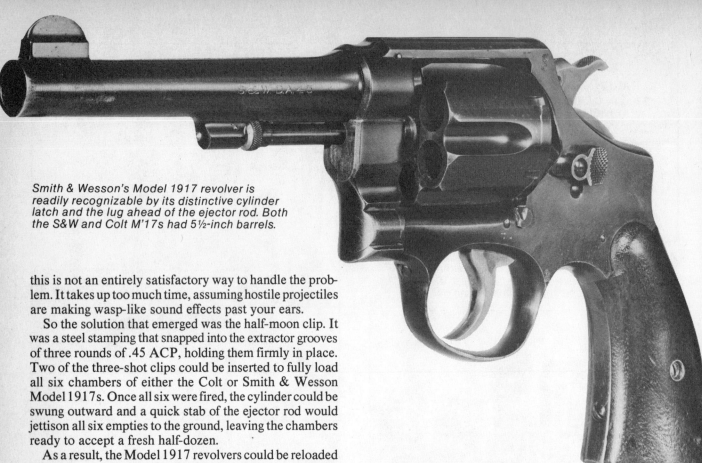

Smith & Wesson's Model 1917 revolver is readily recognizable by its distinctive cylinder latch and the lug ahead of the ejector rod. Both the S&W and Colt M'17s had 5½-inch barrels.

this is not an entirely satisfactory way to handle the problem. It takes up too much time, assuming hostile projectiles are making wasp-like sound effects past your ears.

So the solution that emerged was the half-moon clip. It was a steel stamping that snapped into the extractor grooves of three rounds of .45 ACP, holding them firmly in place. Two of the three-shot clips could be inserted to fully load all six chambers of either the Colt or Smith & Wesson Model 1917s. Once all six were fired, the cylinder could be swung outward and a quick stab of the ejector rod would jettison all six empties to the ground, leaving the chambers ready to accept a fresh half-dozen.

As a result, the Model 1917 revolvers could be reloaded just about as quickly as the Model 1911 autoloading pistol.

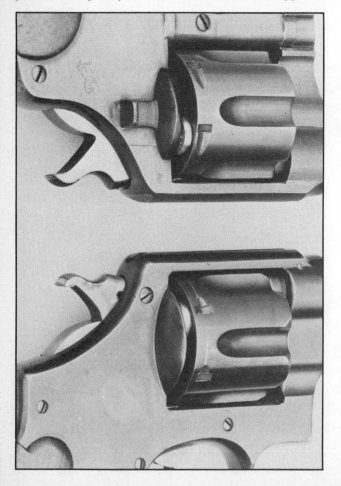

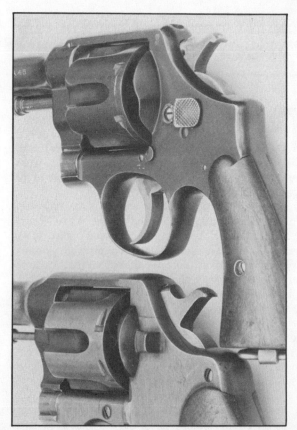

Below left, visible cartridges here are the ones to fire at next pull of the trigger in the Colt (top) or S&W. Below, cylinder latches of the S&W (top) and Colt.

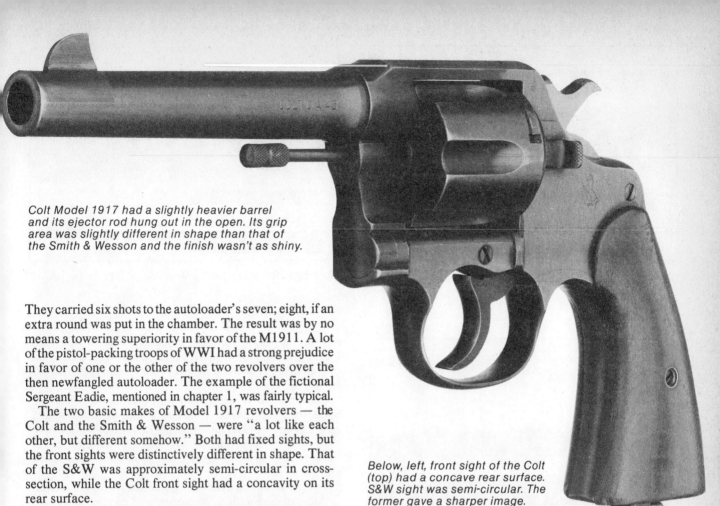

Colt Model 1917 had a slightly heavier barrel and its ejector rod hung out in the open. Its grip area was slightly different in shape than that of the Smith & Wesson and the finish wasn't as shiny.

They carried six shots to the autoloader's seven; eight, if an extra round was put in the chamber. The result was by no means a towering superiority in favor of the M1911. A lot of the pistol-packing troops of WWI had a strong prejudice in favor of one or the other of the two revolvers over the then newfangled autoloader. The example of the fictional Sergeant Eadie, mentioned in chapter 1, was fairly typical.

The two basic makes of Model 1917 revolvers — the Colt and the Smith & Wesson — were "a lot like each other, but different somehow." Both had fixed sights, but the front sights were distinctively different in shape. That of the S&W was approximately semi-circular in cross-section, while the Colt front sight had a concavity on its rear surface.

The Colt was slightly heavier, weighing 2½ pounds to the S&W's 2¼. Both had a uniform barrel length of 5.5 inches but the S&W had right-hand rifling at a pitch of one turn in 14.659 inches compared to the Colt's left-hand rifling at a pitch of one turn in sixteen inches. Both had a bore

Below, left, front sight of the Colt (top) had a concave rear surface. S&W sight was semi-circular. The former gave a sharper image. Below, a closer look at the ejector rods of the Colt (top) and S&W.

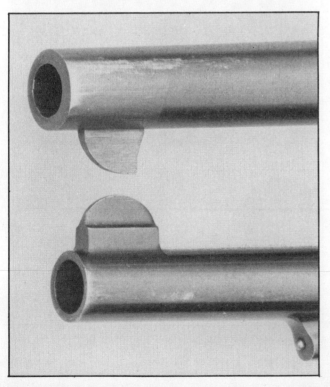

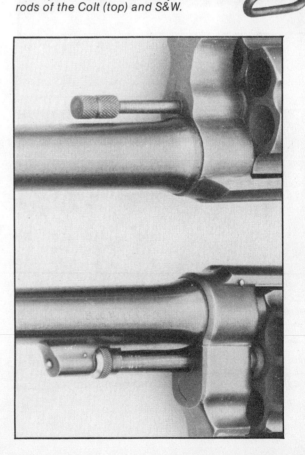

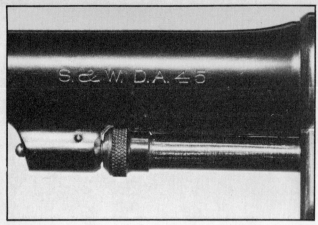

A close look at the S&W ejector rod and marking.

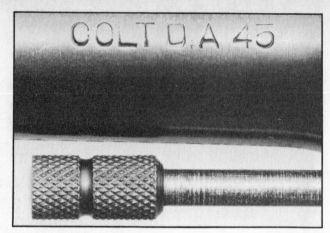

Markings indicating a double-action .45 are on barrel.

"United States Property" is stamped on bottom of barrel.

Above, cylinder locking notch on S&W is positioned above thinnest portion of chamber. Right, notches on Colt cylinder are slightly offset, making it stronger.

diameter of .445-inch, with groove diameters of .452-inch for the Colt and .451-inch for the Smith & Wesson. Total overall length was 10.8 inches for the Colt, 10.79 inches for the S&W.

The Smith & Wesson had a lug on the underside of the barrel to engage the end of the ejector rod; a feature lacking on the Colt. Both had thumb pieces on the left-hand side of the frame for releasing the cylinder, but the one on the S&W was pushed forward; that of the Colt was pulled rearward.

In operation, the cylinder of the Colt rotated clockwise and that of the Smith & Wesson rotated counter-clockwise.

From the personal collection of Smith & Wesson historian Roy Jinks, top and center photos are two views of the same commercial version of the S&W Model 1917. Lower photo is a well preserved straight Model '17.

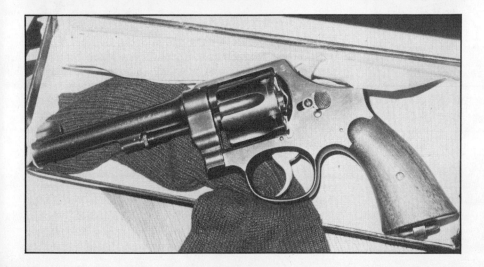

Here are two views of the snubnosed M'17 Colt, presently owned by my brother Ralph. It was given a hard chrome finish and fitted with a Smith & Wesson adjustable rear sight and ramped front sight by John B. Williams of Fullerton, California.

Retired CHP officer Jim Andrews, wearing an RCMP cap to compound the confusion, checks the sights on my S&W Model 25-2 in .45 ACP/AR. Those JHP slugs, peering out of those big chambers, look downright impressive, right?

Thus, on the latter, a cartridge in about the two o'clock position was next in line to fire or the one at ten o'clock on the Colt. This is an important distinction and one that had been an occasional source of problems for users of the two makes.

The cylinder-locking notches on the Smith & Wesson are situated precisely above the thinnest portion of the chambers, thereby weakening the strength of the cylinder significantly; the Colt is somewhat the stronger of the two. So long as the ammunition at hand does not exceed peak presures of 19,900 CUP, as prescribed by the Sporting Arms and Ammunition Manufacturers Institute (SAAMI), that poses no significant problem, as the Smith & Wesson is amply strong enough to handle such stresses. If, however, one proposes to fire reloaded ammunition that may generate

Here are two views of a Smith & Wesson Model 25-5, in .45 Colt, sometimes referred to as the .45 Long Colt. It has a four-inch barrel and S&W's target-type trigger and hammer spur, as well as the full adjustable rear sight and ramped front sight with rod insert. It makes a remarkably nice revolver; compact and handy to carry, with ample power. Sadly, they're not made at present.

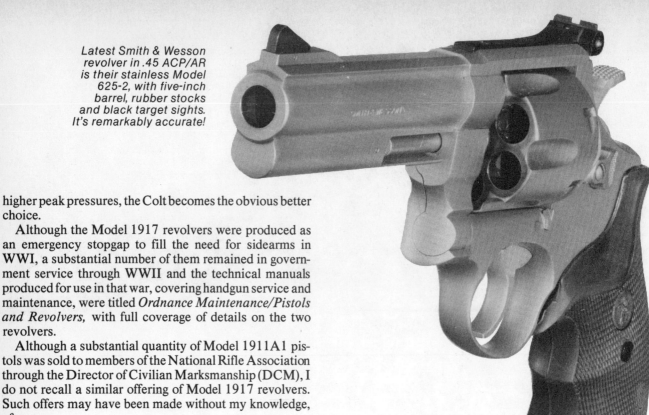

Latest Smith & Wesson revolver in .45 ACP/AR is their stainless Model 625-2, with five-inch barrel, rubber stocks and black target sights. It's remarkably accurate!

higher peak pressures, the Colt becomes the obvious better choice.

Although the Model 1917 revolvers were produced as an emergency stopgap to fill the need for sidearms in WWI, a substantial number of them remained in government service through WWII and the technical manuals produced for use in that war, covering handgun service and maintenance, were titled *Ordnance Maintenance/Pistols and Revolvers,* with full coverage of details on the two revolvers.

Although a substantial quantity of Model 1911A1 pistols was sold to members of the National Rifle Association through the Director of Civilian Marksmanship (DCM), I do not recall a similar offering of Model 1917 revolvers. Such offers may have been made without my knowledge, of course.

In any event, some number of M1917s got into commer-

A more formal portrait of the S&W Model 25-2 being aimed by Jim Andrews, a couple of pages back. This was termed the Model 1955 Target Model when it first appeared as a heavier version of the Model 1950; another fine shooter!

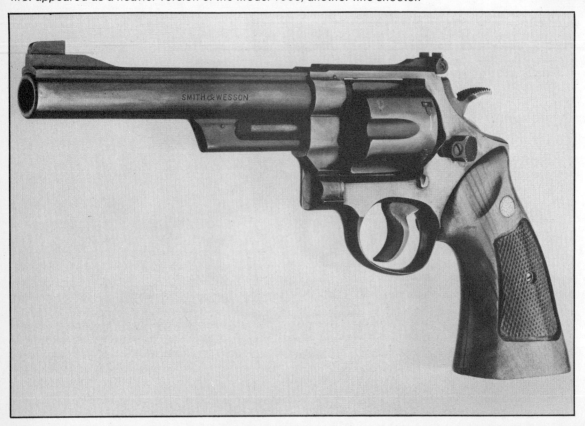

Shown for size comparison, all three off the same photo, from the top, a S&W Model 1917, the Model 25-2 and the Model 625-2, all in .45 ACP/AR.

cial channels. Sifting through an accumulation of old photos turned up a print of me holding a Model 1917 Colt and other photos in the same batch show a 1955 Oldsmobile, thereby dating the photo has having been taken about 1955 or 1956. In those days, such handguns sold in the approximate price brackets of twenty to thirty dollars and I engaged in a brisk amount of horsetrading that saw a great many come and go. It seems probable I kept it for a while, was not overly impressed by its inherent accuracy and swapped it in for some other gun that happened to catch my fancy.

Late in 1963 or early in 1964, I bought another M1917 Colt from Milt Klein in Chicago, paying not much over $20. Its barrel had been cut back to not much more than three inches or so and it had no front sight. I kept that one for a considerable while, eventually fitting some manner of front sight to it and finally bestowed it upon my brother, Ralph, in some manner of fraternal transaction.

I can speak with considerably greater authority about another Model 1917, a Smith & Wesson. Early in the summer of 1965, my wife and I took our vacation and visited some friends in Indiana and others in Illinois. While passing through the latter state, I programmed a stop in Knoxville to meet Gil and Mary Hebard and, in the course of the visit, purchased the S&W Model '17, serial number 43194, for Hebard's asking price of $35.

Several years after that, I encountered Hebard again at a gun show and reminded him of the long-ago purchase.

"If you'd care to get rid of it," he offered wistfully, "I'd be more than happy to refund your thirty-five bucks!"

Above, Mary and Gil Hebard, in their Knoxville, Illinois store, summer of 1965 and, below, the S&W Model 1917 bought from them for a fast $35, here after being fitted with a Bushnell Phantom scope.

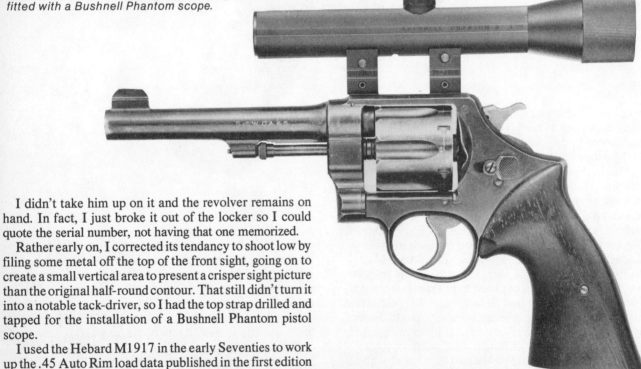

I didn't take him up on it and the revolver remains on hand. In fact, I just broke it out of the locker so I could quote the serial number, not having that one memorized.

Rather early on, I corrected its tendancy to shoot low by filing some metal off the top of the front sight, going on to create a small vertical area to present a crisper sight picture than the original half-round contour. That still didn't turn it into a notable tack-driver, so I had the top strap drilled and tapped for the installation of a Bushnell Phantom pistol scope.

I used the Hebard M1917 in the early Seventies to work up the .45 Auto Rim load data published in the first edition

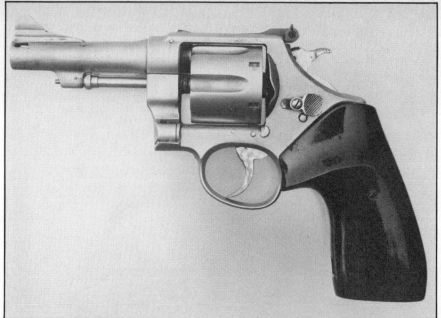

Left, here's how the Hebard M'17 looks in its current reincarnation. John B. Williams of Fullerton, California, trimmed the barrel back to four inches, added adjustable Smith & Wesson sights, hard-chromed it and milled two recoil control vents in the muzzle. I added the Herrett Jordan Trooper stocks. Below, a close look at its serial number.

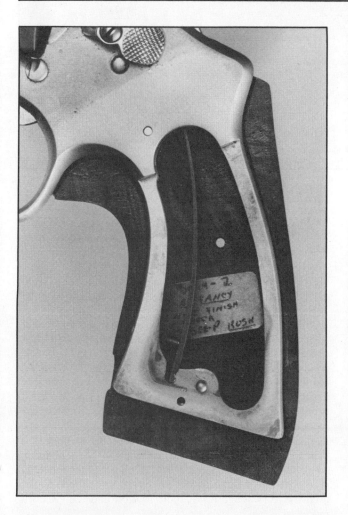

Above, the right-hand half of the Jordan Trooper stocks, from Herrett Stocks, showing how they modify the contours of the original frame. Right, barrel and sight.

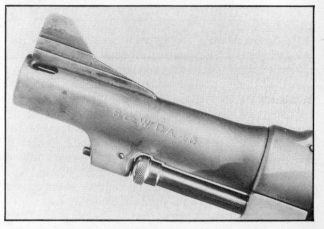

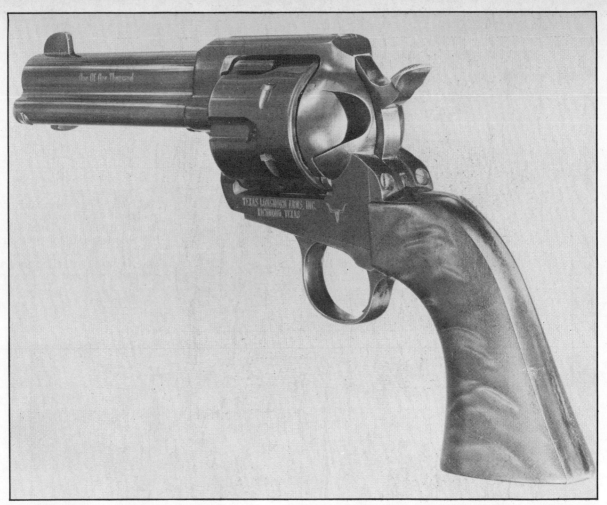

Above, Bill Grover of Texas Longhorn Arms, produces single-action revolvers with the loading gate on the left, where it's vastly more convenient for right-handed shooters. This is not just a mirror-image of the Colt. Left, Grover's gun with a Ruger Blackhawk revolver.

of the *Sierra Manual.* As initially issued, that took the 185-grain Sierra JHP bullet to a maximum velocity of 1300 fps. Later editions have been edited back down to no more than 1100 fps; still considerably more energetic than listings for the cartridge in other data sources.

Some years after that, I turned the gun over to gunsmith John B. Williams of Fullerton, California, for some extensive reworking. He trimmed the barrel back to a length of four inches, installed a new front sight on a ramp, milled the top strap to accept an adjustable Smith & Wesson rear sight, milled a pair of vent slots in the muzzle on either side of the front sight and hard-chromed the entire gun.

I went on to install a pair of Jordan Trooper stocks from Herrett Stocks, all toward the desired end of turning it into a sort of impromptu and unsanctioned .45 Combat Masterpiece.

I like the end result quite a lot. It emerged from all that with a remarkably nice double-action trigger pull. For some reason, there is a pronounced resistance toward cocking the hammer and the single-action pull is one of the hardest I've ever encountered on a revolver; considerably harder than when originally purchased. As a result, I use it primarily for double-action shooting, at which its performance is altogether flawless.

The Colt Model 1917 revolver was based upon that firm's New Service design, introduced in 1897 and discountinued in 1943. After WWII, Colt never resumed the manufacture of large-frame revolvers in calibers bigger than the .357 magnum of their Python and King Cobra models.

Smith & Wesson, on the other hand, continues to produce their N-frame revolvers upon which the S&W M1917 was based, having been originally introduced as the Military Model of 1908 and chambered for the .44 Special cartridge. Collectively termed the Hand Ejector, the design

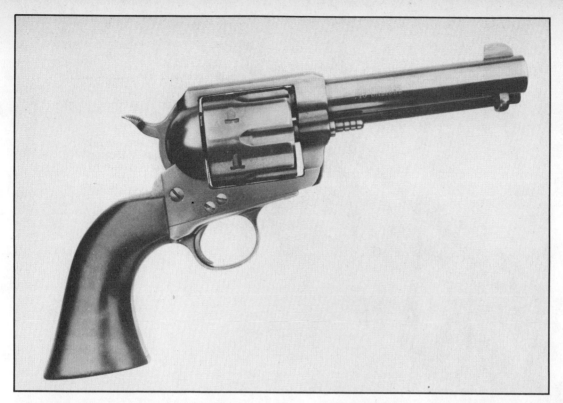

Above and right, Grover's design features a graceful trigger, tucked back where it belongs; a hammer spur that doesn't hide the sights when not cocked and some superb workmanship. This is a 4" in .45 Colt.

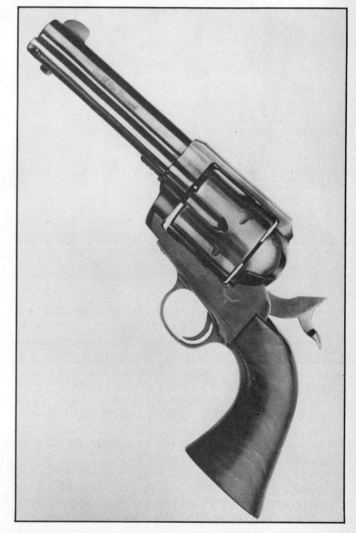

has gone through at least four distinct model changes.

The S&W Hand Ejector, Fourth Model introduced in 1950, was also known as the 1950 Target Model, with the .44 Special version designated as the Model 24 and the .45 as the Model 25, in a numbering system introduced in 1957. The latter came to be sub-designated as the Model 25-2 when chambered for the .45 ACP/Auto Rim cartridges and the Model 25-5, if chambered for the .45 Colt round.

In 1956, the Model 29 was introduced chambered for the then-new .44 magnum, with the Models 27 and 28 respectively identifying the target sight and fixed sight versions of the .357 magnum, which was introduced in 1935. When the .41 magnum appeared in early 1964, the target sight version was termed the Model 57 and the fixed sight was Model 58.

The 1955 Target Model incorporated several changes requested by target competitors, including a heavier barrel and target stocks. With the advent of stainless steel for handgun production, Smith & Wesson added a figure 6 to their model designations to indicate use of that alloy. Thus, when a five-inch version of the .45 ACP/AR revolver in stainless steel was introduced in early 1989, it was designated as the Model 625-2.

A rather small number of the .44 Special Model 24s were produced with four-inch barrels, the 6.5-inch length used for the bulk of production. If they ever made any of the 1950 Models in .45 ACP/AR — later termed the Model 26 — with a four-inch barrel, I've not encountered them. I

Left and facing page, matching profile views of the Smith & Wesson Model 25-2 in .45 ACP/Auto Rim.

think it would have made an interesting modification and the conversion of the Gil Hebard Model 1917 was my own personal effort to find out how such a gun would perform. I don't know if any of the 1955 Models ever were made in .44 Special. Again, I've not encountered any, if they were.

Certainly one of the most familiar examples of the .45 revolver is Colt's Single Action Army or SAA. It was introduced about 1873, more or less simultaneously with the .45 Colt or Long Colt cartridge and, although it has been chambered for various other calibers, the .45 Colt still is by far the most popular.

As with the Colt M1911, any number of clones and lookalikes of the Colt SAA have been produced, both in this country and overseas. Perhaps one of the best known of these is the Ruger Blackhawk, currently cataloged with 4⅝- or 7½-inch barrels in .45 Colt.

At one time, Ruger offered convertible guns that included a fitted spare cylinder for the .45 ACP as well as the .45 Colt much as they continue to produce a .357 magnum Blackhawk with spare cylinder for the 9mm Parabellum. The .45 LC/ACP Blackhawk was a thoroughly pleasing rig, with a lot of versatility. The rimless ACP case posed no problem with it, as the ejector rod of the single-action design punched out the empty cases as neatly as anyone might wish.

I have a .45 ACP cylinder for my .45 Ruger Blackhawk — somewhere. The problem is, right at the moment, I cannot put hands upon it. All too frequently, I have difficulties with equipment seeming to drift over into the Twilight Zone for a time. Usually, the given item returns in time and nearly always after I no longer feel a sharp need for its use.

In this instance, I've little doubt the .45 ACP Blackhawk cylinder will rematerialize, about a week or ten days after I finish working on this book.

A comparable situation existed with my Super-14 Contender barrel in .45 Colt. I had loaned the barrel to a friend, Tom Ferguson, and he had returned it. I remembered that quite distinctly. Again, I kept looking for it as an unattached barrel, perhaps with scope mount and rings in place, alas to no avail.

One day, I was returning some guns to the storage vault, including a few Contenders and I was checking the caliber markings on each. To my unbounded amazement, I found myself holding a complete Contender, fitted with a Redfield scope, the barrel marked .45 Colt. Apparently, I'd finished mounting the barrel to a receiver, had scoped it

and put it away, all without the slightest recollection of having done so. Friend Jim Andrews blames such things on an all-too-common malady he refers to as *CRAFT*. That, he explains, is an acronym, standing for Can't Remember A Flipping Thing.

Be that as it may, I lost little time in making up some loads to try out in the big rig. This is not to be confused with the dual-purpose Contender barrels that handle both the .45 Colt and .410-bore shotshells. In such barrels, the leade of the rifling lies a considerable distance from the bullet as it rests in the chamber. Further, the sights on such barrels are rather rudimentary, being more suited for firing .410 shotshells than single bullets. As a result, .45 Colt accuracy in the .45 Colt/.410 Contender barrel tends to be rather disappointing.

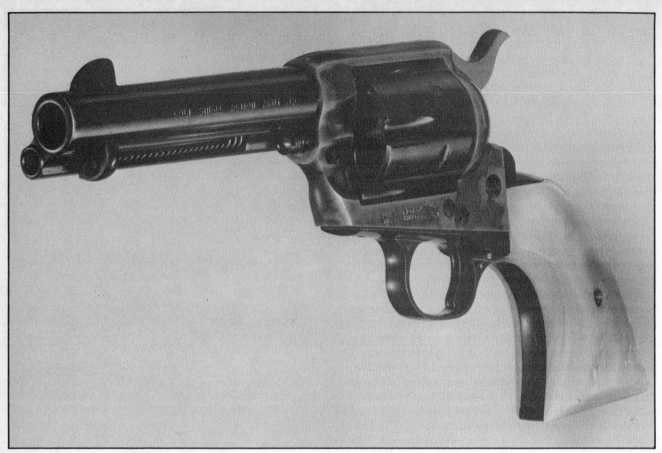

Mention .45 revolver, and most gun enthusiasts will think of the Colt Single Action Army model, here in a four-inch .45 Colt version from the collection of Jack Lewis, with pearl stocks, yet!

Though perhaps not as glamorous as the Colt SAA, the .45 Blackhawk from Sturm, Ruger and Company, is an excellent shooter and has a considerably stronger action. It can be had with a fitted cylinder to handle the .45 ACP cartridge, as well as .45 Colt; I have one but can't find it.

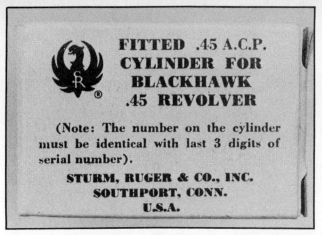

FITTED .45 A.C.P.
CYLINDER FOR
BLACKHAWK
.45 REVOLVER

(Note: The number on the cylinder must be identical with last 3 digits of serial number).

STURM, RUGER & CO., INC.
SOUTHPORT, CONN.
U.S.A.

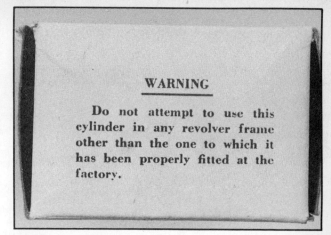

WARNING

Do not attempt to use this cylinder in any revolver frame other than the one to which it has been properly fitted at the factory.

I do, however, have the box in which the .45 ACP Blackhawk cylinder was shipped. Here are two views of it.

The Super-14 Contender barrel in .45 Colt is an entirely different bucket of smelts. It will not accept a .410 shell and I'm grateful for that. In California, possession of one of the .45 Colt/.410 Contender barrels is good for a year in jail, as the state attorney general takes the attitude that it's a sawed-off shotgun and will prosecute accordingly.

The .45 Colt Super-14 barrel displayed accuracy well beyond my most optimistic hopes and some experimental handloads achieved noteworthy velocities. I'm still working to isolate a good load for the heavier bullets and plan to report final results in the chaper on .45 reloading.

Now that Thompson/Center Arms have their long-awaited custom shop — known as Fox Ridge Outfitters — the Super-14 barrels in straight .45 Colt can be ordered and I think it's one of the more interesting possibilities. Unlike the .45-70, recoil of the Super-14 .45 Colt is relatively moderate, considering the ballistics it develops.

For a brief period in the early Seventies, Thompson/Center produced ten-inch bull barrels in .45 ACP and I have one of those. I also have what is believed to be the only .45 Auto Rim Contender barrel in existence. It is a ten-inch bull barrel, also. Warren Center built it up personally to gratify my longing for such a barrel. As a usual procedure, when making up a special barrel for me, he'd produce another for his personal collection. He did not do so with the .45 Auto Rim, however, noting the extractor was a serious challenge. By the time he got the one to function, he felt strongly desinclined to tackle another.

Over the years, various makers have produced single-action revolvers in .45-70 and E.F. Phelps Manufacturing Company, (1703 South Taft Street, Evansville, IN 47710) currently makes one with a choice of eight- or ten-inch

A really capable vehicle for the .45 Colt is this Thompson/Center Contender with a custom Super-14 barrel and 4X Redfield scope on Redfield base and rings. With the right load, it will keep all this inside a 1¼" circle at 25 yards!

At one time, T/C made Contender barrels in .45 ACP and here's a 10" bull barrel in that caliber, with a 2X Leupold scope in Conetrol mounts. It makes a great rig for trying out experimental loads in .45 ACP.

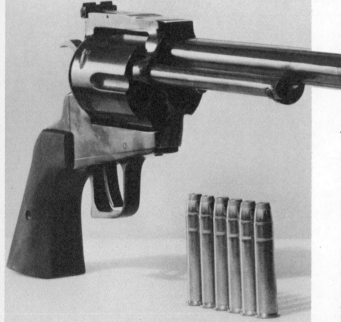

This is the Phelps Heritage single-action revolver in .45-70 Government, also available in .444 Marlin.

barrels, along with another chambered for the .444 Marlin. I have seen the Phelps *Heritage,* as it's called, but have not fired it.

To me, one of the charming things about the non-auto guns in the various .45 calibers is that you needn't concern yourself with functioning through an autoloading action, thereby getting a great deal of leeway for light loads, heavy loads or loads with non-typical bullet weights and shapes. As a further delight, the cases come out when you want them to come out and you needn't court sacroiliac problems by picking them up off the ground.

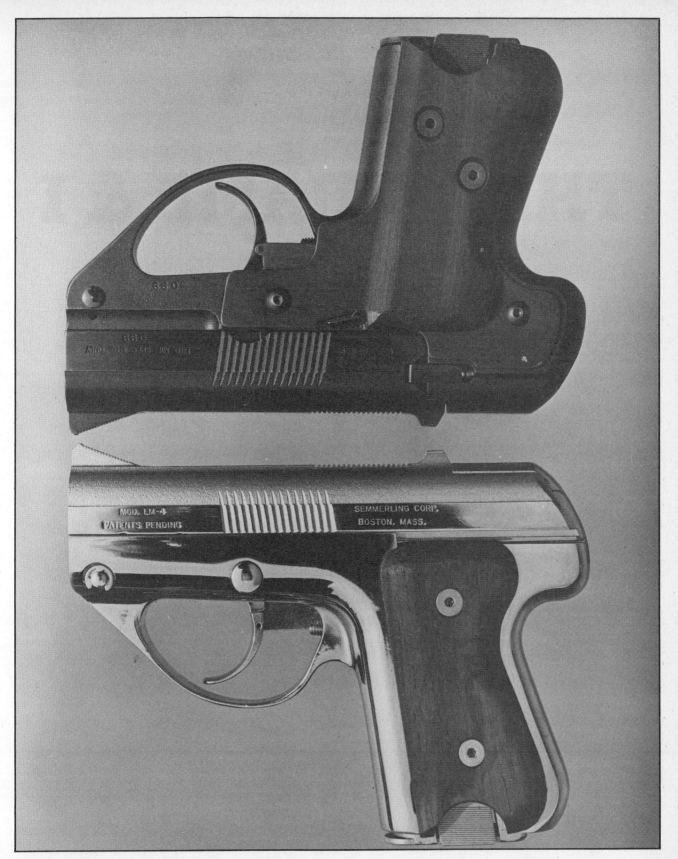

Blued and chrome versions of the Semmerling Model LM-4, which looks like an autoloader, but is not. You fire the chambered round of .45 ACP, then manually shove the slide forward and pull it back to eject the spent case and feed a fresh round from the magazine to the chamber. Trigger is double-action. Currently made and distributed by American Derringer, the suggested retail price is around $2000.

THE O-FRAME & I

Some Purely Subjective Notes,
To Explain Why And How
Someone Can Become Infatuated With A Gun

USAAF Photo

The bulk of gunnery school training was done out of the rear cockpit of North American AT-6s, with air-cooled caliber .30 Brownings in flexible mounts. There was no fire-interrupter to keep you from shooting off the aircraft's vertical stabilizer, but one took care not to do so. A safety belt went through the crotch straps of the parachute harness to keep you from falling out and that saved my personal bacon on one occasion.

Camera film was an awfully scarce commodity in the 1941-1945 era, so I don't have many photos beyond these yellowing prints of Pfc. Grennell in a Martin upper turret (above) and standing next to a waist gun mockup (left), with the obligatory scarf of caliber .50 ammo draped picturesquely about neck.

Y OU JUST said, "The O-*Whaat?*" I knew you were going to ask that; a goodly number of you, at least. Relatively few are aware that, in certain areas in Hartford, Connecticut, any pistols being constructed more or less on or about the chassis of what most of us think of as the Government Model are referred to as O-frames by the people who produce them. It's a term you're welcome to add to your vocabulary.

Sixty years have come and gone since my first encounter with the O-frame and a couple of its stablemates. It was 1929, in the fall of that singularly unfortunate year. I was 5, going on 6, come All Saints' Day and I'd been enrolled in the first grade at Atwater (Wisconsin) District No. 6. Kindergarten had yet to be invented; at least, in that bucolic locale.

You've got to understand the world was different in that time and place. Radio — strictly monaural — was just barely edging onto the scene; an expensive toy for the wealthy and elite, usually powered by batteries, at least in the rural areas. The dim dawn of television was twenty years yet to come, as were all the myriad electronic bemusements of contemporary culture, such as VHS recorders and the like. The automobile was on the scene and one could drive in to the nearest town to view a movie. "Talkies" were just edging up over the eastern horizon.

The first talkie the rest of my family and I ever saw was called *High Society Blues,* a monstrous marvel, at the time. The only scraplet in my personal memory is a brief swatch of lyric: "When nobody comes/To drink our booze/We sort of get those/High Society Blues..."

What I'm trying to say is that, for the average rural family, after the cows were milked and the sun had gone down, there were not a whole lot of interesting things to do. You could strain your eyes reading by the wan orange glow of wick-type kerosene lamps. If you happened to own a crank-up Victrola and some records, you could listen to music, even though you already knew every note, click, hiss and scratch of it.

Along in the winter of 1926-7, after we'd made the pilgrimage from Kansas to Wisconsin, my father discovered an intriguing way to pass the long evenings. He began teaching me to read and write. I recall it as a painful intrusion on my privacy, but he was insistent, as well as a pretty good amateur teacher. As a net result, I was reading the funny papers to myself, well before my fifth birthday and a good year before I launched my formal academic career at good old Atwater District No. 6.

My father kept on with it and I suspect the main reason I didn't start school with a solid grounding in subjects such as differential calculus and spherical trigonometry was due

Despite the fact that Art is my middle name, I make no great claim to skill at freehand sketching and offer these four with such apologies as you may feel they require. Here, I'm about to cut the life-sized rendering of an O-frame out of the end of a discarded peach crate. That's my tongue sticking out of a corner of my mouth, not a fang.

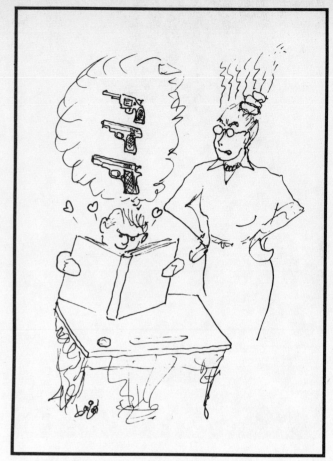

Miss Knudsen took a dim view of my preposterous posturing with the encyclopedia entry on Colts.

to the fact that he was a trifle vague about the details of them.

Thus, I came to encounter my first grade teacher, whose name was Miss Knudsen, at the time. She would return the following year as Mrs. Green, but neither of us were aware of it that year. She launched into the prescribed drill for hammering the bare rudiments of reading and writing into the skull of an unbranded illiterate and found singularly fertile soil.

I, in turn, found the little one-room country school a most fascinating place. They had racks of books in the back of the room and I began to explore them with the keen interest of a Champollion, inadvertently finding himself confined in a quarry of Rosetta Stones.

Among the immensely intriguing volumes in the racks at the back of the school, there was some manner of a set of encyclopedias and I found those highly absorbing.

I suspect I must have gotten to the point of paging through the third volume in the set and, not quite halfway through, I must have come to an entry for "Colt." At any rate, it was illustrated with three line drawings of handguns.

Reading from the top down, there were depictions of the Colt Police Positive, the Colt Pocket Model and — glory, glory be! — the Colt Government Model!

I had been fascinated by handguns to the near verge of morbidity ever since my unrecalled first intimation that such things existed. The pictures of the three Colts and, particularly, that of the Government Model came close to uprooting my youthful mind.

I recall Miss Knudsen took a dim view of my preposterous posturings with the encyclopedia. At length, she determined to shame me out of my silly *schtick* and asked me to bring one of the volumes up and read from it, in front of the entire school. I proceeded to do so fairly briskly, now and then stumbling a trifle over pronunciation of a word I'd never heard voiced to that point. Nonetheless, I did well enough that she never bothered me about it, again. All she asked was that I complete my assigned lessons before returning to my extracurricular activities, and I did my best to comply.

That was my primal encounter with the O-frame and I'll remain convinced — until it's proved otherwise — the

"...a harsh metallic glint in his steely bock beer-colored eyes."

"It hardly took more than one shot to develop a flinch of heroic proportions."

drawing was of a Model 1911A1, rather than of a Model 1911. After all, by late '29, the A1 version had appeared upon the scene, as had the .38 Colt Super. The mind's eye recollects an image of an arched mainspring housing and a neat, short trigger. The mind's eye, I must concede with rueful candor, can remember anything whatsoever, quite regardless of whether it ever happened or not.

The years continued to edge past, with maddening deliberation. It's all a matter of percentile proportions. When you're 6, a year represents something like sixteen percent of your lifespan to date. After you've seen sixty-odd of them come and go, a year gets down to more like .016 percent of the total and thus no longer looms so large in perspective and their passing reminds one of walking along at a brisk pace, holding a stick against a picket fence.

It came to be 1934 and Jimmy Cagney starred in a film — talkies were solidly established, by that time — called *G-Man.* There was a scene wherein he pitched his badge and gun onto someone's desk and stomped off in a towering dudgeon. The gun was some manner of O-frame, presumably in .45 ACP and I may be able to retrieve that scrap of memory, as that film is in the , uhh, "ourchives," in videotape, scavenged off some ante-midnight television program.

By that time, I was sneaking up on my eleventh birthday, a veritable paragon of worldly sophistication and all that. It constituted my second head-on encounter with the O-frame image and it packed a helluva lot of psychokinetic impact.

I must ask a lot of you to accept my unsupported word that, in those days, the penny postcard remained an actuality and would continue to do so until some unrecalled point in the early Fifties. About that time, or shortly thereafter, I encountered my first gunzine. It was called *Hunting & Fishing* and sold for a nickel a copy off the newsstands. I purchased a copy, all my very own and it was by no means a casual impulse, as you may judge by the fact that my cash-flow of the era amounted to exactly seven cents per week.

Then as now, however, one could save money by becoming a subscriber. Rather than splurging sixty cents for a dozen copies, you could send the publisher a quarter and

Left, the man in the center is Robert Lincoln Finklestein, from Wilkes-Barre, Pennsylvania. I regret the names of the other two fellow instructors at the Tonopah ground gunnery range are not retrievable from the depths of foggy memory. In the photo at right, I'm the one on the right, posing with the tommy gun.

What I wouldn't have given for one of these in the 1936 era! It's a life-sized metal replica of the O-frame, with more or less working parts, created primarily for gun fanciers in countries where guns are forbidden.

get the next twelve issues delivered to your mailbox, hot off the press and the ink still a trifle gooey. It took some major maneuvering, but I managed to scrape together the price of a subscription and sent it off.

One of the *H&F* advertisers was the National Rifle Association and you could request a sample copy of their monthly publication, the *American Rifleman,* by sending in a penny postcard. As of about that time, I began receiving the *AR* for an out-of-pocket expenditure of about twelve cents a year.

All the major gunmakers advertised in the *Rifleman* and you could request copies of their current catalogs, so I blew some more penny postcards in that direction.

Fickle memory says the Colt mailing of that era was on glossy paper, rather pinkish in color. They had replaced the picturesque line drawings with straight halftone photographs. All the delectable offerings remained in the line: the svelte Pocket Model, the cute little Vest Pocket .25, the incomparably graceful Woodsman, the capable-looking Police Positive, the hairy-chested New Service and, of course, the Government Model.

The accompanying specifications gave the overall length of the big pistol and, by that time, I'd gotten a grip upon sufficient math savvy to enable me to concoct a scaled-up, life-size drawing of the doughty hand-howitzer and I proceeded to do so. Aha, so *that* was the size of the beast, was it?

Raw material for construction projects was not all that plentiful, nor were there a whole great lot of woodworking tools on hand, but I had been given an inexpensive coping saw and I managed to put hands upon a wooden crate that had carried peaches to the marketplace. The ends of the crate were about three-quarter-inch in thickness.

I managed to transfer the dimensions of my painfully developed life-size drawing to a hunk of wood from the end of the peach crate and used the coping saw to bring it into a rough likeness of its ferrous counterpart.

It still needed a set a stocks and, in feverish scrounging about, I came upon a piece of black Bakelite, one-quarter-inch or so in thickness, that had been the front panel of a defunct Atwater Kent radio. Again, I traced the scaled outlines, coped them out with the coping saw, as best I could cope with the project, beveled the edges with a file and attached them in the proper places.

At long last, I had a tangible replica of my dream-gun, pretty close to life-size and I derived a great deal of deep-down soul satisfaction from clutching the monster in my hand and brandishing it about. I clamped it in my father's bench vise and managed to drill a hole in the muzzle, fairly straight and square, approximately the proper diameter.

Then, as now, Battle Creek, Michigan was the nation's provider of prepared breakfast food and, in those days, you could save up cereal box-tops to barter for any number of desirable items. The box-tops from one particular make of the stuff could serve to procure a Junior G-Man badge. It may have been Huskies or perhaps Grape-Nuts and frankly, Scarlett, I don't give a foop. The thing is, I saved up, sent for one and became duly enbadged.

V-Jay Day had come and gone and I'd finally gotten a second stripe, as well as a rampantly un-GI uniform.

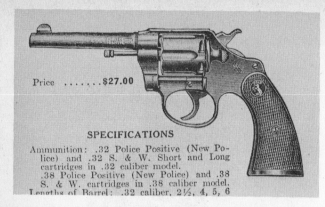

Price $27.00

SPECIFICATIONS

Ammunition: .32 Police Positive (New Police) and .32 S. & W. Short and Long cartridges in .32 caliber model.
.38 Police Positive (New Police) and .38 S. & W. cartridges in .38 caliber model.
Lengths of Barrel: .32 caliber, 2½, 4, 5, 6

The line drawings in the schoolroom encyclopedia would have looked quite a bit like these pictures of the Colt Police Positive, Pocket Model and O-frame, copied from a 1936 Stoeger's catalog furnished by friend Warren Center. Don't those prices choke you? Below, the right side of the imitation O-frame carries a sure-enough serial number for authenticity.

Price $20.50

This is the favorite model for personal and home protection. Ready always for instant action.

Price $36.75

r and Hammer Spur: Checked.
Housing: Checked.
Checked Walnut.
Blued. Nickel Finish **$5.00**

02568

Above, further details on the fake O-frame. The slide locks back and the magazine comes out but there's a reassuring nub in the bore at the muzzle. Right, don't you just love that "Caliver 45" designation?

One of the childhood chores on a Wisconsin dairy farm was to go get the cows from their pasture, at some starkly obscene hour of the early morning, fetching them back for milking, then to do the same thing for the evening milking. As of about that time, the family herd was transferred back and forth at (wooden) gunpoint, by a duly constituted law enforcement officer of the Federal government, replete with Junior G-Man badge carefully positioned on the left side of his blue chambray shirt and a peach crate replica of a Government Model .45 ACP pistol unswervingly clenched in his right hand, a harsh metallic glint in his bock beer-colored eyes.

I view all that, in painfully adult retrospect, as sort of uncomfortably hilarious. Despite that, I still recall it seemed immensely plausible and important at the time. Our priorities tend to shift and settle about as time moves along.

The years came, the years went. I had yet to formulate Grennell's Seventeenth Law Of Subjective Time-Flow, which states, "In nothing flat, it's going to get to be a helluva lot later!" The effect was in force even then, however.

The decade of the Thirties merged inexorably into the decade of the Forties and the global situation become sort of hairy, about that time. I reached age 18 on my personal odometer, exactly three dozen days before the attack on Pearl Harbor.

Franklin Delano Roosevelt was still in the White House and those were the days of the alphabetical government agencies: WPA, NRA, CCC, and NYA, among others. NRA stood for National Recovery Act and was symbolized by a blue eagle insignia, with the proud legend, "We Do Our Part." It had no connection with the National Rifle Association. NYA stood for National Youth Administration.

Due to starting the first grade at age 5 and skipping the second grade entirely, I had graduated from high school in the spring of 1940, several months short of my seventeenth birthday. There was not a whole lot one could do until the eighteenth birthday came and went, so I had to bide my time until early November, 1941. With that to the rear, I got into an NYA program in Racine, Wisconsin, residing at a dormitory, attending classes at Racine Vocational School in aircraft mechanics, getting my room, board and $12 per month to spend any way I saw fit to disburse it.

I stayed with the NYA program for a few months and got some good stuff out of it. For one thing, there was a math instructor at Racine Vocational, named George Kroening, with the unique ability to make any and all students understand the stuff. I shall be grateful to him for the remainder of my allotted days.

After leaving the NYA program, I took a few boring, low-paying jobs and ended up joining the Army Air Force. After a few months, I signed up for training as an aviation cadet, was classified for pilot training and, in preflight training, finally got my hands upon a Government Model .45 ACP pistol, firing it for qualification.

It would be gratifying to report that all that intense motivation resulted in an impressive score. Sad to say, that would be untrue. What I didn't realize, but found out quite quickly, was that the big pistol made a noise that was like a jet of ice water shot into each ear. More, it bucked and twisted violently in recoil. It hardly took more than one shot to develop a flinch of heroic proportions.

My score on that first qualification session was a shameful thirty-three percent, far short of the requirement for qualification as marksman, let alone sharpshooter or expert. It was thoroughly disconsolating.

As many another did in those days, I washed out of flight training. It was iron-bound custom for washed out cadets to be sent to gunnery school. I took my course in that at Harlingen, Texas, and graduated number four in a class of five hundred. They packed me off to gunnery instructors school at Fort Myers, Florida and, after graduating from that I was assigned to instruct on the ground gunnery range at the airfield near Tonopah, Nevada.

Curiously, my shameful performance with the G-Model Colt in cadet preflight was my only encounter to that point. There was no pistol training in gunnery school.

The ground range at Tonopah, however, included a large pistol range and the aircrew members were put through the course on it, firing slow fire at twenty-five yards; timed and rapid-fire at fifteen yards. The targets were six feet square and the 10-ring in the center was six inches or so in diameter. I remain convinced the targets I tried to hit at the San Antonio Aviation Cadet Center — better known in those days as SAADD SAACC — were somewhat smaller.

It was called a Poorman range, presumably in honor of its inventor and Tonopah had one of the few ever set up. A tiny aircraft hung down from a rod and came in on the track for the student to aim at. The steel framework was movable to vary the amount of sight deflection required to hit a pair of targets. I spent a number of months instructing this B-24 Consolidated tail turret setup and did my ears no good at all!

At any rate, I put in some time instructing on the pistol range and, once the students had been put through the course and trucked back to the base, instructors were not all that closely supervised, nor was it necessary to account for every single round of ammunition.

It is possible to become accustomed to nearly anything, even the buck and blast of the G-Model auto. There were a hundred or so pistols issued to the range and it was part of my duties to serve as armorer and keep all of them functioning.

So it came to pass that I selected one particular pistol that seemed to group a little better than the rest. I used a half-round India stone to perform my first-ever trigger job on it and succeeded in coaxing it into a pretty decent pull. As opportunity came along, I practiced firing with that pistol and got to the point where I could produce holes with it fairly close to where I had in mind.

In fact, I fired a qualification course with it and racked up a score well into the expert category. A short time later, just for the heck of it, I did the same, firing with my left hand and scored in the expert category, southpaw. Shooting pistols, I think, is done at least as much with the brain as the hand.

I was still at Tonopah when they dropped the A-bomb on Hiroshima, with V-Jay Day following soon after that. The base commanding officer was determined to celebrate the glad event with a really big parade on the flight line. Everyone would be there, absolutely no exceptions.

You do not, however, leave a ground gunnery range unattended. Someone had to serve as CQ — charge of quarters — and it happened that I drew that assignment. Thus, while all the rest of the field personnel were broiling under the blazing high desert sun of August, I had liberated my pet .45 from its storage locker, and broke out a few boxes of ammo to celebrate the end of the war in my own way.

I set up some tin ammo box liners on the three-hundred-yard line of the rifle range and took my position on the five-hundred-yard line. The object of the impromptu exercise was to walk the hits into the targets, in the manner of artillery fire, by observing the dust puff and aiming higher.

After several shots, I was able to land a reasonable number of hits in the tin liners and, to do so, I had to hold over by what appeared to be about fourteen feet. A lot of years later, with access to computer programs capable of solving such mysteries, I ran the trajectory for GI hardball ammo at two hundred yards and the amount of drop came out quite close to fourteen feet.

Thus it worked out that I regained all my good regard for the Government Model auto, with some to spare. As the postwar years came and went, I bought various specimens, keeping some, trading some and have several examples on hand at present. The foregoing may suggest how all this mass of good regard for a distinctive-looking pistol came about.

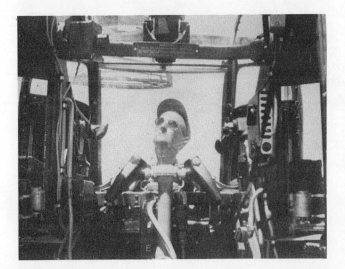

Left, you're looking at a tail gunner's-eye view from the turret on facing page, through five plies of so-called "bulletproof" glass laminations. Above, executed when I was reassigned to the photo lab at Hamilton Field in late 1945, I tentatively titled this photo, "Farewell to Arms."

CHAPTER 9

.45 ACP CARBINES

Improved Performance Is Possible, Though Not Easy!

Simultaneously targeting and chronographing loads through the .45 ACP Uzi pistol. The device at the right is a Brass Catcher, from M.A.M. Products, 153-B Cross Slope Court, Englishtown, New Jersey 07726; it's handy!

LOGIC SUGGESTS a longer barrel should deliver higher velocity with a given load and perhaps improved accuracy, as well. In actual practice, the answer to that one turns out to be, "Sometimes, yes, sometimes, no."

The end results depend heavily upon the burning speed of the powder. In typical .45 ACP factory loads, the powder charge will have been selected to do most of its work within the space of the five-inch barrels that are typical for firearms handling that cartridge.

If you fire the same round in a ten-inch or twenty-inch barrel, the powder charge is apt to have burned completely by the time the bullet is something like six or eight inches up the bore.

There is a tremendous amount of friction involved in driving a bullet through a rifled bore. That becomes acutely apparent if you ever happen to get a bullet stuck in the bore and have to drive it back out with a brass rod or mallet. The frictional resistance is a lot greater with jacketed bullets than with cast ones, but it's considerable, even with the latter.

As the powder charge burns, it is converted into a quantity of hot gas under high pressure. The mouth of the cartridge case expands outward to the limit of the chamber wall, serving to *obturate* or seal against rearward leakage of the high-pressure powder gas.

As the bullet begins to move up the bore, it provides additional volume into which the powder gas can expand and, in so doing, the net pressure of the body of powder gas subsides in proportion. The effect is accelerated as some of the heat of the reaction is passed to the bullet, case and bore walls, cooling the gas and acting to reduce its pressure even further.

Here is where the burning speed of the powder becomes really important. If you load a fast-burning powder such as Hercules Bullseye, it may deliver substantially *less* velocity from a twenty-inch barrel than from a five-inch. Such powders are great in short barrels, not so hot in long ones.

THE MARLIN CAMP CARBINE

One of the most interesting and rewarding shoulder guns chambered for handgun cartridges is the Marlin Camp Carbine. Introduced originally for the 9mm Parabellum, it later was produced in .45 ACP, as well. I have one in each caliber and, if pressed for a decision, would have to admit a slight preference for the .45 over the 9mmP.

To date, I've had slightly better accuracy with the 9mmP. How good? Well, with the 115-grain Hornady No. 3554 JHP bullet ahead of 10.8 grains of Hodgdon H110 powder, five shots at twenty-five yards went into a center-spread of just .250-inch. That works out to a thin slice less than one minute of angle (MOA). The 9mmP carbine was fitted with a Weaver 1.5x-4.5x variable scope on Weaver mounts and rings. Ballistics for that load were 1162 fps velocity and 345 fpe energy, or 1162/345 in the usual manner of quoting.

Hercules Blue Dot was the powder that really got things going with the 9mmP Marlin. The No. 10 *Speer Manual* had specified up to a maximum of 10.2 grains of Blue Dot behind the 100-grain Speer No. 3983 JHP for 1438/459 out of a four-inch pistol barrel. I cut the charge back to 9.5 grains of Blue Dot behind the same bullet and it came out of

The Marlin Camp Carbine well may be the most accurate gun available for the .45 ACP cartridge.

Also available in 9mm Parabellum, the Marlin Camp Carbine is the ultimate fun gun.

the Marlin averaging 1734/668, grouping five shots into a center-spread of .521-inch.

I should note the No. 11 *Speer Manual* still lists a 9mmP load for Blue Dot powder with their 100-grain JHP bullet, but the maximum load has been reduced from 10.2 grains to 9.3 grains.

In the .45 ACP Marlin Camp Carbine, the feed ramp and chamber provide nearly total support to the chambered cartridge. Unlike most pistols in that caliber, there is no significant amount of bare brass hanging over the feed ramp. Thus, the risk of blown case heads should be minimized.

In design, however, the Marlin Camp Carbine is a straight blowback, rather than a system that fires from a locked breech. In effect, that sort of cancels out the generous amount of case head support. The strength of the recoil spring and weight of the bolt are proportioned for typical factory loads and stronger loads would impose undue and unwanted stress upon the action and working parts.

Despite the rather steep feed ramp, the Marlin .45 ACP tends to feed nearly any bullet quite reliably. About the only stoppages I've encountered have been due to loads with insufficient powder, incapable of driving the bolt back far enough to eject the spent case, cock the action and pick a fresh cartridge off the top of the magazine. It even feeds the Lyman No. 452423 cast semi-wadcutter bullet quite reliably, with its broad, flat area at the nose. Ordinarily, that is considered strictly a bullet for use in revolvers.

Speaking of magazines, the one used in the .45 ACP Marlin is essentially a duplicate of the one for the Model 1911-type Colts and Colt magazines will work just fine in it.

The best group I've fired with the .45 ACP Marlin to date used the Remington No. R45AP4 factory load with its 230-grain FMJ round-nose bullet. Average velocity was 842 fps, good for 362 fpe. Five shots at twenty-five yards drilled into a group with a center-spread of .357-inch, translating to 1.363 MOA.

You will note that hardly represents more velocity and foot-poundage than one might expect from a Model 1911-type pistol. It gets back to the earlier observation about how most factory loads are designed so the powder charge achieves nearly complete combustion about the time the bullet is five inches out of the muzzle. Barrel length on the Marlin Camp Carbine is about 16⅜ inches. It seems probable the bullet reaches a higher velocity at some point between five inches and the muzzle, but frictional resistance slows it down before it emerges.

The problem of obtaining noteworthy performance from the .45 ACP in a straight blowback carbine stems from the rather low pressure ceiling decreed for the .45 ACP by the Sporting Arms and Ammunition Manufacturers Institute (SAAMI) of 19,900 copper units of pressure (CUP). The 9mmP, along with the .38 Super, operate at pressure ceilings of 35,700 CUP and provide quite a bit more elbow-room for experimental ballistics.

Speaking in loose generalities, it is difficult to achieve velocities much beyond 2000 fps with a straight-sided case, regardless of the barrel length or case length. The .45 ACP is a straight-sided case and is relatively short. It was designed to move a 230-grain FMJ bullet out of a five-inch barrel at something like 780-820 fps or so and it performs that function quite acceptably.

In conversation with Marlin's Tony Aeschliman, I asked if he had any plans for producing the Camp Carbine in .38 Super. He replied that the .38 Super was one of his own personal favorite cartridges, but he was uncertain on a couple of points: Would it show any appreciable gain in performance over the 9mmP in a barrel of that length and would it sell enough carbines to justify the tooling and production cost?

You can improve ballistics quite usefully if you switch to a bottleneck cartridge case and you might think the obvious possibility is the .38-45 Clerke that is made by necking down a .45 ACP case to accept bullets of .355-inch (9mm) diameter.

I hate to rain upon your picnic, but I doubt whether that would be a good caliber for the Marlin Camp Carbine due to the fact that the carbine action is not locked at the instant of firing. I'm inclined to suspect a Marlin Camp Carbine in .38-45 Clerke would encounter somewhat the same problem as I encountered in the Uzi carbine in 9mm Action Express. We'll discuss that further in just a bit.

I've long been a firm believer in the need for wearing shooting glasses while shooting. The Marlin Camp Carbine seems to have a habit of directing unburned powder particles back in the shooter's face, making eye protection exceptionally important when firing it. The effect is noticeable when firing it off the right shoulder and somewhat more so when firing from the left one.

On a load with 12.5 grains of Accurate Arms No. 7 (AA-7) powder, behind the 185-grain Nosler JHP bullet, average velocity from the Marlin .45 ACP camp carbine is 1278 fps, 671 fpe, and it groups about one inch in center-spread at twenty-five yards. That is a +P load in .45 ACP. Accurate Arms' Marty Liggins reports that 11.0 grains of

AA-7 behind the 185-grain Nosler JHP delivers right at 20,000 CUP and should be considered the maximum load at standard pressure and is to be approached with caution in the given gun. With 12.5 grains, pressure would be about 23,200 CUP.

The load of 12.5 grains of AA-7 was put up in unfired brass cases from PMC, using Federal 150 primers. Examination of the fired cases showed moderate pressure signs on the primers, but no bulging in the case head area, even when fired in typical M1911-type pistols.

I merely report results on that load with 12.5 grains of Accurate Arms No. 7 powder; I do not recommend it for use by others. You should be aware that some makers of .45 ACP pistols, in the general pattern of the Colt Model 1911A1, use barrel blanks produced by investment casting and others use two-piece barrels, with the lower shank attached to the barrel proper by welding, brazing or other methods. Such barrels do not possess the strength and durability of barrels machined from forgings and may fail under even moderate amounts of stress.

THE UZI CARBINE AND PISTOL

Initially, the Uzi semi-automatic carbine and autoloading pistol were made in 9mm Parabellum. Later, versions of each were produced to handle the .45 ACP cartridge. Still later, barrels and magazines were offered to use the .41 Action Express and 9mm Action Express.

In working with the original .41 Action Express — a rebated head case, with head dimensions of the 9mmP and a body sized to accept bullets of .410-inch diameter — I experienced no noteworthy problems.

The .41 Action Express had been the brainchild of Evan Whildin, vice president of Action Arms Ltd. He then went on to the next logical step and necked the .41 Action Express case back down to accept bullets of .355-inch diameter again. The result was a cartridge packing a lot more pizazz than the 9mmP or the .38 Super.

How much more? Well, in working with a five-inch barrel for it in the faithful old Colt .38 Super that has been a staunch friend and companion since the fall of 1969, I got the 88-grain Speer No. 4000 JHP going out of its muzzle at an average velocity of 1923 fps. I can remember that figure without undue effort as it's the year of my birth and, with that bullet weight, the wee slug starts out packing 722.76 foot-pounds of kinetic energy.

If you're reaching for writing materials, I can save you the cost of a postage stamp; no minor trifle, these latter years. I am not going to release the data for that particular load. I might make up a few more and fire them, but I don't want anyone else doing it on my say-so.

My reason for cranking all this into the discussion is to note that I fired a somewhat reduced version of that load in the Uzi carbine, out of a 9mm Action Express barrel in the basic 9mmP receiver. The ejected cases made for some really thought-provoking contemplation. The original bottlenecks were almost entirely ironed back to .41 Action

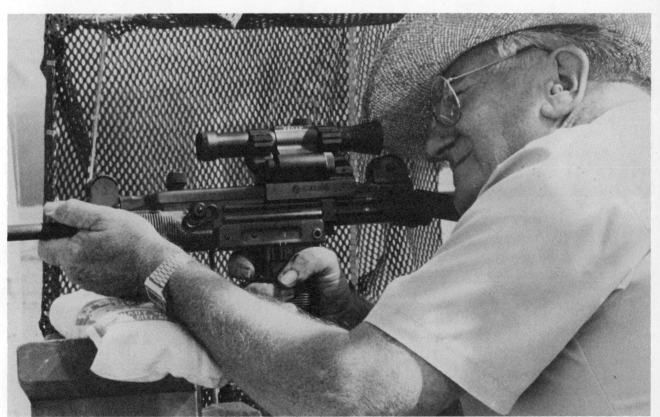

Firing the .45 ACP Uzi carbine, again with the handy Brass Catcher policing up the empty cases.

With its collapsing skeleton stock, the Uzi carbine in .45 ACP is quite compact. The notice shown below is stamped on top of its receiver and should be heeded!

ALTERATIONS TO THIS FIREARM ARE UNSAFE AND ILLEGAL. READ MANUAL BEFORE OPERATING

Express configuration!

What had happened was pretty obvious. As the pressure built up in the chamber, the bullet went down the bore and the case started backing out of the chamber. Pressure of the powder gas continued to seal the case mouth to the chamber wall but, as noted, the case was moving rearward.

Fortunately, the bullet made its exit from the muzzle, thereby venting the pressure vessel before the case eased free of the chamber to do the same thing at the other end. Even so, it was a pretty near thing. Since that time, my intrepidity in making up loads for straight-blowback actions has become severely eroded. In fact, I've gotten downright trepid about such things!

The Uzi carbines and pistols have a certain charm and charisma, if you can overlook their slightly Darth Vader appearance. The carbines, in particular, are capable of delivering respectably decent accuracy, even with the open iron sights that require a tool resembling an old-fashioned skate key for adjustment. If you mount one of the Action Arms red-dot sights or a moderate-power scope, they are capable of dotting in clannish little groups that will brighten your eye and tend to make your coat sleek and glossy.

There are two basic receivers, the carbine and the pistol and each is available in 9mmP or .45 ACP configuration. The two for 9mmP will accept barrels for the .41 and 9mm Action Express, as well. Magazines to feed the two Action Express cartridges may pose minor problems, but I'd hope they have those under control by this time.

Using the Uzi carbine in .45 ACP, there is no slightest problem. The sixteen-round magazines for it hold that

Although it accepts the longer carbine magazines, the magazine supplied with the Uzi pistol is more compact.

many cartridges and feed them with admirable reliability.

As with the .45 ACP Marlin Camp Carbine, the potential is somewhat hamstrung by the innate limitations of the cartridge. Factory loads are designed to get in their best performance in barrels not much over five inches in length. Ballistics can be improved by judicious reloading, but always by keeping the low — 19,900 CUP — pressure ceiling of the cartridge and the hard need for coping with the limitations of the straight-blowback action, firmly uppermost in mind!

A GI CARBINE IN .45 ACP?

The M1 Carbine, introduced in WWII, along with its funny little cartridge the size and shape of a cigarette butt, appears to be one of the more universally adored and admired firearms, as viewed by the massed ranks of shooting sportspeople in the USA. As originally issued, it is capable of decent performance, both as to accuracy and ballistics. It was conceived as a weapon that would offer certain advantages over the existing Model 1911A1 pistol at the cost of greater weight and reduced portability.

The GI carbine fires a bullet of .308-inch diameter, compared to the .451-inch diameter of the .45 ACP cartridge. Respective cross-sectional areas are .074- and .159-square inch: roughly a two-to-one ratio, with the fine edge in favor of the considerably older pistol cartridge.

In all fairness, it must be conceded that it's easier to score a hit upon a given target with the GI carbine than with the Government Model pistol. A small bullet that hits its intended mark delivers more useful effect than a much larger projectile that misses.

All of which seems to hoist the basic question: If the GI carbine were capable of firing the .45 ACP cartridge, what might be its resulting potential?

As it turns out, it's possible to convert the beloved GI carbine to handle the — at least arguably — beloved .45

Firing the GI carbine converted to .45 ACP by J.W. Carlson of Crofton, Nebraska: another real fun gun!

ACP cartridge within limits. In fact, I have one of the converted carbines on hand.

The conversions are performed by J.W. "Doc" Carlson, (304 West Harold, Crofton, NE 68730). If it's done on a carbine furnished by the customer, Carlson's current fee — subject to change — is $125, including return shipping charges to addresses within the contiguous forty-eight states.

Discussing it with him, he said one of the problems lies in getting the old steel magazines. It may or may not be necessary to perform slight modification of the magazine lips to make the .45 ACP cartridge feed properly. That's no big thing with the older steel magazines, but one can't do much with plastic magazines.

As converted, the carbine won't self-load with typical .45 ACP factory ammunition. Thus you have, in effect, a straight-pull bolt-action and I don't regard that as entirely to the bad. For one thing, it's much simpler to keep track of the empty cases.

Carlson says it's possible to get the action to function, but you have to work up special loads for the purpose, adding, "Heaven help you, if one of those loads gets into a .45 pistol!"

I asked if he'd ever thought of converting to the .45 Winchester magnum. He said no, but it seemed like an interesting idea. When he started doing the conversions, the .45 Win mag wasn't even a gleam in Wildey Moore's eye. Carlson has, however, worked some up for a cartridge he calls the .38-40 Rimless and says those can be made to work the action in pretty good fashion.

FEDERAL ENGINEERING MODEL XC-45

This is an unusual but highly efficient design, produced by heli-arc welding for the basic assembly. Available in 9mmP as well as .45 ACP, the Model XC-450 has a 16¼-inch barrel with integral flash-hider vents at the muzzle. Standard finish is a full phosphate black and teflon finish is available as an option.

Supplied as standard is an adjustable Williams peep-type rear sight that's adjustable for windage and elevation. If desired, a scope or red-dot sight can be installed quite easily to capitalize upon the impressive degree of accuracy

The Federal Engineering Model XC-45 is remarkably accurate and efficient.

Above, fired case at left is a 9mm Action Express that orginally looked like the one at right. Fired in the Uzi carbine's non-locking action, the bolt began moving to the rear as the bullet was still in the bore, ironing out the neck. Below, testing setup with the Oehler Model 35P chronograph and target at 25 yards and the Marlin Camp Carbine in .45 ACP on portable shooting bench.

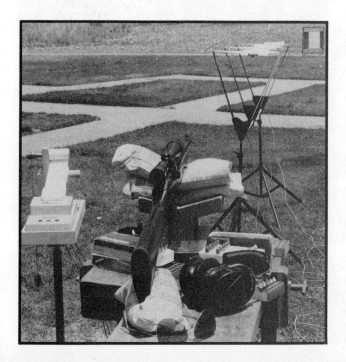

of which this carbine is capable.

The Federal Engineering Model XC-450 is a straight blowback design, but the combination of a somewhat stronger recoil spring and heavier bolt make it capable of handling some remarkably energetic reloads. In firing some experimental reloads, I was able to get some 185-grain Nosler JHP bullets out of its muzzle at 1630/1092. That is a considerably greater amount of velocity and energy than I've obtained with the .45 ACP cartridge to date. Again, I do not care to quote the exact details of the load because, for one thing, there would be the obvious hazard that such loads could be fired in some other gun inadvertently — and with most unfortunate consequences.

The fact remains that the Model XC-450 displayed really exceptional accuracy, particularly after being fitted with a scope sight. Like many other autoloading firearms, it benefited from some amount of initial breaking-in. At first, it has occasional stoppages with ammunition carrying bullets other than the traditional 230-grain FMJ round-nose design. After a hundred rounds or so, it was feeding just about everything put through it, with stoppages scarce to non-existent.

The XC-450 has been supplied with two magazines holding thirty-two rounds of .45 ACP each, plus a serviceable padded carrying case. It disassembles and reassembles readily into four small components for transportation or storage.

Further details on this interesting carbine may be requested from its designer/builder, Richard Krieg, at Federal Engineering Corporation, (2335 South Michigan Avenue, Chicago, IL 60616).

CHAPTER 10

James E. Clark — Pistolsmith Extraordinary

Here's An Artisan Who's Been Right Up There At The Top Of The Heap, Almost Since The Game Began!

Now there's a smile you couldn't remove with a belt grinder! It was taken in 1958 when Clark was presented with a gold inlaid Smith & Wesson target pistol for winning the national championship.

JIM CLARK shot National Rifle Association Bullseye competition for twenty-eight years, retiring from competition in 1975. Clark won the National Pistol Championship in 1958 and is the only civilian ever to accomplish this feat. He was the fifth man in the U.S. to break 2600 and the fourth to break 2650. He has been fully active in the pistolsmith business since 1950.

That's what is says on page 3 of Clark's catalog covering the pitolsmithing service he offers. It's $1 per copy from Clark Custom Guns, Incorporated, (11462 Keatchie Road, Keithville, LA 71047). It goes on to catalog seventy-two wins racked up by the cheerful Clark in the interlude from 8/7/49 through 5/28/65 and I'd be willing to bet he forgot to mention a few along the way.

In 1985, the American Pistolsmiths Guild awarded Clark a trophy proclaiming him American Pistolsmith of the Year. Bagging double brass rings as the best pistol shooter in the country and its top pistolsmith is a unique coup, accomplished by James Edwin Clark and by no other known human being. I would say it serves as more than adequate excuse to feel a bit chesty about things and would have to add that Jimmy Clark is just about the last person in the world I'd want to get really ticked at me.

Friend Jimmy and his lovely wife, Bernice, had been my dinner companions at many a banquet where Clark, along with Harry Reeves, has been a sort of perennial nominee for the Outstanding American Handgunner Award and I'd dearly love to see both of the genial gents get the IHT — for Instant-Hernia Trophy — so they could share my own relief at becoming a non-nominee from then on. It is highly gratifying to be a nominee — the first time. By the eighth nomination, I can privately confide, you reach the point where you'd really sooner cut seed potatoes. If you've never engaged in that singularly untidy activity, the irony may be lost upon you. Both Clark and Reeves have been nominees many more times than I was and both could outshoot me, their eyes shut and hands in pockets.

Mrs. Clark works in the office in the shipping-receiving department and they have a son, Jim Clark, Jr., who's also a pistolsmith and shooter. The younger Clark racked up his first listed win in 1971, his twenty-eighth in 1988. Give him time and he may catch up with his sire, but that's a tough row for anyone to hoe, though his genes should be helpful.

The story of Clark's early years constitutes one of those triumphs over bleak adversity through sheer guts and perseverence. He was born on the fifteenth of February in 1923, down in Fort Worth, Texas. When he was 3 years old, his father deserted his mother and her brood of three. She struggled to keep the family intact as best she could, working as a seamstress. After a time, she remarried and, from Jim's viewpoint, everything didn't start coming up

The same Jim Clark, in more contemporary times. The cheerful expression is one he usually wears.

Clark is at left here, with
our mutual good friend,
the late Skeeter Skelton.
The accompanying account
of Clark's career is adapted
from an earlier coverage
by Skelton, probably the
best practitioner ever to
write about guns and
the people who shoot them.

roses, as of that moment.

His stepfather wouldn't allow Jim to own or fire guns during the lad's early years. The children had no toys other than what Jim was able to construct and share with them.

In that context, I can't help recalling some of the background material on the early years of John M. Browning, covered back in Chapter 2. Discussing his life and career in his twilight years with someone, Browning observed that, had he been born into a wealthy family, he doubted if he would have invented any guns whatsoever and he well may have been right.

Put another way, when the basic alloy is just right, adversity can serve as the tempering agent that, somehow, produces an uncommonly remarkable human being. Browning certainly was one example and Clark is another. Does this mean we should set up homes for over-privileged children and systematically mistreat the wee nippers so they'll grow up to be the leaders and innovators of generations to come? I hasten to note that I'm being facetious... probably.

Despite being 8½ months older than myself, Clark made a more routine passage through the school system and

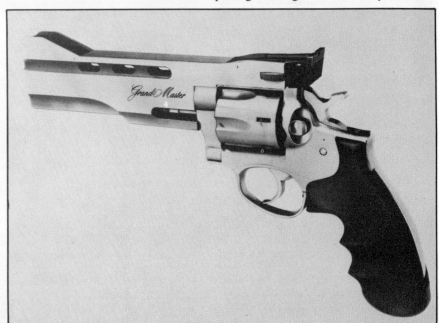

Clark's Grand Master
re-work of a Ruger
double-action revolver.

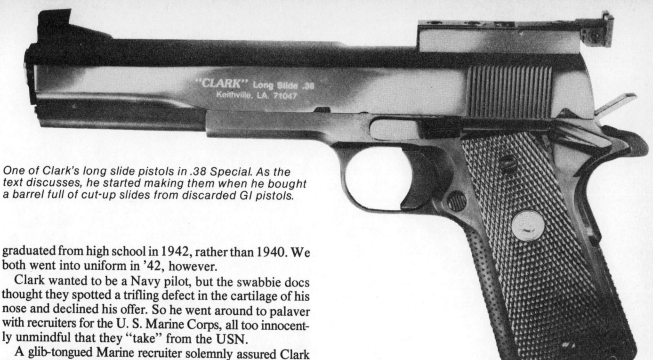

One of Clark's long slide pistols in .38 Special. As the text discusses, he started making them when he bought a barrel full of cut-up slides from discarded GI pistols.

graduated from high school in 1942, rather than 1940. We both went into uniform in '42, however.

Clark wanted to be a Navy pilot, but the swabbie docs thought they spotted a trifling defect in the cartilage of his nose and declined his offer. So he went around to palaver with recruiters for the U. S. Marine Corps, all too innocently unmindful that they "take" from the USN.

A glib-tongued Marine recruiter solemnly assured Clark that, if he'd only sign the paper and hold up his right hand, he'd go off to pilot training, straight as a shot. So Clark signed up and they zipped him off to training...as a rifleman.

Clark's family had moved to Shreveport, Louisiana, in 1939, about the time he got into high school and his favorite course had been mechanical drawing, getting nothing but straight As for that on his report card. He'd also joined the ROTC and became the captain of its rifle team. Thus, the USMC's arbitrary assignment wasn't all that grotesque. All they really did was nail the feet of a would-be birdman to terra ever-so firma.

the scope in his pack and later, on unpacking it, discovered it had been demolished by a shell fragment, even though he didn't have so much as as scratch.

He discarded the sightless Springfield in favor of a scavenged M-1 Garand and an M1911A1 pistol, dealing himself into the surrounding fray. After a time, he acquired another Lyman-scoped Springfield from a sniper who'd collected some punctures and was being retired from com-

Another Clark long slide, this time a combat version in .45 ACP chambering with low-profile target sights.

Clark got through USMC boot camp and was assigned to Camp Elliot, California, for scout/sniper training with the newly organized 4th Marine Division.

Graduating with honors from that program, Clark saw service at Roi-Namur and Saipan with the division. Scout/snipers serve as sort of the eyes and flashing fangs of combat USMC groups; a spectacular but small band of specialists. Most of Clark's duties were carried out well in advance of the American lines.

He was issued a Springfield with a 10x Lyman target scope sight and came to like the rifle, meanwhile feeling somewhat less warmth toward the unwieldy and painfully vulnerable scope. During the Saipan landing, he stashed

Here's a Clark Custom Combat pistol with Clark's unique slide guide fitted on the forward end of the receiver, beneath the slide. The accessory is doubly useful as it has provisions for taking up wear in use.

The road below was all a-crawl with Jap troops engaged in a frantic bugout. Clark managed to get his new scoped Springfield sighted in for the generous distance and fired over three hundred rounds, scoring nothing but hits after he'd "found the range." It seems likely he accounted for more enemy soldiers than he would had he gotten his original wish and won his wings.

Clark put in twenty-one days of combat before catching a rifle bullet in the shoulder as he attempted to rescue a wounded partner. He was sent to the hospital and his left arm was paralyzed for six months. He spent the next year in various stateside Naval hospitals before receiving a discharge in 1945.

Returning to Shreveport, Clark enrolled in college, majoring in architecture and took a job after classes, working part time in a local gun shop.

bat, thus putting Clark solidly back into business as a scout/sniper.

As Clark's unit came up on the small village of Garapan, Clark had lost three different spotters to enemy fire. All by himself and unattended, he perched alone upon a cliff, a thousand yards or so above a road leading out of the village.

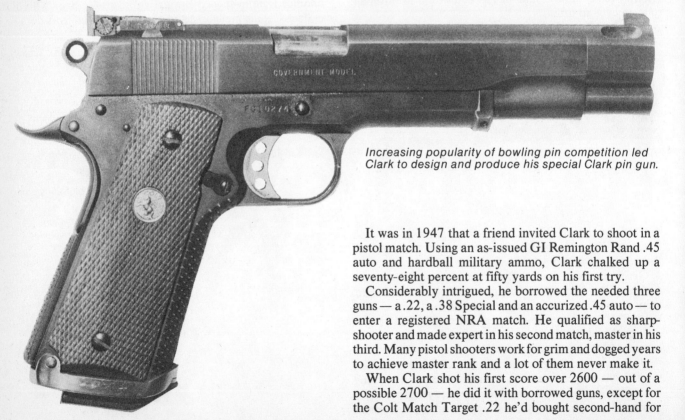

Increasing popularity of bowling pin competition led Clark to design and produce his special Clark pin gun.

It was in 1947 that a friend invited Clark to shoot in a pistol match. Using an as-issued GI Remington Rand .45 auto and hardball military ammo, Clark chalked up a seventy-eight percent at fifty yards on his first try.

Considerably intrigued, he borrowed the needed three guns — a .22, a .38 Special and an accurized .45 auto — to enter a registered NRA match. He qualified as sharpshooter and made expert in his second match, master in his third. Many pistol shooters work for grim and dogged years to achieve master rank and a lot of them never make it.

When Clark shot his first score over 2600 — out of a possible 2700 — he did it with borrowed guns, except for the Colt Match Target .22 he'd bought second-hand for

$50. It was 1950 when Clark broke 2600 and 1960 when he became the fourth man to top 2650.

With the outbreak of the Korean War, Clark was called back into service in 1951 and spent considerable time at Camp Pendleton, California, doing accuracy jobs on Marine competitors' .45 pistols. He encountered a .38 Super Colt that had been converted to handle the .38 Special wadcutter and was thoroughly fascinated by the prospects he saw in it.

Upon his discharge in late 1951, Clark went back to Shreveport with a Sheldon lathe and milling attachment he'd purchased for $600 from a Marine gunner. His friend Bill Gooch — the same one who had introduced him to pistol shooting in the first place — loaned him money and helped him set up a building.

Clark arranged a bank loan and bought twenty .38 Super Colts, converting them to handle the .38 Special midrange wadcutter cartridge. He ran an advertisement in the *American Rifleman* and it drew a heavy response from interested would-be customers. The Clark name quickly became known among pistol competitors and there has been heavy demand for his products and services ever since.

Despite the time and effort of maintaining a successful business, Clark continued as an active competitor. Goaded by the heavy traveling entailed in match shooting, Clark learned to fly and bought an airplane, thus finally realizing a long-term ambition.

During the years as a match competitor, Clark spent upward of $10,000 a year on match fees, travel expenses and practice ammunition. There are some who do not need a great deal of practice, but Clark admits he is not one of them.

His top place in the U.S. open pistol championship in 1958 was a singular achievement, as Clark was the first

Clark's son, "Jimbo," is a master pistolsmith and a prominent combat shooter — a real chip off the block!

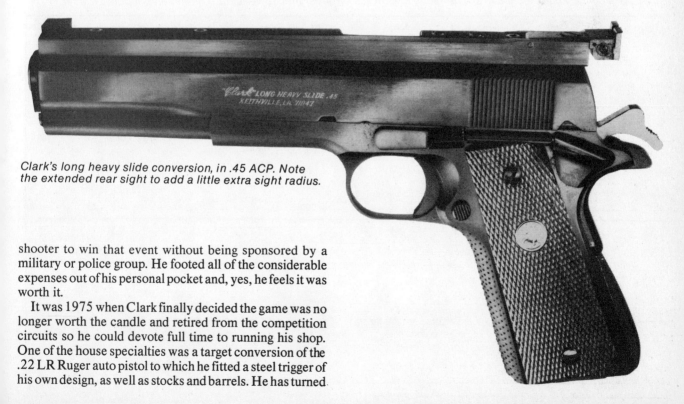

Clark's long heavy slide conversion, in .45 ACP. Note the extended rear sight to add a little extra sight radius.

shooter to win that event without being sponsored by a military or police group. He footed all of the considerable expenses out of his personal pocket and, yes, he feels it was worth it.

It was 1975 when Clark finally decided the game was no longer worth the candle and retired from the competition circuits so he could devote full time to running his shop. One of the house specialties was a target conversion of the .22 LR Ruger auto pistol to which he fitted a steel trigger of his own design, as well as stocks and barrels. He has turned

Jim Clark Jr. checks the sights on a Clark pin gun.

front of the magazine well and the relieved area at the lower edge of the chamber. Second, it supported the case head and thus prevented the occasional problem from blown case heads. Clark now manufactures such barrels entirely in his own shop.

Another Clark innovation was the long-slide conversion and that came about rather fortuitously. Visiting a war surplus store in Arkansas, Clark came upon an entire oil drum full of GI pistol slides that had been cut in two by the government in the process of deactivating service pistols. Clark bought the entire lot of destroyed slides for a dime

A closer look at the Clark slide guide, with the two set screws used in taking up slack resulting from wear.

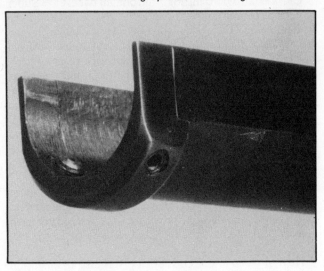

out close to 30,000 such guns, along with nearly a quarter-million .45 accuracy jobs and .38 Special Colt conversions.

As time permitted, Clark made a number of experiments aimed at improving performance of the .45 ACP Colt. Among the things he discovered was that six inches probably represents the ideal length for the barrel. He began using Douglas barrels that incorprated an integral feed ramp of his own design The novel concept served two vital purposes: First, it cured a lot of the feeding problems that stem from the juncture between the feed ramp at the upper

Clark pin gun features a barrel extension, low-profile target sights, rowel-spur hammer and stippled frame.

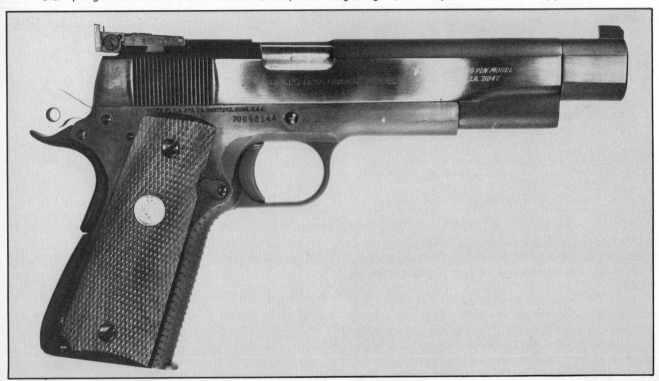

Above, Clark's long slide conversion of the .38 Special couples the fine accuracy and light recoil of the cartridge to the convenience of the auto action to make a top-flight target pistol. Left, an early example of Clark's pin gun, with a muzzle brake and padded magazine floorplate.

apiece and spent the next several years turning them into long slides. With the supply finally exhausted, he had them made from scratch by an outside vendor.

With the advent of bowling pin competition in the mid-Seventies, Clark came upon another area of endeavor. He produced what probably was the first auto pistol expressly designed for that challenging event. As refined and finalized, the Clark pin gun has a coned sleeve at the muzzle extending in front of the slide and the same width. At the buyer's option, it can have recoil-control vents or it can be plain, with a choice of 5½- 5¾- or 6-inch barrel lengths. Several other helpful features can be had such as a bevel around the base of the magazine well, stippled front strap, low-mounted sights by Millett, Bo-Mar or others, extended ejector and a lowered ejection port.

Traditionally, part of the accurizing of the GI pistol consists of squeezing the sides of the slide into a close fit with the receiver rails. Clark will do that number if the customer

insists, but prefers his modified version of an approach invented by John Giles. It has two locking adjustment screws in a housing welded to the lower front of the receiver. The screws bear against the slide when the pistol is locked up in battery. After some amount of extended use, play may develop, but it's a simple matter to unlock the two screws, take up the slack and lock them back up again, good as new.

Clark is an enthusiastic hunter and has taken dozens of deer, using an iron-sighted Model 29 Smith & Wesson with an 8¾-inch barrel, along with a great many smaller game species bagged with assorted other handguns.

Credit where due: Much of this biographical information on Clark has been taken, at his request, from an earlier article by the late Skeeter Skelton. I extend my grateful thanks to both!

We'll be discussing Clark's barrel with the integral feed ramp in greater detail in the next chapter.

CHAPTER 11

BLUE LAIG'S
CHINESE REMINGTON RAND

*How A Model 1911A1 Went Overseas, Fell
Upon Hard Times, Found Its Way Back Home
And Ended Up Better Than New!*

The facing page gives you starboard and port views of Andrews' repatriated and resurrected Remington Rand.
In the photo above, he's happily squirting a burst out of my customized AMT long slide, by way of comparison.

I'VE BEEN corresponding with Colonel Claud S. Hamilton since shortly before he retired after a career in the field artillery, back in the early Seventies. I'd also been writing to Tom Ferguson and, in the course of things, the three of us got into the habit of sending copies of letters to each of the other two. Bill Corson got absorbed into the informal little *kaffeeklatsch* and was a lively member until his untimely passing in late 1982.

The several branches of the Army each have their distinctive colors, used for cap braids and the piping along the outer seams of trousers for the full dress uniform. Red is the color for the field artillery and Hamilton, who traces his origins to Georgia — USA, not USSR — became informally known as Red Laig.

When Jim Andrews turned up and got assimilated into

the group, it turned out his service had been with the infantry and their piping color is a light shade of blue, so we busted a magnum of champagne across his prow and christened him Blue Laig, though he prefers *Pierna Azul.* Having done time in what has come to be termed The Old Brown-Shoe Air Force, whose cap-braid colors were royal blue and gold, I've been known to sign off my own contributions as *Pierna Azul y Oro.* You're quite right: Anybody who'd go that far probably wouldn't stop there!

Andrews is as hopelessly infatuated with the M1911 design as I am, perhaps even more so and that's chokingly difficult to believe. In the course of the...uhh...choruspondence, he mentioned he had just gotten an interesting .45 back from being refined by a nearby pistolsmith and asked if I'd like the loan of it to try out and test. It took a remarkably

Here's a close look at a cartridge chambered in a standard M1911A1 barrel. Note the considerable amount of unsupported brass case head exposed.

Andrews, who shares my fond regard for the Hensley & Gibbs 938 conical-point bullet, found it had to be seated to about this length to feed reliably in his gun.

small amount of arm-twisting before I gave in.

The pistol arrived with a brief letter outlining its known history and other pertinent details. The serial number dates it as having come off the production line at Remington Rand in Syracuse, New York, in 1944 and it was shipped to China some time after that.

It returned home long after WWII in a shipment Pacific International picked up from China, but there's no way of establishing whether it was Taiwan or Mainland China. Andrews purchased the pistol in 1986, presumably for an attractive price. The entire pistol was thickly swaddled in rust.

The rifling was fairly well shot out of the barrel and it appeared to have fired a large amount of corrosive-primed ammunition without ever having been cleaned. Potassium chlorate has been the implacable nemesis of uncountable .45 autos down the years.

The only surviving usable parts were the frame, slide, sear and magazine release. It was necessary to soak the entire pistol in solvent for several days in order to remove or, at least, soften the crud and corruption sufficiently to detail-strip it.

There was light pitting on the frame and somewhat heavier pitting on the slide. On the left side of the slide, the pitting was deep enough to require draw filing that wiped out nearly all of the rollmarking before getting down to a smooth surface. Following that, the entire slide was sandblasted lightly, then Parkerized.

"It was rebuilt first as a standard .45," Andrews recalls, "and, while good, was not outstanding. In late 1988, I was given the Clark barrel and Dale Martenia, at Quality

The same cartridge as on the facing page, here put into the Clark barrel to show how nearly everything ahead of the extractor cut is backed up by solid steel.

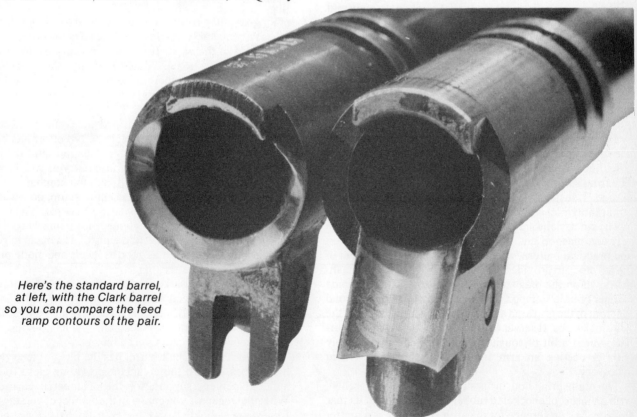

Here's the standard barrel, at left, with the Clark barrel so you can compare the feed ramp contours of the pair.

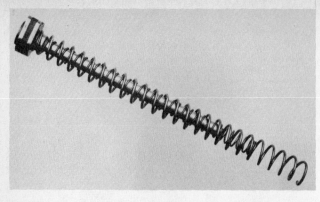

In setting it up to handle .45 Super loads, Ace Hindman furnished one of the coaxial spring sets, with a buffer on the full-length recoil spring guide rod to ease strain.

Gunsmithing, (5165 Auburn Boulevard, Sacramento, California 95841), rebuilt the pistol entirely. I called Ace Hindman and got a .45 Super kit, which Martenia installed.

"If we consider June to be the middle of the year, this is the gun's forty-fifth birthday and I can only say I wish I could have handled such heavy loads when I was 45! Everyone calls it my Chinese gun."

As received, the inscrutable oriental Remington Rand retains its Parkerized finish, though it's not nearly as greenishly repellent as the typical GI finish; more of a soft bluish-gray. It has about as nice a trigger pull as ever titillated my index finger and I fancy myself something of a connoisseur when it comes to trigger pulls.

The front sight is a neat blade that's not apt to snag and there is a Wichita adjustable rear sight neatly inletted into the slide to make a fairly low profile. The hammer now sports a rowel spur in the manner of Colt Commanders and there's a beavertail grip safety to allow clearance for the rowel spur on the hammer. The thumb safety has an extended, wider engagement area for the thumb. When cocked and locked, the safety sweeps down in a delightfully crisp and positive manner with a casual flick of the thumb.

The auto carries an aluminum trigger, midway in length between a short and long Colt trigger, with three transverse holes and a trigger stop in the manner of a Colt Gold Cup. The front surface of the trigger is smooth and flat from side to side. I suspect the trigger contours contribute to the remarkably pleasant trigger pull.

The stock slabs are of a dark wood in a color somewhere between maroon and burnt umber, checkered in a plain and practical pattern, with a relief cut at the upper front of the left stock to provide some welcome clearance for mashing down on the magazine release button. There is some manner of little stamped sheet metal insert wrapped around the front of the grip area and held in place by pressure of the two stock slabs. It serves to provide a positive non-slip surface where a bit of roughness may be helpful, probably without costing an arm and a leg. I think it's a neat accessory.

The mainspring housing is straight, rather than arched, with an insert of checkered rubber or Neoprene on its rear surface. My preference for the arched housing is a matter

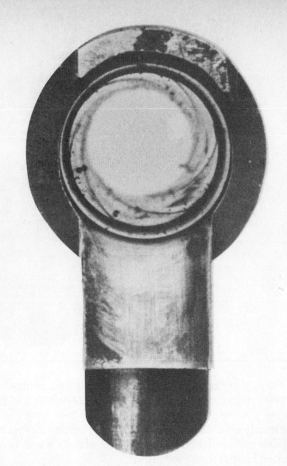

This gives you a look into the breech and up the bore of the Clark barrel and you'll note it has right-hand rifling.

of long-standing record, though I'd have to admit this pistol has a remarkably comfortable — and comforting — feel when held in the hand. It just sort of snuggles down and makes itself at home. Mindful of my blast-deadened auditory equipment, there have been times I could have sworn I could hear it purring softly. I could be wrong about that. I'm not, but I *could* be.

The pistol at hand was conceived and created as a combat pistol, rather than a target pistol. No effort has been spared to maximize its efficiency in the grim game of playing marbles for keeps. It should also carry its weight well for use in the various forms of simulated combat.

The *piece de resistance* of the entire setup, however, is the Clark barrel backed up by the .45 Super kit. The result is a .45 auto that does not whimper for pampering. That ties in with the total *gestalt* of the pistol. It's made to go in harm's way, dishing out as good as it gets and, quite probably, a whole lot better.

The hardware is Parkerized and the woodwork is starkly functional. If it collects a few dings and gouges in the line of duty, it's not going to break the owner's heart. Rather, they would serve as battle scars, establishing its no-nonsense, watch-your-step-Buster overall image.

This particular Clark barrel has the integral feed ramp that slopes up into the chamber, providing close to one hundred percent support for the chambered cartridge. What that means is you can — in the manner of the starship *Enterprise* — boldly go where few if any have gone before

The Remington Rand, fieldstripped to show the parts in their relation to each other.

and, with a bit of luck, you can get away with it! Up to a certain point, not yet precisely established, you can use regular .45 ACP brass for warmer loads, so long as you take care not to let such loads stray into some other pistol incapable of standing the stiffer gaff.

Just about any factory .45 ACP load you choose to stuff into the magazine will roll through the Chinese Remington Rand like unto Schlitz through Schultz. I've yet to find any factory fodder capable of hanging it up and I've tried just about everything I can put hands upon. In short, it boasts the credentials of a pedigreed combat pistol, the primary criterion of which is that it launches a bullet every time you pull the trigger, until the hopper runs dry.

However, it is by means of judicious and canny reloading that this particular pistol can be brought to really interesting levels of performance. Andrews has come to share my fervent infatuation with the cast bullets from the Hensley & Gibbs No. 938 mould. They have conical points with an included angle of seventy degrees and they drop from the mould weighing anywhere between 175 and 180 grains or so, depending upon the composition of the casting alloy.

In the normal mill-run routine of things, the H&G 938 can be seated with its shoulder flush with the case mouth and it will feed every week in the world. In the celestial Remington Rand, a load seated thus will get you a stoppage with every single shot.

However, by seating the 938 out just a little bit farther to a cartridge overall length of 1.250 inches, every last indication of problem feeding dries up and blows away. When seated to the suitable length for the given gun, the H&G 938 is a super-reliable feeder and, even better, it tends to produce good groups in nearly any gun, with nearly any load.

The powder charge Andrews has come to prefer for use in the Chinese Remington Rand is 12.5 grains of Accurate Arms No. 7 behind either the Hensley & Gibbs 938 cast bullet or the Nosler 185-grain JHP factory bullet, either load sparked by the Federal No. 150 primer. I am fond of that load, myself. In fact, I may have touted him onto it. With the H&G 938 at 177 grains, that load gets about 1140/511 and, with the 185-grain Nosler JHP, more like 1080/749. It's not necessarily the planet-wrecker special of all time, but it does tend to make its presence noted. That is not a suitable load for use in stock, mill-run .45 autos that have not been beefed up to handle it and it should not be used in such guns.

Remington's .45 ACP +P load, with its 185-grain JHP bullet, will come out of the Chinese Remington Rand at right around 1126/521 and the pistol will handle it with cheerful insouciance.

It would be entirely natural for you to wonder if, by installing the stronger recoil springs of the .45 Super kit, the pistol might have lost its ability to work with the lighter, target-level, .45 ACP factory loads. It has been my experience that a pistol thus modified will retain a high degree of reliability with the lighter loads, thereby giving it a useful amount of all-out versatility.

John W. Quintrall is the proprietor of Quality Gunsmithing and Dale Martenia was the gunsmith who did the final fitting and assembly of the Chinese Remington Rand. Quality Gunsmithing has an interesting brochure of general information on such matters, called *The Combat .45 Auto*. If you send them a business-length self-addressed envelope and enough stamps to carry two ounces of first class mail, I'm sure they'd be happy to send you a copy of it.

One of the things they stress rather heavily is that one never should mash down on the slide stop to let the slide bang forward on an empty chamber. To do so is to run an unacceptable risk of absolutely ruining the exquisite trigger pull. Having reveled in the sensuous pull on Blue Laig's Chinese Remington Rand, I'll confess I'd regard that as awfully close to a capital offense!

CHAPTER 12

THE .45 SUPER AND .451 DETONICS MAGNUM

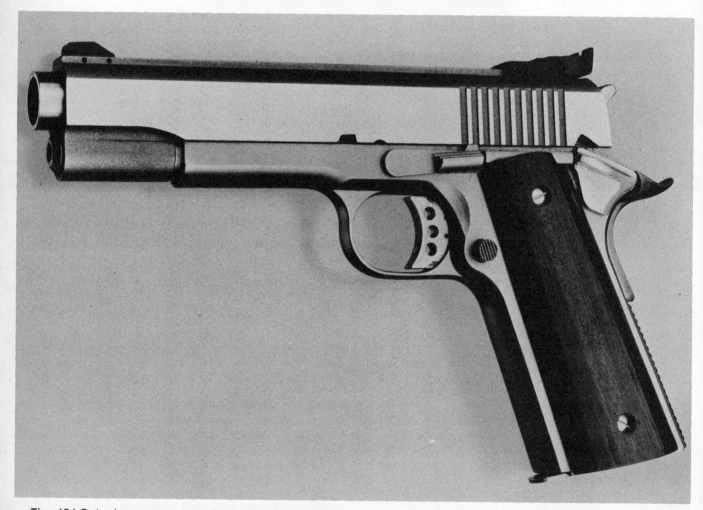

The .451 Detonics magnum was developed as a proprietary cartridge by Detonics for use in their pistols, such as this Scoremaster. As shown, it carries a five-inch, custom-fitted barrel in .45 ACP, rather than the original .451 D-mag barrel, which is six inches in length. It performs quite well with the .45 Super loads, but does even better with the .451 D-mag. Unfortunately, .451 D-mag cases are sold out.

ICAME up with the concept of the .45 Super cartridge in a roundabout way and continue to have somewhat mixed emotions about it. I was motivated to a large extent by frustrations over the fact that there is hardly any load data for the .45 ACP cartridge that gets any manner of bullet up into four-digit velocities. A few have been listed, just barely over 1000 fps, but following editions of the same manual tend to cut them back to the high-900s, if that much.

The critically vulnerable Achilles' heel of the .45 ACP cartridge is the portion of the case head of the chambered round that hangs unsupported over the feed ramp. There is absolutely nothing but a small amount of brass between the roaring stress of the burning powder gas and the magazine well. It does not take a lot of pressure to blast through the weak brass, unleashing a lot of high pressure gas into the magazine well.

I have experienced that particular catastrophe twice. Back in the latter Sixties, someone sent me a 9mmP barrel to use in my Government Model .38 Super. I contemplated the extravagant clearance of the feed ramp, in-

stalled it in the pistol and took the sensible precaution of firing the first round of a factory 9mmP load without the magazine in place.

It was well I did so. Factory 9mmP ammo is held within the pressure limit of 35,700 CUP, prescribed by the Sporting Arms and Ammunition Manufacturers Institute (SAAMI) and the brass cases in 9mmP are designed to withstand that much strain. Even so, the factory load blew the head of the case and all that suddenly vented powder gas split the bejeepers out of a really lovely set of Jay Scott simulated pearl stocks that happened to be installed on the .38 Super at the time.

The palm of my right hand — I'm a natural northpaw — smarted and stung for a little while and that was the end of the problem. I returned the custom barrel, with a thanks-but-no-thanks letter.

I think it appropriate at this time to enter a note about the choice of handgun stocks, if you contemplate firing loads that might tend to go in harm's way. The wrap-around set of M1911-type stocks marketed by Pachmayr are moulded around steel plates that cover both sides of the handle area

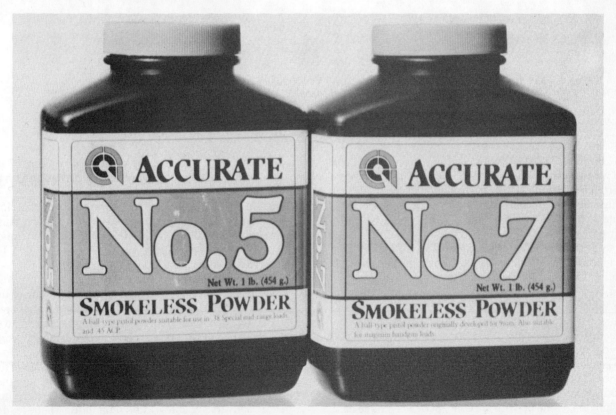

Two powders that perform quite well in both the .451 D-mag and .45 Super are Accurate Arms No. 5 and 7. Accurate Arms No. 9 doesn't quite reach the velocities of AA-7, but it delivers excellent accuracy.

When the primers in standard .45 ACP cases start looking like these, it is a strong indication you have reached the back-off point on your powder charges or, in higher probability, you've gone beyond it!

of the receiver. The steel plates, encased in rubber, can go a long way toward withstanding the blast of high-pressure gas from a ruptured case head. Put another way, if it gets through the steel plate of the Pachmayr stocks, you've got a problem, but it would have been much worse with any other type of stock.

The Pachmayr rubber stocks manifest all the fetching elegance of black rubber and not one tiny bit more. A shooting friend, Ed Greisberg, tends to refer to them as "rubber-uglies." As you may have inferred from previous discussions, I am partial to woods of attractive color and grain pattern, tending to favor such woodwork on my personal pistols. Even so, when engaged in experimental development of loads that may pose the risk of blowing a case head, I have no esthetic qualms at all about installing a set of the Pachmayr stocks, call them what you will.

Some few years ago, the Detonics firm, up in Bellevue, Washington, came up with the concept of a cartridge case of stronger head construction that was somewhat longer than the nominal .898-inch of the basic .45 ACP. They

had a quarter-million of the cases made up by one of the major domestic ammunition producers, to a case length of .945-.947 inch.

Loaded rounds in the new case were termed the .451 Detonics magnum and were reputed to operate at pressure levels as high as 34,000 CUP, perhaps with a bit of tolerance to spare. Detonics went on to produce pistols in .451 D-mag, as well as conversion kits for fitting existing M1911A1 pistols to handle the new cartridge.

I put in some amount of experimental surveying of the .451 D-mag, without ever quite getting to the point where I felt I had reached the limit of its capability. In the course of that, I brought it to performance levels considerably beyond that of the .45 ACP.

My pistol for the .451 D-mag was and still is one of the Detonics *Scoremasters,* with a six-inch barrel for that particular cartridge. The designation is adequately justified. It delivers accuracy I find a bit hard to believe, despite the fact that I'm sitting there, pressing the trigger.

I sent the basic pistol back to the factory and paid for

This is the headstamp on the .451 Detonics magnum case which, alas, has gone to join such ephemeral artifacts as the penny postcard, dinosaurs, dodo birds, Lucky Strike green and the two-bit haircut.

having a five-inch barrel in .45 ACP factory-fitted. With that particular barrel, I've managed to fire five-shot groups off the sandbags on the bench, at a distance of twenty-five yards, with a center-spread as tight as .755-inch. That is about the best I've been able to do with the .45 ACP cartridge out of handguns and I've done only a little better out of the Marlin Camp Carbine in the same caliber.

The work with the .451 D-mag and the fairly rewarding results of it made me wonder about the possibilities of a personal problem in applied ballistics with which I wrestled on various past occasions, without hardly any noteworthy success.

I refer to the .38-45 Clerke cartridge, made by necking the basic .45 ACP case down to accept bullets of 9mm/.355-inch diameter. When working with the .45 ACP case, one is perforce hobbled down to the 19,900 CUP pressure ceiling prescribed for that brass by SAAMI. If you remain below that pressure level, you do not get any overly satisfactory ballistic results from the cartridge. Indeed, there is some amount of difficulty in getting the

autoloading action to function reliably.

I conjectured upon the possibilities of making up .38-45 Clerke cases from .451 D-mag brass so as to get free of the hampering limitations of the .45 ACP case. I tackled the project and came out of it with results at least as good as I'd dared to hope for; perhaps even better.

That, in turn, illuminated still another small light bulb above my head. If the approach worked for the .38-45 Clerke, why not try making .45 ACP brass out of .451 D-mag brass?

In the process of doing that, I encountered some interesting facts about the length of .45 ACP cases. They are supposed to be .898-inch in length. In actuality, it's all but impossible to find one that really measures quite that long. Typical examples will mike-out to .893, perhaps as much as .895 or .896-inch. As the cases are reloaded, again and again, they tend to shorten somewhat from the original length.

At the time, I had four different pistols capable of firing the .45 ACP cartridge and a bit of cut-and-try trimming

Here are four more powders I've used with some amount of success in exploring the possibility of extra-effort .45 ACP loads. Others, not shown, include Hercules Blue Dot, Herco and IMR 800-X.

turned up the fact that all four pistols would lock up quite nicely on a case with a length of .905-inch. A Smith & Wesson Model 25-2 revolver would not work with cases longer than .904-inch and a ten-inch T/C Contender bull barrel in the discontinued .45 ACP chambering would not lock up with cases longer than .902-inch.

I set up the Forster power trimmer base on the bed of my drill press and, after a bit of patient adjusting, got it to trimming the .451 D-mag cases back to .905-inch, rapidly and with little effort. To speed the inside/outside neck deburring, I made up a small adapter to hold the Lee deburring tool, with a .375-inch shank. I used it in my Black & Decker variable speed reversible (VSR) electric drill, held in a bench stand. Between the Forster and Lee tools, it shaved a lot of time from making up the cases. A control knob on the electric drill enabled me to throttle it down to a moderate number of revolutions per minute for better control of the chamfering.

Once I got into loading the trimmed cases, it didn't take long to find out the brass at the necks was somewhat thicker than that of typical .45 ACP cases. If you wanted to seat the heavier bullets deeply enough to allow the loaded round to work in the magazine, there would be a bulge in the outer case wall, corresponding to the base of the bullet. The obvious solution to that was to go into the neck with a reamer of .450- to .451-inch diameter, to a depth that would eliminate such bulges.

I did not have a reamer of that size at the time, so did most of my work with the bullets up to about 200 grains.

In the course of testing the Detonics Scoremaster with its six-inch .451 D-mag barrel installed, I had worked up a progression of loads with Accurate Arms Nos. 7 and 9 powders behind various of the lighter bullets.

All of the following loads were put up in the unmodified .451 Detonics magnum cases, using CCI-300 standard large pistol primers and five rounds of each were chronographed out of the six-inch barrel. Charge weights are listed in grains, with the five-shot average given as velocity/energy. The first series was with the 185-grain Sierra No. 8810 Match bullet:

Grains	Powder	Vel./Energy
9.4	AA-7	641/169
10.3		776/247
11.0		878/317
12.1		999/410
13.1		1098/495
14.1		1229/621
15.0		1320/716
15.7		1371/772
16.2		1384/788
16.6		1414/821
12.9	AA-9	831/284
13.9		954/374
15.0		1043/447
16.0		1135/529
17.0		1175/567

Switching to cast bullets from the Hensley & Gibbs No. 938 mould, at a weight of 175 grains, all other factors the same, the averages ran:

Grains	Powder	Vel./Energy
15.0	AA-7	1410/773
15.7		1420/784
16.6		1520/898
17.0		1557/942
18.3	AA-9	1384/744

As discussed, the black rubber stocks from Pachmayr may not be the prettiest, but the steel plates moulded into the rubber on each side afford welcome protection in case of a load that blows the head of the case.

Earlier, I had conducted some tests with the .451 D-mag barrel and conversion kit in a standard Model 1911A1, made by Remington Rand in WWII and was left with an indelible memory of fairly severe recoil with it. For reasons not readily apparent, the recoil of comparable loads in the Scoremaster seemed quite a bit milder.

Bullet seating depth seemed to have a strong influence upon reliability of feeding, as well as upon typical accuracy, both in the Scoremaster and converted M1911A1. With the H&G 938 bullet, it's my usual custom to seat the bullet shoulder flush with the case mouth. Getting it to feed in the .451 D-mag required seating it .045-inch farther out of the neck. That made the difference between won't-ever-feed and feed-every-time and it turned out the bullets seated deeper grouped to about one inch in center-spread for five shots off the sandbagged bench rest at twenty-five yards. The loads with the bullet seated .045-inch farther out showed a typical spread of 2.25 inches or so, under the same conditions.

In much the same way, things tended to turn out that you could get gratifying accuracy or blistering ballistics, but rarely if ever with the same load. For example, the load that grouped to .755-inch of spread out of the five-inch .45 ACP barrel in the Scoremaster on the trimmed-down .451 D-mag cases — the .45 Super, to use my private term for them — had the 200-grain Hornady No. 4515 jacketed semi-wadcutter bullet ahead of 8.1 grains of Winchester 540 powder and it only averaged about 780/270; hardly up to typical .45 ACP performance!

I published my first discussion of the .45 Super early in 1988 and the idea seemed to tickle the fancy of quite a few readers. Detonics was retailing the basic .451 D-mag cases at about thirty-seven cents apiece and the last of their original quarter-million went out the door inside of a little over a year after the first published discussion of the .45 Super. From what I've been able to find out, it's highly unlikely that any more .451 D-mag cases will be made up; at least not on orders from Detonics

As long as the cases were offered in the original .945-inch length, for use in matching chambers, the annual sales volume was rather modest despite the manifest fact that it was an excellent cartridge. Once the suggestion had been made to use it for boosting .45 ACP performance in guns of that chambering, it didn't take long for the supply to run dry.

I've observed the shooting public tends to get quite bright-eyed, if offered a way to upgrade performance in guns already on hand in substantial quantities. If it's necessary to buy a new gun in order to use a new cartridge, apathy stretches farther than the eye can see. In that regard, the 5mm Remington rimfire comes to mind — along with a lot of others.

It would be painfully incorrect to assume each and every firearm capable of handling the .45 ACP can handle hot .45 Super loads with equal ease and safety. For but one example, I would not fire *any* +P .45 ACP load in any Model 1917 revolver, be it by Colt or Smith & Wesson. They've learned a lot of useful things about metallurgy since the harried days of 1917.

I don't think there is any place for hot .45 Super loads in the Marlin Camp Carbine, much as I admire the graceful little i-dotters. As we've discussed, the action is a straight blowback and that means the case may be easing out of the chamber before the bullet gets out of the muzzle. That can result in the kind of adventure no one needs nor wants. The same would apply to Uzi pistols and carbines in .45 ACP, for the same reason.

I'd be inclined to practice some amount of moderation when it came to feeding +P loads through contemporary Smith & Wesson Model 25-2 or 625-2 revolvers. Their metallurgy is scrupulously state-of-the-art, but they still have that locking notch in the thinnest part of the chamber and I learned long ago to avoid force-feeding even the S&W Model 29 revolvers in .44 magnum, let alone any

One fairly rapid and satisfactory approach for removing .040-inch from the .451 D-mag case neck to make .45 Super cases used this RCBS case trimmer with their power conversion kit for an electric drill.

with more steel bored out of the chambers. If you've a yen to hot-rod an N-frame S&W revolver, get their Model 57 in .41 magnum and exercise sober discretion, even with that.

I regard it as a deplorable pity T/C Arms dropped the .45 ACP as a chambering for their Contender single-shot. Perhaps it may be possible to get a .45 ACP Contender barrel by way of their new custom shop, Fox Ridge Outfitters. For the present, I have a ten-inch Contender bull barrel in .45 ACP and would not part with it for any price a sane person might offer nor would I sell it for any price to a buyer who wasn't sane.

Even so, the upper permissible pressure limit for a T/C is determined by the case diameter at the head, to a considerable extent. A larger head gives the chambered case more area and more pressure applied to that much area produces more strain on the action; just that simple.

It is possible to coax some thoroughly impressive ballistics out of the T/C Contender which is, at least arguably, the world's most versatile handgun. You can do it, for example, with the .45-70 Government cartridge and that has an even larger head diameter. What it has, also, is quite a bit more volume to accommodate the powder charge and that can make a significant difference in the level of peak pressure to which the action is exposed.

Victor Borge, the Danish pianist/humorist, used to be much given to commenting, "The trouble with pancakes is,

in the first place, they should be waffles!" Somewhat the same observation applies to the extraction of impressive ballistics from the .45 ACP case. The head construction should be stronger and it'd be ever so helpful if the case could be lengthened to about the same dimension as the .45 Winchester magnum.

How about the Ruger Blackhawk? Various sources of load data carry +P .45 Colt listings for use only in the T/C Contender or Ruger Blackhawk. Be advised that standard .45 Colt loads are not supposed to exceed 15,900 CUP and the hotter loads, as given in the eleventh edition of the *Speer Manual,* do not exceed 25,000 CUP.

As noted earlier, I have a fitted .45 ACP cylinder for my Ruger Blackhawk, but I'd not subject it to the hotter .45 Super loads, some of which generate peak pressures considerably in excess of 25,000 CUP.

Does that imply that hot .45 Super loads should be restricted to any and all Model 1911-type autoloading pistols? No way, Jose! There are M1911-type auto pistols in the hands of the shooting public that are every bit as weak and fragile as any of the guns mentioned previously, indeed, even wimpier. The past couple of decades have seen the appearance of a number of different M1911 clones and, by way of pruning production costs, some of the makers machine the barrels from investment castings, rather than from forged steel billets. It's done for the sake of holding the retail prices to a more attractive level and there's no slightest

that such things have happened.

In view of the foregoing, I would hope you begin to share my qualms and concerns about the fabrication and employment of +P .45 ACP ammunition and, in special specific particular, *homemade* .45 ACP +P loads.

SAAMI decrees an industry maximum pressure for the .44 magnum of 43,500 CUP. I note that by way of giving you a comparative yardstick by which to evaluate the situation. The thing about being an experimental ballistician is that, every now and then, you have to stick your neck out and go in harm's way. It's neither reassuring nor all that much fun. In fact, you tend to break out with the cold cobblies, every time you stop to think about it.

I've had reports to the gist that some of my experimental .45 Super loads develop peak pressures on the order of 44,000 CUP, slightly in excess of the hottest sanctioned .44 magnum loads. At that spooky level, you get a 185-grain Nosler JHP bullet out of a five-inch barrel at about 1500/925 and a bit.

Curiously enough, examination of the ejected cases didn't trigger all that much alarm. True, the primers were

Another procedure, which worked even better, used the power trimmer base from Forster, installed in the shop drill press. The photo was taken by high-speed electronic flash while the chuck was spinning.

question as to the importance of cost control in these inflation-stricken times.

Other makers produce the basic barrel, then attach the lower lug by electron beam welding, silver soldering, brazing or perhaps with recycled chewing gum that has been processed by a patented technique. The resulting barrels do not have structural integrity on a par with barrels machined from solid forgings. Most will handle typical .45 ACP factory loads without coming apart. Their salvation lies in the fact that most .45 ACP factory loads are loaded to somewhat *less than* the 19,900 CUP SAAMI maximum levels.

If you commence firing striving .45 Super loads through one of the more marginal barrels, you may not even get the first magazine emptied before the barrel splits, doing regrettable things to the slide, perhaps to other hardware and human meat within the near neighborhood. I've had reports

This is what can — and will! — happen if you start pushing your luck with regular .45 ACP cases, even if produced by a highly reputable maker, as this was.

This round of .451 D-mag carries the 200-grain Speer No. 4477 JHP, affectionately termed the Flying Ash Tay. It shows little if any bulge at the base of the seated bullet, despite not having been neck-reamed.

somewhat flattened and cratered, but the heads did not display any detectable bulges in the area not supported by the chamber walls. What all that proves, rather redundantly, is that anyone who feels he can gauge peak pressures by looking at fired cases is only deluding himself.

Two of the most popular and widely used centerfire handgun cartridges in this country are the .45 ACP and the .38 Special. We've had +P .38 Special ammunition for the past several years and some striving stuff termed +P+, as well. Not all handguns chambered for the .38 Special cartridge are capable of coping with +P loads, let alone the +P+ variety.

Standard working pressure for the .38 Special, according to page 398 of the eleventh edition of the *Speer Manual,* is 18,900 CUP: an even one thousand less than even the painfully hamstrung .45 ACP. They quote a pressure level of 22,400 CUP for the +P .38 Special loads and refrain from discussing the +P+ variants.

Within the recent past, I've been checking out one of the really striving .38 Special loads, the *ThunderZap,* pro-

Three cast bullets used in experimental loads include, from left, H&G 68 and 292, Lee's Micro-Band.

duced and marketed by Richard C. Davis, (Box 578, Central Lake, Michigan 49622). Davis, who developed, manufactures and distributes the Second Chance ballistic vests that have saved the lives of more police officers than any comparable product, worked up the ThunderZap as his personal entry toward making the short-barreled .38 Special revolvers a force with which to be reckoned. The load launches a plastic hollow-point projectile weighing 32 grains and it's said to average 2800 fps from a four-inch barrel.

I have two lots of the ThunderZap loads. Davis sent the second batch after discovering the first had been primed with standard small pistol primers, rather than the magnum-type primers that were used in making up the second batch.

Fired out of my Smith & Wesson Model 36 Chiefs Special two-inch, five of the first batch of ThunderZaps averaged 2157 fps, with a low of 2112, a high of 2200 and an extreme spread of 88 fps, the empty cases extracted from the chambers with no difficulty.

Five rounds from the second batch of ThunderZaps, fired from the same small revolver, averaged 2301/376, but the spent cases had to be driven from the chambers with a short brass rod and a mallet, suggesting that, if firing that load, it would be a good idea to accomplish all the urgently needed work in the first five shots. I don't plan to fire any more of the second batch in the Chiefs Special, because I think they're a little too rich for its blood.

Getting back to the nominal topic of +P loads in .45 ACP, there are some interesting alternatives to be explored. Jim Clark's custom barrel, with its integral feed ramp, leaves little of the chambered case head unsupported and somewhat the same can be said of the Smith & Wesson Model 645, 745, 4506 and 4516. With such barrel and chamber configurations, it may not necessarily require a case with stronger head construction to obtain higher velocities. It may be possible to do quite well with standard .45 ACP cases, particularly on the first loading in virgin brass.

The key consideration in such applications is what the firing of such loads will do to the affected components of the pistol. As you begin venturing beyond conventional ammunition specifications, several buckets of snakes slither onto the scene.

When Detonics used to market a kit for converting standard M1911A1 pistols to handle the .451 Detonics mag-

From left, a full-length .451 Detonics magnum, .45 ACP and .45 Winchester magnum. You'll note the extractor groove is narrower on the outer pair, which sometimes makes a tight fit in shell holders.

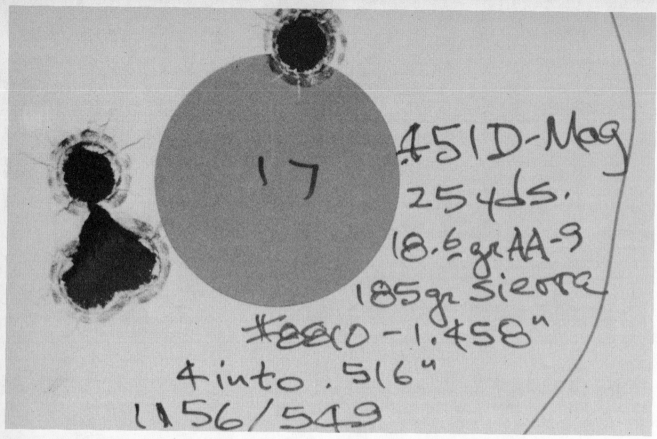

Handwritten on target:
17
.451D-Mag
25 yds.
18.6 gr AA-9
185 gr Sierra
#8800 – 1.458"
4 into .516"
1156/549

A 5-shot, 25-yard group, fired from the 6-inch, .451 Detonics magnum barrel off a sandbag rest saw three go into one tiny cluster at lower left. Even with the apparently mandatory flier, it's not all that bad. As was noted, AA-9 powder develops moderate velocity, 1156/549 in this case, but tends to group quite well.

num, they supplied a new firing pin spring, as well as a stronger recoil spring assembly with two coaxial springs. As I understand it, the stronger recoil spring helps to absorb the substantially stronger recoil impulse, but once compressed and released, it drives the slide forward so rapidly the inertia firing pin may not be arrested and controlled by the standard firing pin spring. Supposedly, it can pick up enough inertia on the forward trip to override the firing pin spring and set off the primer of the next chambered round.

What you have, as of about that moment, is a handheld submachine gun in .45 ACP caliber and, once fired, it will keep on firing, full-auto, no matter if your finger is on the trigger or not.

On two distinct and widely separated occasions, I've had the experience of firing full-auto guns that weren't *sup-*

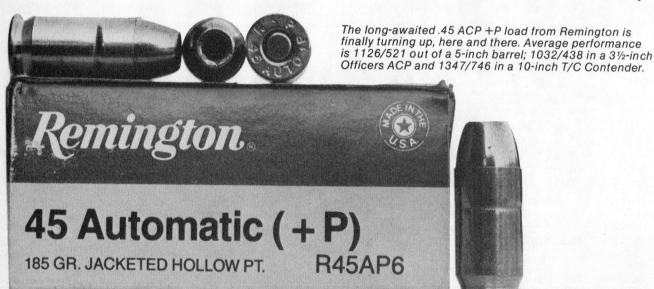

The long-awaited .45 ACP +P load from Remington is finally turning up, here and there. Average performance is 1126/521 out of a 5-inch barrel; 1032/438 in a 3½-inch Officers ACP and 1347/746 in a 10-inch T/C Contender.

Remington
45 Automatic (+ P)
185 GR. JACKETED HOLLOW PT.   R45AP6

Ace Hindman built me this highly customized and ornately decorated .45 Super, which comes close to being much too pretty to shoot!

posed to be full-auto. I can solemnly testify that it's enormously discombooberating, distracting and scary as all get-out. You hang on to the bucking, stuttering gun as best you can manage and you become convinced the (unprintable, expletive deleted) magazine is *never* going to run dry.

I quietly note that to apprise you working with exalted-performance .45 ACP ammunition can involve thoroughly unpleasant consequences: that one among possible others. It is not a promising field for the casual dilettante to dabble about in.

I also should note that, if the pistol at hand is a Colt of the Series '80 design, releasing pressure on the trigger will arrest any runaway performance such as that described. In the Series '80, unless pressure is maintained on the trigger, the firing pin will lock up so it cannot course forward and set off a chambered round, no matter how rapidly the stronger recoil spring propels it. The Series '80 modification gives you a trigger pull that is not quite as sensuously crisp and delightful as the Series '70 and earlier versions. Despite that, I'm inclined to view the Series '80 with considerable favor and forgive its slightly more twitchy trigger.

Rather frequently at trade shows, people spot my name tag and come up to say they'd really like to have a job like mine: "Nothing to do but shoot, all day!" I make every effort to keep a straight face and mumble suitable platitudes — a platitude is an imaginary line, running crosswise to plongitudes — but the sad truth is, my day-to-day routine involves a lot less firing of firearms than anyone would be apt to imagine.

Thus, it came to be that I got the idea of making up extra-effort .45 ACP loads from cases with stronger head construction. I published details on the basic concept and, with the ongoing press of toppling deadlines being how it is, have not got back to do the follow-up investigations I'd dearly like to get in. Since that time, I've had phone calls from people who claim to have hatched the idea before I did, wanting credit for the inspiration, but not feeling inclined to give their names. Well, no one ever claimed it was supposed to be simple, right?

A southern gunsmith, Ace Hindman, (1880½ Upper Turtle Creek Road, Kerrville, Texas 78028), read my original writeup on the .45 Super and went on to take the ball and run with it. He has worked out all the necessary details on beefing up M1911-type pistols of suitable credentials to cope with the fuss and fury of the hotter load without problems. He can also "Superize" the .45 ACP Smith & Wesson autoloaders and reports gratifying results

with those, as well as with the Colt Delta Elite in 10mm Auto.

I hereby transfer any claim I may have to guru-hood on .45 Supers along to Ace Hindman, at the address given, having no delusions as to his knowledge of the subject exceeding my own. I'm convinced it does.

All of the foregoing discussion on the .45 Super and the .451 Detonics magnum that sired it may be more than slightly academic, in view of the curtailed availability of .451 D-mag cases. Beyond any doubt, some of the original quarter-million remain intact in the hands of reloaders and shooters. If one has a barrel chambered for the .451 D-mag, the obvious course is to leave it at the original length and use it in that format. I think the case is more capable and predictable in .451 D-mag than when whittled back to .45 Super.

In the present marketplace, *sans* .451 D-mag cases, the only other obvious alternative for making up extra-strength .45 ACP brass is to use the .45 Winchester magnum as the parent case. Be duly advised the .45 Win mag is stronger in the head than most or all .45 ACP cases, but it is *not* as strong as the .451 Detonics magnum.

Within recent times, Remington has announced a load in .45 ACP +P that carries a 185-grain JHP bullet. It is entirely natural to assume that one could use the spent cases from that load to make up further .45 ACP +P loads but that would be faulty logic, unsupported by facts. The brass cases used in the Remington +P loads are no stronger

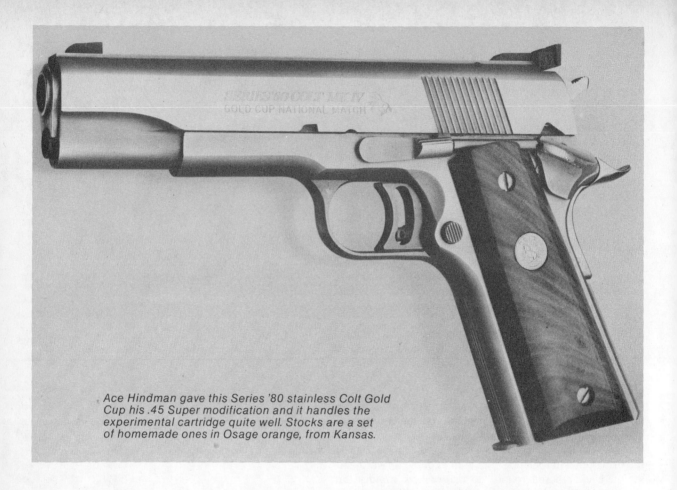

Ace Hindman gave this Series '80 stainless Colt Gold Cup his .45 Super modification and it handles the experimental cartridge quite well. Stocks are a set of homemade ones in Osage orange, from Kansas.

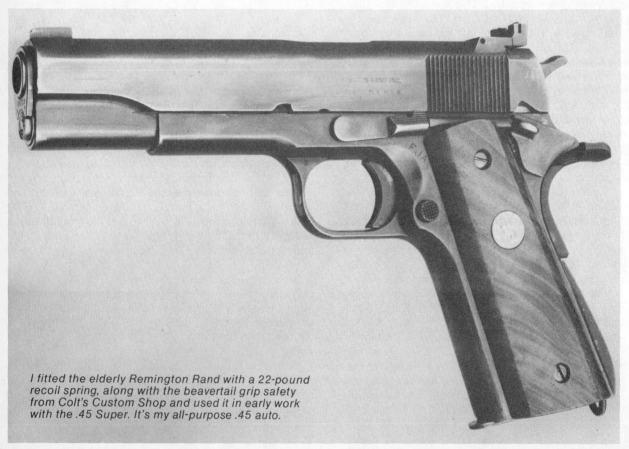

I fitted the elderly Remington Rand with a 22-pound recoil spring, along with the beavertail grip safety from Colt's Custom Shop and used it in early work with the .45 Super. It's my all-purpose .45 auto.

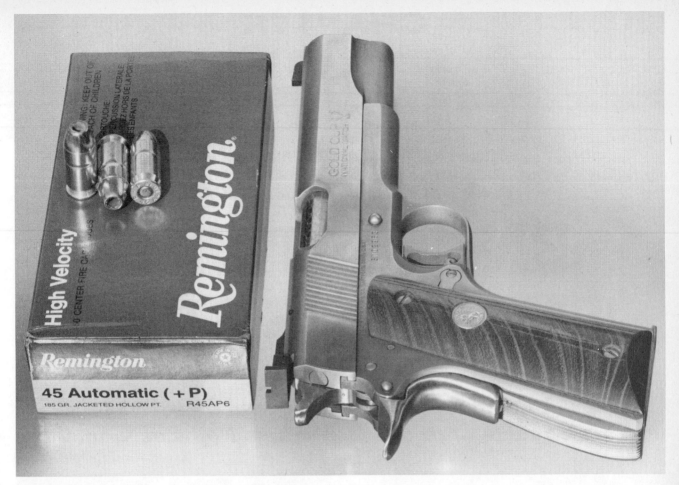

Here's the other side of the stainless steel National Match Gold Cup shown on the facing page and you'll note it now sports an arched mainspring housing — awfully hard to come by in stainless steel, but well worth the intrepid scrounging. Having been set up to handle the .45 Super cartridge, this pistol takes to the Remington +P .45 ACP load like a contented baby kitten lapping up thick cream. One can hope the day may be approaching when the elderly .45 ACP cartridge is brought up to its full potential which, indications suggest, is awesome.

in head construction than the brass employed in other Remington .45 ACP loads.

The fact remains: Despite all the wonder cartridges such as the 10mm Auto, .41 Action Express and the like, the shooting public — which includes the gun-buying and ammo-buying public — retains a lot of keen-eyed interest in .45 ACP ammunition that will perform better than the long-term, typical 780/311 performance of the traditional military hardball load with its 230-grain FMJ/RN bullet.

The ammo-maker who comes up with a hotter .45 ACP load in a stronger brass case that will be capable of being reloaded to superior performance levels is going to intrigue the living daylights out of the ammo-buying public and, in so doing, will earn the heartfelt gratitude of corporate stockholders.

Down the line, gunwriters have been the movers and shakers that forced cartridge development to new and needed levels. In the early Thirties, Philip Sharpe agitated

for the appearance of the .357 magnum cartridge and saw it appear upon the scene. Some years down the line, after milking .44 magnum performance out of guns nominally chambered for the .44 Special, Elmer Keith managed to sweet-talk the industry into coming up with the .44 magnum. Later, Keith took an elegant encore and sired the .41 magnum.

There is no way of guesstimating the returns banked by the makers of guns and ammunition from Sharpe's suggested .357 magnum, but I think it's safe to say they have been profuse and prodigious. The same applies to the .44 magnum, introduced in 1956 and, perhaps to a lesser degree, to the .41 magnum that tripped onto stage in early 1964.

Up here in the scruffy end of the Eighties, we're still waiting for someone to bring .45 ACP autoloaders up to the performance levels they are capable of achieving. I think it is the great untapped bonanza remaining to be claimed.

CHAPTER 13

A NOVICE ENCOUNTERS THE .45 SUPER

*A Longtime Shooter/Reloader Discovers
This Capable Cartridge Is A Whole New Ball Game!*

Andrews and I, hamming it up when he and his wife visited the Grennell domicile. If you can't make out that lettering at the bottom of the bulletin board, it's a photo of a theater marquee advertising a billing of films that read, "Pope/Romancing/Top Secret/Ghostbusters." My twisty mind can't resist such things!

Here's Ace Hindman and, despite Andrews' proffer of nomination, I'd say he's the real guru of .45 Super!

(Author's note: I first encountered the affable Jim Andrews when he wrote to request clearance to use in his classes a small treatise I had written on trigonometry. A retired officer of the California Highway Patrol, Andrews teaches accident investigation, with an accent on the use of skid marks to establish the facts of the matter. Apparently, that involves some amount of trig and the average student goes into an irreversible state of blind funk when encountering the stuff. In my book, ABC's of Reloading, *Third Edition, I'd included a simplified boildown of the basics of trigonometry and Andrews felt it was just what he needed to give his students an elementary grasp of the concept.*

(I gave my consent to quote the pertinent wordage, under certain conditions, and it was the start of an enjoyable and rewarding friendship. I'm pleased to be able to include Andrews' account of his early work with the .45 Super, feeling it gives a representative viewpoint of a fairly typical shooter coming to grips with this interesting but challenging cartridge. — DAG)

FOR OVER forty years I have had a tumultuous affair with the Colt Government Model, of various calibers, and have reloaded my own ammunition for even longer. Until I made acquaintance with the .45 Super I would have been incensed if someone had called me a novice. I now freely admit that I was a novice regarding this wildcat handgun cartridge.

In 1988, I became interested in the articles written by Dean Grennell and Tom Ferguson about this long overdue concept. I contacted Mr. Grennell and through him started corresponding with Tom Ferguson and Ace Hindman of Ace's Custom .45's about the Super. In December of the same year I sent a Government Model to Ace for conversion to the 45 Super. Ace sent me the information necessary to prepare the cases and load the cartridge. All one had to do was reduce the length of the .451 Detonics case and ream it to a depth determined by Ace. Simple? No way. Ace had measured the depth of the chamber in my barrel after he had fitted it and sent me the length to which to trim the cases. When this man says "trim to .900-inch,"

Andrews demonstrates his favored grip and stance with a mill-run example of one of his many .45 autos. No matter what he says the man's no tyro around .45s!

he means just that — no more, no less.

A phone call to Detonics, a check, two weeks wait and I had cases and the proper reamer. Now to work.

In a painfully short time I determined that the reloading equipment I possessed was not capable of the precision necessary. No problem, I purchased a case trimmer of impeccable name and found it had un-impeccable manners when it came to holding within three thousands of an inch.

A call to Ace resulted in a package containing a short-based Forster trimmer. He said it was just the ticket and it was. Following his instructions to the letter resulted in a couple of hundred cases trimmed to the proper length. Now to ream them. Oh oh! Something is wrong. The cases are getting hot, galling and the reamer has turned blue and is dull. No problem, — just a call to Detonics for another reamer and I'm back in business. What — they no longer have reamers.

A frantic call to Uncle Dino — notice it has gone from Mr. Grennell to Dean to Uncle Dino — produces a slightly less than vicious chuckle and a new reamer. This time I used my head. I called Ace and told him my problem. He didn't chuckle or make any comment on my novice mistake. I was told how to make a mixture of alcohol and cutting oil. It worked — oh, how it worked. The cases were cut cleanly and reamed to the proper depth without a hint of trouble.

Ace's instructions require a specific primer to be used. A visit to the store where I buy reloading supplies was fruitless, they were out of this brand. Pacific Bell's Yellow Pages informed me that there are eighteen stores in the Sacramento, California, area which handle reloading supplies. Eighteen phone calls informed me there were no primers of this brand to be had. One kind soul was nice enough to tell me that the packaging was in the process of being changed and that they should be back in the pipeline within a month.

The kind soul was close. Six weeks later I bought several thousand of the needed large pistol primers. In this period I had not been idle. I started to make up a couple of dummy

Above, Andrews turns one loose from the .45 shown on the facing page and you can see the flying empty. Below, this is Andrews' first .45 Super, built on the pistol he supplied to Hindman; frame is nickel plated.

Here's the other side of the .45 Super shown on the previous page. Though Andrews appreciates fancy stocks, you'll note he opts for the practical Pachmayr rubberwork on this one, but it goes well with the mixture of bluing and electroless nickel plating.

The short-base Forster trimmer solved the problem of trimming to the necessary precison, but doing it by turning the crank proved overly tedious in the long haul, causing Andrews to go for the rig on next page.

It's hardly surprising Andrews ended up with the Forster base in the drill press. Here, it's set up for inside-reaming the case necks. Subsequent phone conversation revealed his formula for reaming fluid. It's three parts of denatured alcohol to one part of plumber's cutting oil, removed afterward by hot, soapy water and final rinse.

cartridges. A problem quickly made itself known. Prior to this I had loaded all my .45 ACP ammunition on my Star reloader. This machine is so old that it was purchased new with two heads, .38 Special and .45 ACP, for less than $250.00. Price one today and you will quickly see what I mean about old.

I purchased a set of well-known dies for the .45 ACP and discovered that the neck expanding punch was both too long and too thick for the bullet Ace specified. This was not a big problem. The punch, a couple of the bullets and I were off to see an old shooting buddy, Gene Spenser. Gene is not only a shooter and gunsmith but a tool and die maker. The punch, after Gene was done with it, expanded the case to the base of the bullet when seated at the proper depth and left a lip large enough at the mouth to start the bullet squarely. When I told Gene that it seemed to work like a Lyman M-type die, his only comment was "You noticed."

After we had lunch, Gene took one of the bullets and busied himself at his bench. He told me to go out and get some cold beverage and named his brand. When I got back he handed me a bullet seating punch which matched the ogive of the bullet to be used. Gene sent me on my way without offering one of the six cold beverages. He also didn't charge me anything for his labor, so I'm way ahead.

When I got home from seeing Gene, my pistol was there. Ace's work can only be described as beautiful. The fit of the metal was such that as the slide went into battery it made a "clank" and it was locked tight. I couldn't wait, so it was off to the Capitol Pistol Club, a new indoor range, to try it out. Using regular .45 ACP, both factory and reloads, the gun functioned flawlessly. As beauty is in the eye of the beholder, so accuracy is dependent on the shooter. In spite of my old eyes and hands, this gun was accurate. The groups were keepers and I kept them.

A few hours at the bench produced some .45 Super ammo and the next day it was back to the range. After the first few rounds, the chronograph I was using packed it up, again. A few calls and I knew what I had to have for testing. I had a long talk with my sons and an early Father's day present was ordered. One week later, accompanied by a new Oehler Model 35P chronograph, I was off to the range. Two shots into the first string the Oehler started recording only 0's. I re-read the instruction book and tried again. Same result. When I got home I called Oehler Research in Austin, Texas. Mr. James Bohls listened to my tale of woe and told me he would send me another unit to try.

Three days late it arrived and it was back to the range. This unit worked perfectly. So did the Super. The "light" loads with a 185-grain JHP bullet averaged 1150 fps. The

Above, Andrews' Star loader on its downstroke. Left, using the RCBS Rock Chucker press to seat one of the Hensley & Gibbs conical point 938 bullets in Super case.

top loads averaged 1375 fps with the same bullet in my gun. That is out of a Hindman-modified Government Model with a five-inch barrel. The recoil was slightly more than factory 230-grain hardball and not as much, in my opinion, as hardball ammo in the light Colt Commander.

Since then, I have fired over 1500 rounds of various .45 Super loads. One load provided by Dean sends an H&G 938 cast bullet over the skyscreens in excess of 1350 fps.

I was a novice in reloading this cartridge when I started. My years of experience allowed me to solve some of the problems that arose. Dean Grennell, Ace Hindman and Tom Ferguson were more than helpful in providing the knowledge they had gained in the development stages of the cartridge.

Hindman specifications for the individual pistol called for a trim length to .900-inch, meaning just that!

A question you are apt to ask is, can I recommend this cartridge to others? The answer is yes, with a big *caveat*. It is not for the inexperienced or the person who approaches reloading in a cavalier or precipitant fashion. This is not a mix and match job of reloading. It requires one to follow directions to the letter, the use of the components as directed and a pistol modified with the parts designed and made by Ace Hindman.

Do I like the .45 Super? The answer is simple — I now have two and the third is in the building stage. Do I think the average shooter should have one? You have to answer that question. This cartridge, in a properly modified gun, is knocking on the door of magnum performance and pressures. If you cannot shoot a good group with a standard .45 ACP, you will not be able to use the Super to its potential. If you cannot load ammunition to exact specifications, you could quickly find yourself in trouble.

Prior to the advent of the .44 magnum, many of us old folks found happiness with a heavy-loaded .44 Special. Elmer Kieth was our guru. Many, who were not careful, discovered there was a limit to the strength of the guns then available. This pistol and cartridge is no different. With care one can have an outstanding combination. I have not mentioned loading data for a good reason. Somewhere out there is one person who would not follow the caveats and as sure as night follows day an accident would result.

Dean, I am no longer a novice and you may be a guru.— *James R. Andrews*

According to Rob Wilkinson of the Star Machine Works, the current cost of Andrews' Star loader would be about $935 plus $155 to $345 to tool up for the second caliber.

CHAPTER 14

"OLD SMOOTHIE"

*Noted Knifemaker Bob Loveless
Has His Own Ideas About How A
.45 Auto Should Look And Work!*

Robert W. Loveless takes a thoughtful look up the sights of his highly customized Colt Commander. He set out to make the pistol as painless and comfortable to fire as possible and did so without compensators.

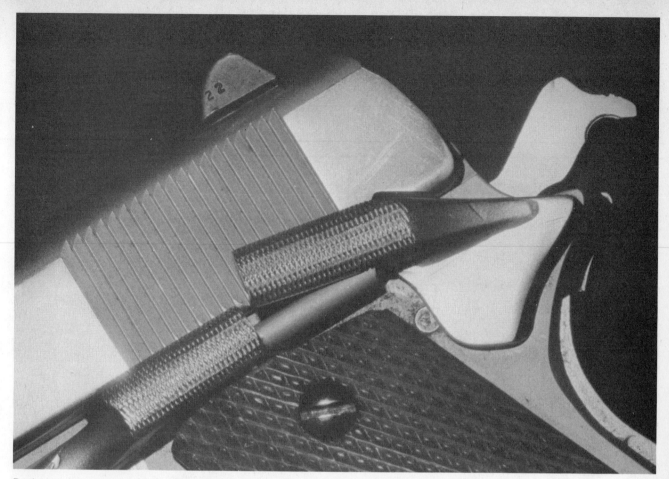

Both the slide stop and safety have been given extended working surfaces and checkered for positive action. Here, the hammer is cocked and the safety is on. Note the bite-free treatment of tang and hammer spur.

ROBERT W. LOVELESS is something of a living legend in the field of custom knives and his designs have had a profound influence on the work of many other makers. Quite apart from fancy cutlery, he has a keen interest in guns of every description and handguns in special particular. Once into that category, he shows little partiality between autoloaders and revolvers, owning and doting over several examples of each.

Some years back, Loveless took Jeff Cooper's course in applied pistolcraft at Cooper's Gunsite Ranch in Arizona. It involved the firing of a substantial number of rounds and Loveless was using an alloy-frame Colt Commander in .45 ACP, unmodified at the time. His right hand took a severe mauling and, as that is the member that earns his living, he was concerned.

"It took me a while to figure it out, but I finally decided the way to keep the gun from hurting me was to cut away or remove all the parts that dig and gouge," he recalls.

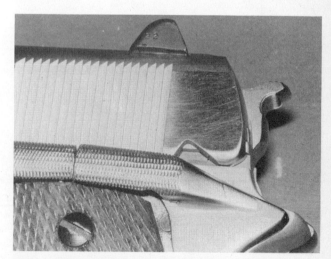

With the safety down, it and the slide stop meet in a neat straight line. Note the rounding of edges and corners, done by way of defanging the little kicker.

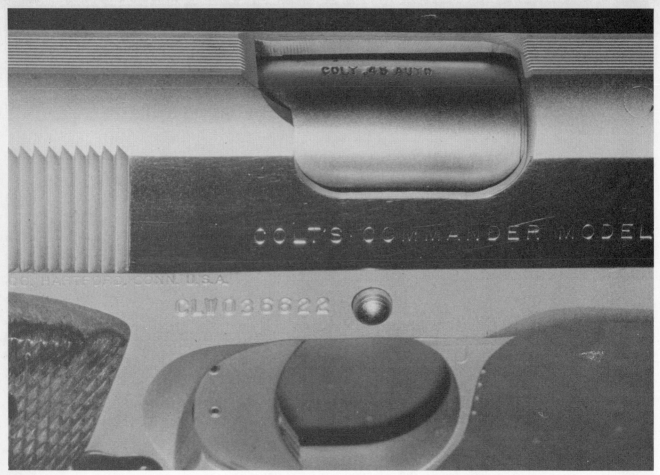

Treatment of the ejection port is pretty straightforward. Commander is the alloy frame model.

It would be difficult indeed to fumble getting the safety down and ready for action with this rig!

The result was a defanged Commander he calls Old Smoothie, completely free from sharp corners and rough edges. The lower portion of the rowel hammer spur has been removed, along with quite a bit of the grip safety tang. As a result, the pistol is incapable of nipping the back of the hand that holds it. That's a big step forward right there.

"My favorite carry mode always has been inside the belt, over my right kidney," Loveless notes. "For that reason, I like a gun that just sort of slips into place there and makes itself at home. If you have any sharp corners or edges, they hang up and you can't tuck them under the belt."

Old Smoothie has some other unusual features, apart from being painstakingly smoothed. The slide stop and safety lever have been re-done in the Loveless manner and manipulating them leaves one favorably impressed to the point of wishing Colt made them the same way. The accompanying photos describe them far better than words can. The rear of the slide stop meets the front of the safety, with no more than a small gap between them. The operating surfaces are half-round in cross-section, well checkered so even the sweatiest thumb still can work either in a totally positive manner.

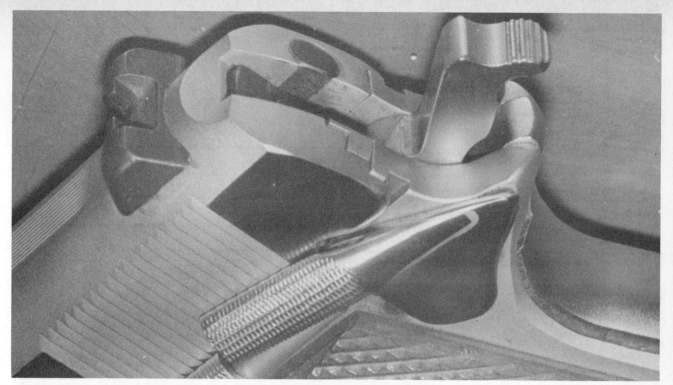

Just enough of the rowel hammer spur has been left to permit easy cocking. Rear sight's a Loveless design.

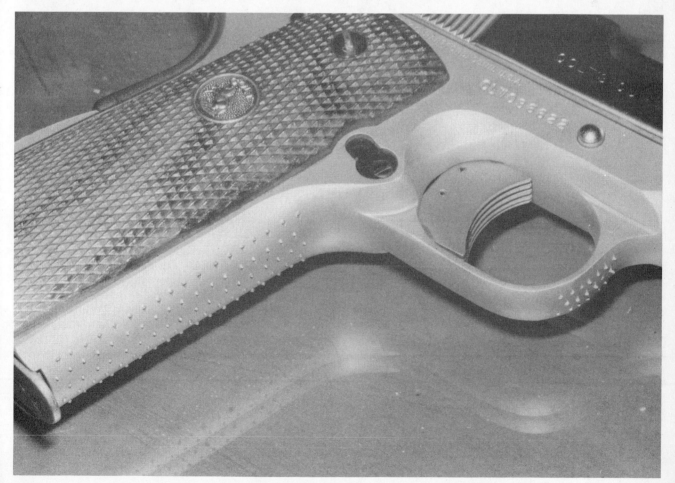

Both front strap and front of trigger guard are lightly stippled. Checkering is an alternative option here.

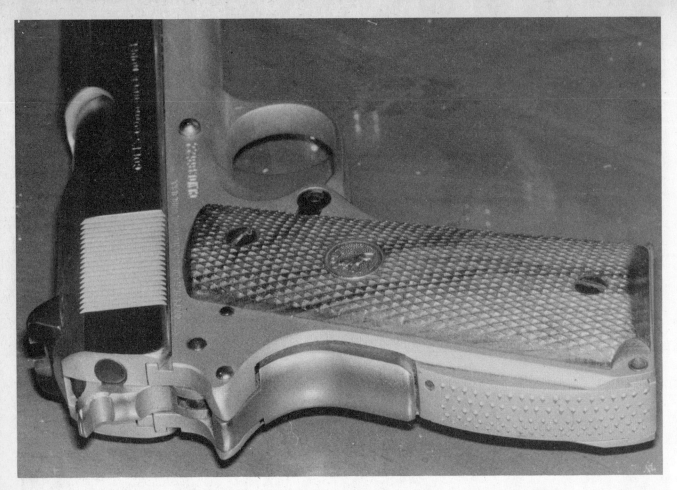

The mainspring housing has been reworked to put the bulge higher, so as to duplicate the feel of the S&W Model 39 which, Loveless feels, is in a class by itself. Stippling here matches that on the front strap.

The mainspring housing has a contour quite different from that of the standard Commander. I asked Loveless if he'd modified it to that shape from an existing housing and he confessed he couldn't remember.

"My idea there was to bring the main part of the bulge up to position it more strategically in the palm of the hand," he recalled. "In the present configuration, it bears a closer resemblance to the shape of a Smith & Wesson Model 39 and I regard that as one of the best-feeling guns ever produced. I may have just made the housing from scratch."

On Loveless' personal Old Smoothie, the rear of the mainspring housing, front strap and a portion of the front of the trigger guard are sharply stippled to discourage finger slippage. He has made up reasonably accurate facsimiles of Old Smoothie for other shooters, but he will perform the modification only on the alloy-frame Commanders, not on the steel-frame Combat Commanders. He feels the added

weight on the latter defeats the primary purpose and nullifies the basic concept.

Should the owner of an alloy Commander prefer checkering, rather than stippling, or desire any other special features and treatments, nearly any possible option can be negotiated and executed. Quizzed as to the probable cost of the operation, Loveless responded it would run in the ballpark neighborhood of $400 to $500, including hardchrome finish and return shipping costs.

The Loveless gun has a long trigger, with a vertically grooved front surface, but he's not a fanatic about that. As a matter of fact, he recalls, he used that particular trigger, because it happened to be on hand at the time he was putting the pistol together.

Loveless has some cogent comments on .45 auto pistols and those who shoot them. I think they bear quoting. He feels that one should not become totally dependent upon

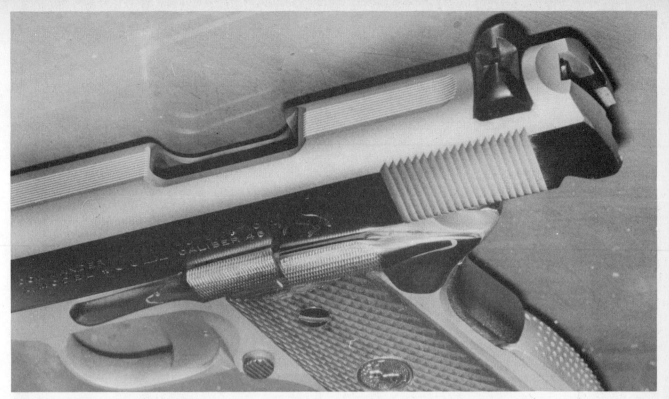

Ten lines milled in the top of the slide simulate the effect of a rib, but without the bulk and weight. Loveless concedes this is a purely cosmetic touch, but he sees nothing wrong with looking good.

Loveless can't recall if he modified this mainspring housing from an existing one or built it from scratch. If you look closely, you'll note considerable metal was removed from the lower corner, leaving neat look.

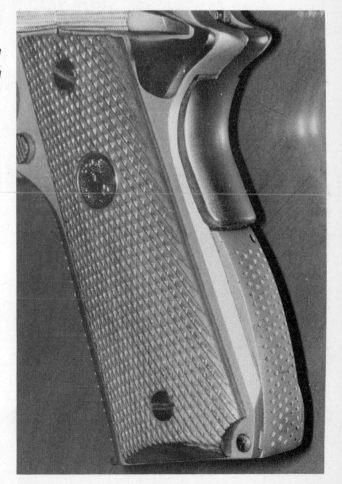

any one particular pistol or set of configurations. Short triggers/long triggers, straight housings/arched housings, short barrels/long barrels, alloy frames/steel frames and so on down the line. Loveless feels good *pistoleros* — or *pistoleras,* comes to that — should be able to give a good account of themselves with whatever gun comes to hand. Thinking it over, I believe he has a pretty good point.

Old Smoothie has a number of custom features that, as Loveless freely concedes, are purely cosmetic touches. They include the serrations down the top of the slide and what he calls the "Browning cuts" at the front of the slide to give that area the ambience of the Browning 9mm Hi-Power. If nothing else, the so-called Browning cuts make it easier to stuff the muzzle under the belt and inside the waistband, as do the beveled edges at the front of the slide.

"I see nothing all that shameful about cosmetics," Love-

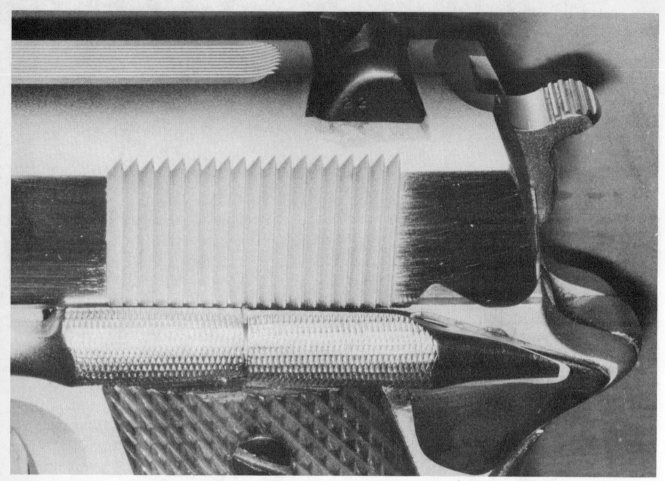

Although there are nice straight lines and square corners in the notch, the outer rear sight contours are comfortably rounded, always toward the end of producing a pistol that's smooth and easy to carry.

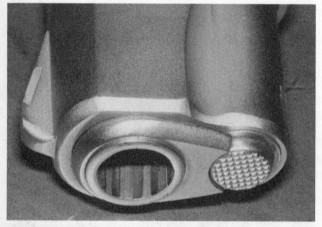

Loveless likes to shove the muzzle under his belt to pack Old Smoothie over his right kidney. Contouring of the slide, sight and barrel bushing help out on this.

less opines. "A gun with a pleasing appearance tends to be valued proportionally and an ugly gun tends to get traded off for something that looks nicer."

However, before you rush to pack your lightweight Commander for shipping and write the check, be further advised we are talking about one of the custom knife-makers whose work is in hot demand. The pistolsmithing projects have to take a number and wait their turn, exactly as do the knife orders. As of the summer of 1989, Loveless estimates the turn-around time to be somewhere between eighteen and twenty-four months.

Additional information can be requested from Robert W. Loveless, Box 7836, Arlington Station, Riverside, CA 92503 and a self-addressed stamped envelope is appreciated.

 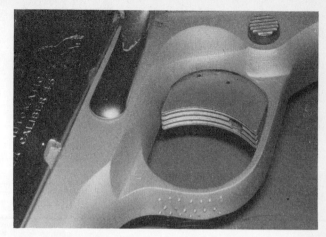

Left, note how the front portion of the slide has been milled to resemble the same area on a Browning M35 Hi-Power 9mmP. Right, not all that finicky, Loveless installed the long trigger because he had it on hand.

The craftsman views his work and finds it good. "Eat yer heart out, Sammy Colt!" he murmurs.

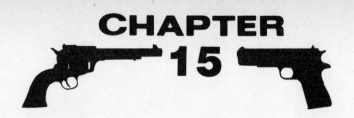

CHAPTER 15

RELOADING .45 AMMUNITION

How To Bypass Steep Ammo Prices And Tailor Cartridges To Fit Your Fancy!

Opposite, the Dillon RL550B press set up for .45 ACP. The shell plate is advanced manually, as in the photo above, which takes a lot of the confusion and pesky frustration out of operating a progressive press. The powder measure dispenses powder only when there is a case in position to receive it and the powder measure is infinitely adjustable, holding its adjustment in use.

AN EMPTY centerfire cartridge case — provided it is Boxer-primed — commands an innate value much higher than what it might bring as scrap metal. Such cases can be reloaded: resurrected to good-as-new status, perhaps capable of performing even better than they did when first taken out of the factory box.

The process of reloading a fired case involves a few simple steps, and it only seems forbidding if you've never done it. As originally manufactured, the cartridge case mouth held the base of the bullet in a secure grip. When the cartridge was fired, the case walls were forced outward into tight contact with the chamber walls, springing back only slightly as the bullet left the muzzle and the pressure fell back to that of the normal atmosphere.

Reloading involves removing and replacing the spent primer, restoring the case to its original dimensions, putting in a new powder charge and seating the bullet.

The usual procedure is to employ a loading press, together with loading dies and a shell holder properly dimensioned to handle the given cartridge. Most loading presses will accept dies and shell holders for a vast multitude of different calibers. Thus, you can buy the one press, then merely add die sets and shell holders as your needs may dictate.

Left, Lee Precision's Pro 1000 progressive loading press has a case sensor to prevent the feeding of primers unless there's a case to receive it and an automatic case feeder. Since this photo was taken, they've added a case collimator to keep the tubes filled with cases. Right, the case mouth expander actuates powder measure.

Some shell holders will accommodate many different cartridges. The one for .45 ACP, for example, can be used to load rifle cartridges in .22-250, .30/06, .308 Winchester, 6mm Remington and a teeming host of others.

At the same time, it may be possible to load more than one caliber with the same die set. For example, a set of .45 ACP loading dies can be used to load the .45 Auto Rim — though you'll need a different shell holder for it — and, quite possibly, the .45 Winchester magnum, .45 Colt, .451 Detonics magnum and .45 Super. Using the same die set for various cartridges will involve readjusting the dies in the press head.

Let us discuss the separate steps involved in reloading:

CASE RESIZING/DEPRIMING

Usually — though not always — the resizing die incorporates the depriming or decapping pin (synonymous terms). Some die sets have the depriming pin on the case

mouth expanding die that is used in the next step. Let's not worry unduly about the matter and go on to cover the theory behind the resizing and expanding of cartridge cases.

Making cartridge cases involves some amount of manufacturing tolerance from one given maker and from maker to maker. As just one example, the cases used in making Remington .45 ACP ammunition, with the R-P headstamp, tend to be somewht thinner at the mouth than some other makes. The objective, in reloading, is to restore the case mouth to dimensions that will grip the base of the bullet securely.

The usual approach is to size the case down a little too far, giving it an undersized inside diameter (ID) at the neck. Then, as the next step, the case is pressed up over a suitably dimensioned plug in the expanding die to restore it to the dead-perfect ID that's the object of the game.

Sizing, I should note, involves forcing the oversized fired case up into a die that has a lower opening that will

I make these small loading blocks that hold ten cases, sizing the holes for various calibers. They are handy for making up five or ten rounds of a given load to take to the range for testing and I like being able to look down into the necks and inspect the level of the powder charges for uniformity before going on to seat bullets.

compress the case and neck back down to a smaller ID. Loading presses supply the operator with a really tremendous amount of leverage and mechanical advantage to take a lot of the sweat and strain out of the operation.

There are two basic types of resizing dies: hardened steel and carbide. Hardened steel dies cost less, but require the cases to be lubricated on the outside to prevent galling and scratching. At some point along the way, the case-sizing lubricant must be removed from the case to keep it from imposing unwanted stress to the firearm action at the time of subsequent firing.

Most carbide resizing dies have an insert of tungsten carbide. Redding uses titanium carbide, which has a somewhat smoother microsurface. The great advantage of the carbide resizing dies is that one need not apply case-sizing lubricant and, thus, need not remove it at a later point in the operation.

Carbide sizing dies are available for straight-sided and slightly tapered cases. They are less frequently encountered for bottleneck cases, though C-H Tool & Die Corporation can supply carbide dies for the .223 Remington. However, when carbide dies are used with bottleneck cases, the cases must be cleaned grit-free and lubricated.

As noted, the old primer may be punched out in the case-sizing step or the next one. If you don't own a reloading press and are about to go shopping for one, I suggest you devote some attention to what the given press does with its expelled primers. Some presses catch spent primers neatly for future disposal. Other presses tend to carpet the floor with spent primers. Even if you don't reload barefoot, policing up hundreds and hundreds of spent primers off the floor gets damned tedious.

CASE MOUTH EXPANDING

Most die sets have expanding plugs that bring the case mouth ID back up to within about .002- to .003-inch below the intended bullet diameter. The plug then provides a taper that flares the edge of the mouth to an angle of

You need a shell holder, which slips into a slot on the head of the press ram. This is the Lee Precison No. 2 size, which fits the .45 ACP and several other calibers for handguns and rifles.

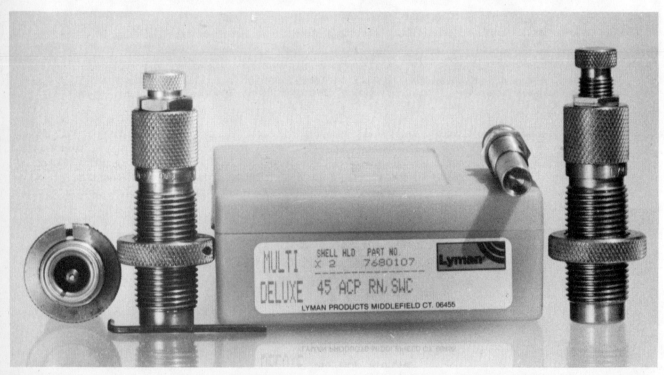

This is Lyman's Multi Deluxe die set for .45 ACP with tungsten carbide resizing die and two different stems for the bullet seating die. Mouth expanding die is Lyman's M die with detail illustrated later.

Here's a good close look at the business end of the Lyman resizing die from the facing page. You can see the insert ring of tungsten carbide in the mouth, to resize without lubrication, and the decapping pin.

perhaps thirty to forty-five degrees. The idea is that you adjust the expanding plug to the point where the press cycle leaves a tiny flared area at the mouth; this enables you to seat the bullet without gouging metal off the sides of its base. Bullets with gouged bases do not group worth rancid hockey pucks.

There is, however, a truly elegant solution to the matter and my main regret is that I didn't think of it myself. I refer to the Lyman M die, which positions an expanding plug with the lower portion about .003-inch smaller than bullet diameter, merging gently into an upper portion that's about .003-inch larger than bullet diameter.

When using the Lyman M die, the preferred strategy involves a patient postioning of the die and punch in the press head, with the objective of getting perhaps 1/32-inch at the outer end of the mouth expanded to the larger diameter. With that done, the base of the bullet can be finger-seated into the expanded mouth, after the powder charge has been dropped and the bullet can be seated with really exquisite precision.

Expanding plugs to fit the Lyman M die are easy and simple to make, if you have access to a metal lathe and even a modest amount of know-how in running it. The plug shanks are threaded 10-32. After shaping the plug to dimensions of your taste, cut off the workpiece, reverse it in the headstock and face off the rear surface. Put a counter-bore bit of suitable size in the tailstock to make a small locater hole that prevents the drill bit from skating about. Substitute a No. 21 drill bit, then replace that with a 10-32 tap.

Do not attempt to tap the hole under power on the lathe. The workpiece and/or drill bit will move in the chucks, ruining one or both. Rather — with power off and clutch out — bring the tailstock and tap up against the workpiece and rotate the headstock a turn or three by hand to start the tap into the workpiece nice and straight. Then loosen the tailstock chuck, move the tailstock to the right, loosen the headstock and take the workpiece and tap over to the bench vise to finish the job with a tap wrench and, perhaps, a small spritz of *Rapid Tap* or a similar cutting fluid to ease

Although it's possible to reload the .45 Winchester magnum with .45 ACP dies, after a fashion, RCBS has this set expressly tailored for the cartridge, with a tungsten carbide resizing die, shown here.

the effort and get cleaner threads.

Flush out the tapped hole with the small plastic tube on a can of Outers *Crud Cutter*, then cut a short piece of 10-32 threaded rod to serve as the shank, smoothing the cut ends to make them turn in freely. Anchor the shank in the plug with a drop or two of Stud N' Bearing grade *Loctite*.

PRIMER SEATING

Primers come in diameters of .175- and .210-inch, respectively termed small and large. Both sizes are available in two basic types known as pistol and rifle. With no more than a few exceptions, one uses large pistol primers when reloading for most of the .45 handgun cartridges.

A further branching of primer types is that most makes, sizes and types are offered in standard and magnum versions. The magnum primers are intended for use with powders that are relatively difficult to ignite and/or for loads apt to be fired when the outside temperature is relatively cold.

Rifle primers require a slightly deeper primer pocket than pistol primers. Cases nominally made for use in rifles — the .45-70, for example — have primer pockets dimensioned to accept large rifle primers and large pistol primers should not be used in them.

Most loading presses incorporate some manner of arrangement for the seating of primers. You may decide to use the primer seater on the press or, again, you may not. There are various alternative ways to seat primers including hand-powered seaters such as the RCBS Posi-Prime, the Lyman 310 tong tool or the Lee Auto-Prime. The last can be adapted for use in loading presses and it makes a convenient, speedy way to seat a lot of primers in a lot of cases with minimal physical effort.

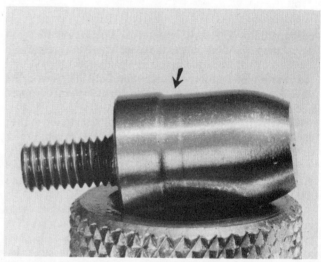

Left, the Lyman M-type expander die has been disassembled to illustrate its construction. The 10-32 shank on the expander plug turns into the end of the 9/16-18 central stem and is secured in adjustment with the locking ring on the stem and the matching ring on the die body. Right, a closer look shows the area of the plug that is slightly greater in body diameter than the bullet diameter to provide easy insertion.

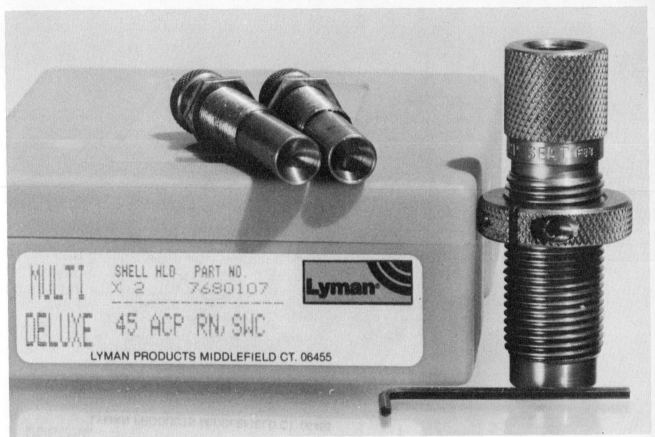

Seating die of the Lyman Multi Deluxe set has stems to fit both round-nose and semi-wadcutter bullets.

Primers need to be seated in their pockets firmly, but not brutally, so as to deform the primer cup and crush the wafer of priming mixture. If you seat primers with excessive force, you are quite apt to obtain erratic ignition, or perhaps no ignition at all.

CHARGING THE POWDER

The powder charge is selected after thoughtful reference to one or more reliable sources of loading data. Some of the makers and distributors of powders supply booklets of loading data at no charge through their dealers or on direct request from the maker or distributor. Such firms include IMR — formerly Du Pont — as well as Hercules, Hodgdon, Winchester and Accurate Arms.

Then there are the manuals and handbooks published by makers of bullets, reloading equipment and, in the example of Hodgdon, powder distributors. These are hefty books, usually bound in hard covers and definitely not available free of charge. No matter; they're worth the asking price and somewhat more than that. Such books are available from Hodgdon, Lyman, Nosler, Sierra and Speer. All are good to have and it conveys a pleasant sense of luxury to have all of them available.

If you have more than one such book and commence comparing the listings, it may trigger some amount of puzzlement and confusion, because the listings for a given caliber, powder and bullet weight are rarely, if ever, identical.

That's hardly surprising. What would be surprising is if it were otherwise. Each block of data under each cartridge and bullet weight was worked out by one or more lab technicians, working under controlled conditions and putting down the numbers to the best of their judgment.

One technician, with whom I'm reasonably well acquainted, was given the assignment to work up a whole new batch of load data for inclusion in a book. There was hardly any time available and vastly less money. I'm told he did most of the drill by making up loads at pretty close to the listings in an earlier book, going on to fire them across the chronograph and writing down the velocities thus obtained. For what interest it may provide, the velocities he got had no discernible correlation to the velocities listed in his drafted-volunteer source book, so the entire project came up smelling more or less like roses.

Be all that as it may, you need to have a source book for load data. It's ever so much more reassuring and safer than

A 1970 vintage taper crimp die from RCBS turns the case neck flare back in for reliable feeding, without putting undesirable strain upon the base of the seated bullet. Bullet base is not scraped on leaving the case.

It's a good idea to check cartridge overall length by trying a few in the magazine you plan to use, making sure they go in and feed out without undue binding.

making up your own as you go along.

One of my basic precepts is never to give a negative order. Putting that on hold for just a bit, do not start out with the top load in any given data source. There are a great many variables involved and, if they all end up pointing in the wrong direction, you can be in bad trouble when you go to fire the resulting reloads, or if someone else fires them.

Each and every individual gun is a law unto itself. You may encounter some who dispute that, but my own experience says it's almost painfully true. Powders of the same make and type vary from lot to lot, sometimes to a really dismaying extent. Powder scales and powder dispensing devices may show variations from the accepted norm. Two bullets may register identical weights, but one may build up more back pressure than the other. Going from one make and type of primer to another can produce significant fluctuations in muzzle velocity and peak pressure. For that and other good and sufficient reasons, it is a good idea to start fairly low and work up cautiously, ever on the alert for danger signals that you are venturing into the regions of unsafe pressures.

It may prove helpful to remove the barrel from an auto pistol for use as a checking gauge to make sure the reloaded cartridges chamber easily and properly. Cases should drop in of their own weight and the case head should be flush with the rear surface of the barrel hood, as here. This is a special gauge, once made by Bar-Sto Precision from barrels that somehow didn't pass inspection, no longer available, sad to say.

BULLET SEATING

With a charge of powder in the load-ready case, you are ready to seat the bullet selected before you consulted your reference sources and picked out the powder charge. If the case mouth has been prepared with a Lyman M die, you can put the load-ready cases in a loading block, drop the powder charges into the cases and go on to visually inspect the level of the powder in each case under a good light, with a critical eye. If they pass muster, you can start the base of a bullet into the mouth of each case before going on with the bullet-seating steps.

The beauty of that particular *modus operandi* is that it gives you an absolutely positive assurance that every case has one and only one powder charge.

The considerations in seating the bullet include assuring the cartridge will fit into and operate out of box-type magazines for autoloading pistols or, alternatively, that the nose of the seated bullet will not project ahead of the chamber face in revolvers, even if it's the sixth round to be fired and thus subjected to the recoil stresses generated by the first five.

There is a technique that works fairly well for adjusting the bullet seating die, providing the bullet you propose to seat is similar in size and shape to bullets used in factory loads. It involves using a factory load to make the tentative setting of the seating die, subject to minor readjustments as may be necessary to seat the bullet at hand.

Before installing the seating die, put the factory load in the shell holder and run the press ram to the top of its stroke. Back the seating stem up out of the seating die by several turns: You don't want it to touch the bullet nose yet.

Turn the seating die down into the press head, until you feel the die body make contact with the mouth of the case in the shell holder. Tighten the locking ring on the die to hold the die in that setting. Now turn the seating stem down, until you feel it make contact with the nose of the bullet, and tighten its locking ring to hold the stem in place.

Use that setting to seat the bullet in three or four charged cases, then check to make certain they can be loaded into the magazine without the bullet nose rubbing against the front of the magazine.

With the bullet seated and mouth taper-crimped, the load can be rechecked for satisfactory fit in barrel.

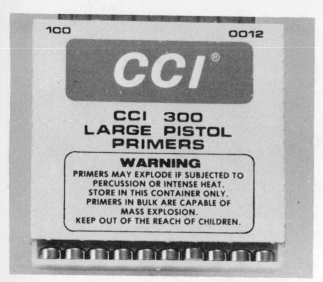

Primers come in large or small, rifle or pistol and standard or magnum types. The CCI-300 is a standard large pistol. Treat them with care, per label warning!

Seating stems are available to fit the noses of most bullets. If a fitted stem is not available, try packing a small amount of paper towel or aluminum foil up into the cavity of a seating stem, perhaps with a small amount of cast bullet lubricant to hold it in place. In seating a few bullets, the filler material will mould itself to accommodate the shape of the bullet nose.

When loading cartridges for auto pistols such as the .45 ACP, it's helpful to have a barrel of the given caliber to serve as a chamber gauge. Hold the barrel muzzle-down and drop a round of the reload into the chamber. It should drop down into place of its own weight and the rear face of the case should come up flush with the rear surface of the barrel hood.

Depending upon the amount of flare you put in the case mouth when you ran it up into the expanding die, it may be necessary to run the reload into a crimping die to turn the flared neck back into a smaller diameter that will fit into the chamber without resistance. There are two basic types of neck crimp: the roll crimp and taper crimp. Roll crimps are used for cartridges that will be fired in revolvers, so as to resist bullet migration due to force of recoil.

A taper crimp is preferable on cartridges to be used in auto pistols and you only need to apply enough to make certain the cartridge chambers easily. Excessive taper crimping should be avoided, because it reduces the diameter of the base of the seated bullet. The brass case neck is slightly elastic and will expand a little, as the cartridge is pulled back out of the taper crimp die. The cast bullet or the lead core of a jacketed bullet is quite inelastic and will not expand back up to the same diameter. Thus, excessive taper crimping weakens the hold of the case neck against the bullet base and, for that reason, should be avoided.

It remains to pack the reloaded cartridges into suitable containers and label them in such a manner that gives the pertinent details of the load: make/weight/type of the bullet; kind of powder and charge weight; make and type of primer; and so on. Failure to identify details of the load will leave you frustrated on future encounters, as you're not apt to be able to remember the exact recipe you used.

HIGH-PRODUCTION PRESSES

In the foregoing discussion, the press was assumed to be a single-station design in which you remove the resizing die to install the expanding die and so on. Presses are available that have a turret at the top, rather than a single die station. The turret is capable of holding three or more dies, perhaps the powder measure, as well. The case can be left in the shell holder and the turret rotated to bring the next die into use, enabling you to complete a reload in a series of steps.

Going a step beyond the turret presses, we have the progressive presses, with multi-station shell holders so several operations are carried out simultaneously with each cycle of the operating handle. The press may advance the turret of the shell plate automatically by means of a linkage to the operating handle; or it may require manual indexing by the operator.

The obvious attraction of the progressive press is the speed of production. The disadvantage is the need for alert attention at all times to prevent missing or double powder charges, missing primers and similar defects.

SAFETY IN RELOADING

Powder is a highly flammable substance that will burn with a quick flare if ignited without being confined. Take care to replace the covers on cans of powder. Keep the lid in place on the reservoir of the powder measure and avoid leaving powder exposed to possible ignition. Clean up all spilled powder, but *do not use a vacuum cleaner to do so.* Sparks from the motor can ignite the powder granules.

Do not smoke in the reloading area and do not allow anyone else to do so. Wear shooting or safety glasses at all times when reloading. Be mindful that primers in bulk are capable of a mass detonation and handle them carefully.

Do not store quantities of powder near the loading area nor in the vicinity of bullet casting operations. Keep one or more fire extinguishers in instant availability and readiness.

Exercise common sense and good judgment in reloading as well as in shooting.

Here are four manuals/handbooks. Missing is the No. 25 Hodgdon Manual, which I couldn't put hands on at the time. (Sorry, Uncle Bruce!) IMR, Hercules, Winchester, Scot and Accurate Arms all have booklets of load data for free distribution and a new manual is due for publication shortly from Nosler Bullets.

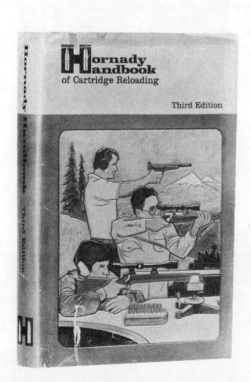

CHAPTER 16

BUILDING A
PARA-ORDNANCE/SERIES '80 .45

The Project Is Full Of Challenges,
But The Resulting Gun Is A Doozy!

Doozy is short for Duesenberg, a legendary automobile of the Twenties and Thirties and I think the resulting pistol merits the term. Despite appearance, the handle is only a trifle larger than that of the standard M1911.

Here's my first pistol construction project on the A.R. Sales frame, with a Springfield Armory slide that carries a Smith & Wesson rear sight and the Caraville Double Ace System. I doubt if there's another like it!

I'VE BUILT 1911-type autos before and found it fun. I'll never forget the sense of mounting panic, the first time I got a 1911A1 reduced to its component parts and started trying to get them all back together again. That would have been at some time in 1944 and, over the years since, I've taken more .45s apart and put them back together than I'd care to have to count.

In the early Seventies, I got an alloy receiver from A.R. Sales and used it as the foundation for an unusual pistol that incorporated a Springfield Armory slide off a WWI pistol, with a Smith & Wesson target sight off a revolver installed on it, plus a Caraville Double Ace device that cocks the hammer for firing if the lever that replaces the grip safety is squeezed in and held. A.R. would give you the serial of your choice, provided someone hadn't beaten you to it, so I got DAG-938: my initials plus the military occupational specialty (MOS) number of an aerial gunnery instructor.

A.R. Sales is no longer in business but, within the past year, Para-Ordnance, (3411 McNicoll Avenue, Scarborough, Ontario M1V 2V6 Canada), introduced a new receiver for use with existing parts for Colt Government Models and all true copies. Like the A.R. Sales receiver, it's made of tough aircraft-grade aluminum alloy and given a hard-anodized finish in flat black. Unlike all other .45 autos, it accepts a staggered-column magazine that holds thirteen rounds of .45 ACP, also available from Para-Ordnance.

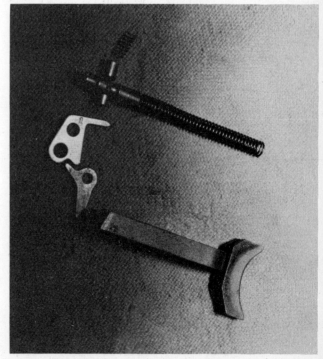

I apologize for the quality of this photo, but it shows the Series '80 parts in their correct relationship.

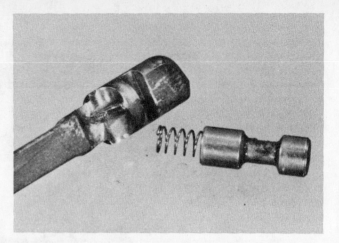

The photo at left shows what Tussey means by the Para-Ordnance having a more straightline feed than most M1911 pistols, thus requiring little by way of feed ramp modification. Photo at right shows the ledge on the extractor that retains the firing pin plunger (10) and plunger spring (33). Getting them out of the assembled slide can prove to be a rather nettlesome chore, though reassembly is a little easier. You do not use force!

The Para-Ordnance (P-O) receiver comes as a kit, with a magazine release and trigger dimensioned to work with the thicker magazine. The plunger tube is integral to the frame, as are the stock screw bushings, and it requires a special size of stock screws, of which four are supplied. The kit comes with a triangular filler piece that can be used with the pre-Series '80 parts and components.

For various reasons, I chose to go with the Series '80. If you put a round in the chamber, a full P-O magazine gives you fourteen rounds, the equal of two standard magazines and a spare P-O magazine offers the ability to get off twenty-seven rounds with minimal delay.

Carrying a pre-Series '80 1911-type with a loaded chamber involves some hazards, even if the hammer isn't cocked. If dropped on the muzzle or struck on the muzzle with sufficient force, the inertia firing pin can be driven forward hard enough to set off the chambered round.

In the Series '80, the firing pin is locked against forward movement until and unless the trigger is pulled. Even so, Colt cautions against carrying the Series '80 guns with loaded chambers and so do I. It's an area where the owner needs to make the decision. If it seems likely a situation might arise where the gun needs to get into action with minimal delay — and minimal audible noise — wiping down the thumb safety on a cocked-and-locked 1911 is as fast as anything is apt to get. Under certain desperate circumstances, carrying with the chamber empty can be more dangerous than the loaded/cocked-and-locked approach but, as noted, that's the owner's decision to make.

The Series '80s were introduced about that year, but I didn't get one until about mid-1986 when I bought the stainless .45 Gold Cup that has come to be one of my special delights. Even then, I didn't take it apart and work on its intimate gizzardry all that much. I substituted a stainless arched housing for the straight one and that was about the end of it.

At some point before or after that, I had occasion to detail-strip a Series '80 and found the project a real bucket of snakes, particularly as it involved reassembling it. The trigger bar lever (part No. 57) rides on the sear pin (48), to the right of the sear (45) and disconnector (5). The plunger lever (31) pivots on the hammer pin (16), in a special niche to the right of the hammer (15) and the pin goes through the lower of its two holes.

If you don't have the exploded view handy — and I didn't, at the time — it can be a real Chinese puzzle, just figuring out how those two pieces are supposed to be installed and which end goes where. That's why I'm supplying the exploded view and parts list here. They can prove ever so helpful when the going gets sticky.

The original Model 1911, as I recall, had forty-nine parts, including the frame or receiver. Going to the target rear sight, Gold Cup trigger with its trigger stop and the Series '80 parts, you have fifty-eight parts. I find it helpful to have a pair of tweezers for coaxing the plunger lever and trigger bar lever into place for pinning. I never needed tweezers to assemble a .45 before, but I do now.

So I got a Series '80 slide assembly, a National Match

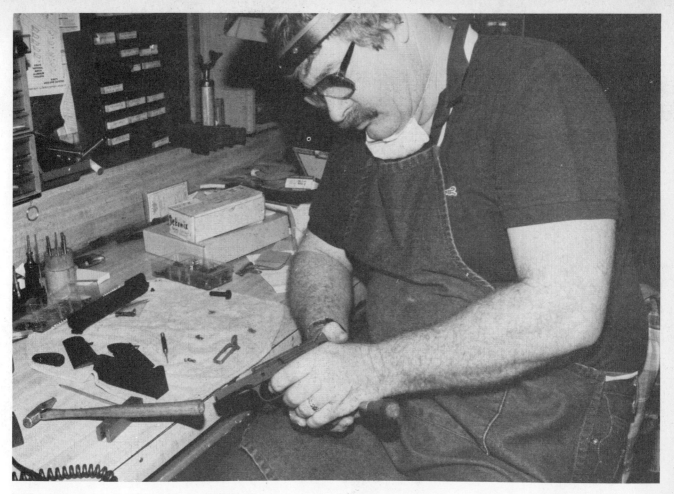

Here's the genial and highly competent Terry Tussey at the bench that has produced a great many .45 autos.

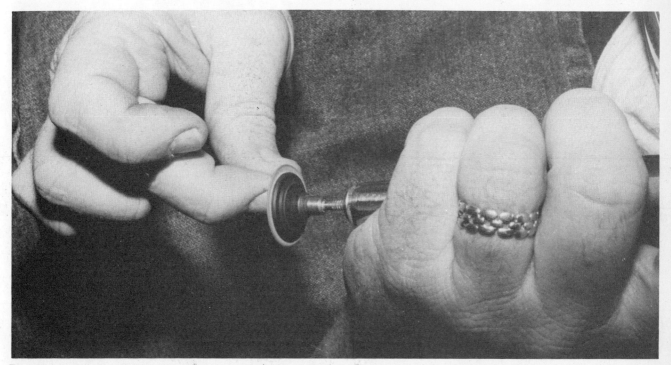

Tussey has this handly little flexible-cord grinder for polishing and finishing. Grit is 320 or smaller.

Firing pin plunger can be used to hold the pin forward...

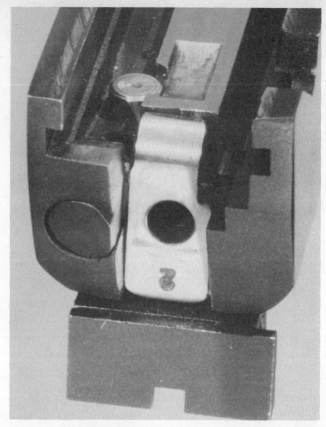

...permitting hand insertion of the firing pin stop.

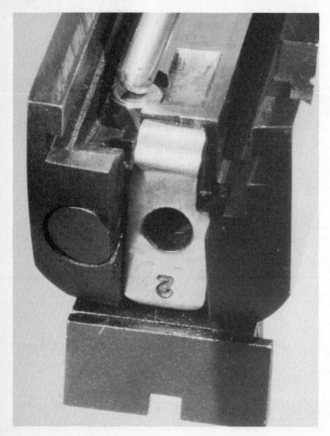

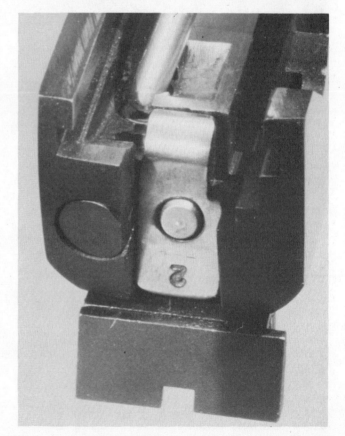

With that done, use a tool to press lightly on the plunger and the firing pin pops into place; a neat trick!

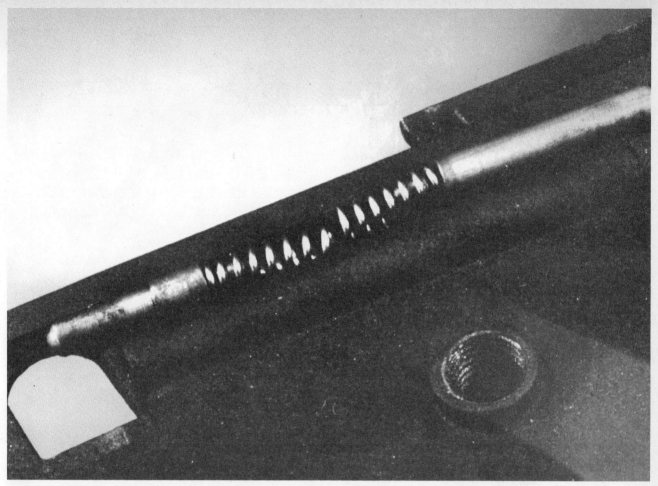

Here's the slide stop plunger (52), plunger spring (32), and safety lock plunger (44) all in their proper position above the integral plunger tube (34) of the Para-Ordnance frame. Push them in from the rear. The little kink in the center of the plunger spring is supposed to be there, as it holds them all in place.

Gold Cup version, with the Elliason target rear sight and all the trimmings. Then, for once, I did something smart. I set up an appointment with old friend Terry Tussey, whom I've known since about the time the crust of the earth was commencing to cool. For the past several years, Tussey has been a full-time professional pistolsmith and I regard him as a darned good one. He has worked on other guns for me and his work is utterly flawless.

Tussey has built enough pistols to make the *Exxon Valdez* ride low in the water — well, almost — and I figured he could impart some helpful advice as we went along, which turned out to be correct. What's more, he stocks all those pesky little parts I didn't happen to have.

It was Tussey's first encounter with the Para-Ordnance receiver and he was most favorably impressed by its precision and overall excellence of workmanship. That's not surprising. I know several other pistolsmiths and I've yet to encounter one with a single bad word for the Para-Ordnance. Since that time, Tussey has built up a P-O for his own use and several for various clients and he says, for fast, instinctive shooting, the P-O ranks right in there with the regular Colt, which he regards as the pistol he shoots best of all.

The Para-Ordnance frame takes special stocks and stock screws and this shows their inner/outer contours.

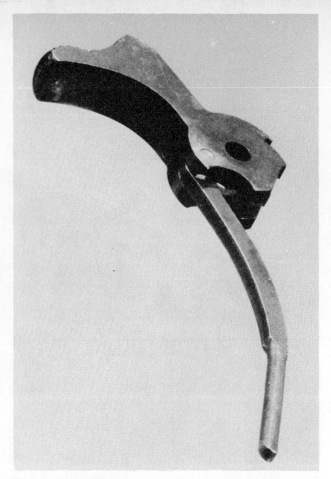

Tussey polished the barrel feed ramp mirror-bright, but removed as little actual metal as possible, left. Above, the hammer (15), hammer strut pin (18) and hammer strut (17), assembled. You can see where Tussey polished the area around the end of the pin.

Tussey's general approach in assembling a pistol is to polish every surface that rubs against — or is rubbed against by — another surface as the pistol operates, *but without removal of any more metal than can be helped.* This is done with 320-grit abrasives or even finer. An area that gets special attention is the standing breech or bolt face. The cartridge head slides upward against that as the action goes into battery and a smooth surface does a lot of good things for overall reliability.

Tussey also noted that one of the best approaches for the person who wants to build a Para-Ordnance is to take another pistol — known to be operating well — and simply shift its pertinent parts over to the P-O frame. That way, it's much easier and there's no need to worry about parts fitting properly: If they worked on the original frame, they'll work on the P-O frame and you have the added advantage of being able to see how it all goes together before you start moving parts across.

I think that has the sound of a good idea and second the motion. I'd have done just that, if only I'd thought about it in time. As noted, however, the only other Series '80 I had

on hand was the stainless Gold Cup. That would have resulted in a rather garish appearance and, besides, I'm awfully fond of the Gold Cup as it stands.

Here are several of Tussey's thoughts and pieces of advice on the general subject of putting a .45 together from parts:

"Use a good quality extractor, such as those made by Caspian, Wilson or Colt. Make sure the tension is proper: not too tight and not too loose. If tight, it will bind as the action closes. If too loose, it will cause several types of ejection failures. Polish the part of the extractor tip that slides over the rim of the case, but don't change the basic dimensions.

"It's advisable to install a new firing pin spring, as supplied by Wolff, Wilson or Colt, particularly on pre-Series '80 guns. A weak firing pin spring may allow the gun to fire if dropped on the muzzle, or if the slide goes forward too fast. It can also allow the firing pin to stick forward in the port, causing the firing pin stop (12) to drop and tying up further operation.

"Check the barrel in the frame, making sure the feed

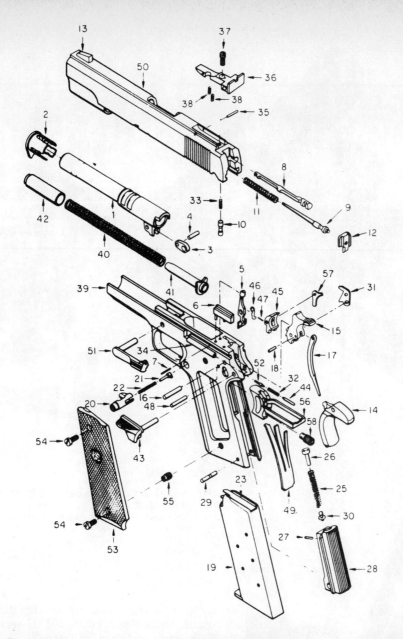

1—Barrel	21—Magazine Catch Lock	41—Recoil Spring Guide
2—Barrel Bushing	22—Magazine Catch Spring	42—Recoil Spring Plug
3—Barrel Link	23—Magazine Follower	43—Safety Lock
4—Barrel Link Pin	24—Magazine Spring (not shown)	44—Safety Lock Plunger
5—Disconnector	25—Mainspring	45—Sear
6—Ejector	26—Mainspring Cap	46—Depressor
7—Ejector Pin	27—Mainspring Cap Pin	47—Depressor Spring
8—Extractor	28—Mainspring Housing (flat)	48—Sear Pin
9—Firing Pin	29—Mainspring Housing Pin	49—Sear Spring
10—Firing Pin Plunger	30—Mainspring Housing Pin Retainer	50—Slide
11—Firing Pin Spring	31—Plunger Lever	51—Slide Stop
12—Firing Pin Stop	32—Plunger Spring	52—Slide Stop Plunger
13—Front Sight	33—Plunger Spring F/P	53—Stock Set (Walnut)
14—Grip Safety	34—Plunger Tube	54—Stock Screw (4)
15—Hammer	35—Rear Sight Leaf Pin	55—Stock Screw Bushing (4)
16—Hammer Pin	36—Rear Sight Leaf	56—Trigger Assembly
17—Hammer Strut	37—Rear Sight Elevation Screw	57—Trigger Bar Lever
18—Hammer Strut Pin	38—Rear Sight Elevation Spring (2)	58—Trigger Stop
19—Magazine Assembly	39—Receiver	
20—Magazine Catch	40—Recoil Spring	

This exploded view and parts list covers the Series '80 Model 191A1 and/or National Match Gold Cup. It is similar to one of the pre-Series '80 pistols, but not identical in every respect. It is useful information to have!

Removing the magazine catch (20) lets you remove the trigger (56) but, on the P-O frame, you must remove the stock panels (53) in order to get the trigger out.

Magazine catch is removed by pressing inward and turning the catch when it lines up with the slot. The .45 carries most, if not all, the tools needed for its disassembly and the tip of the sear spring can serve.

ramp of the barrel does not overlap the feed ramp of the frame. There should be about 1/32-inch gap between the frame ramp and chamber ramp.

"It was not necessary to throat the feed ramps on the chamber or frame. It's more of a straightline feed than most such guns. The barrel ramp was polished. The frame ramp was not polished nor were any parts of the frame polished or touched, so as to preserve the hard-anodized surfaces.

"Getting into the trigger, fit the disconnector against the trigger that's supplied with the P-O kit. Put the sear and disconnector in and put the pin through. If it's a Series '80, install the trigger bar lever at the same time. Make sure the disconnector is lying against the trigger bow. Use *only* a Colt disconnector. If the disconnector doesn't touch, it may require a little relief in the window, *below* the visible part of the hole, allowing the disconnector to come forward. The window is that sort of square hole in the center of

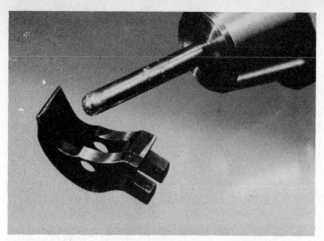

Tip of the brass rod points to the area on the "inside of the moon" that is relieved on latterday sears, per text.

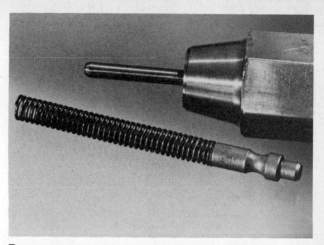

Tussey recommends starting with a new firing pin spring (11). Note relieved area in Series '80 type.

the disconnector and you can increase the window size to let the disconnector come forward. It is essential that the disconnector *does* touch the rear of the trigger bow.

"The sear should be a Colt and a late model with the extra bit of metal relieved from the upper, inner surface — the "inside of the moon" — a feature of commercial sears since the late Fifties or early Sixties. That is especially important if you're going to use the Gold Cup hammer, or hammers by Wilson, Ed Brown or Chip McCormick, because those hammers are not safe with any other type of sear.

"Those particular hammers cock a little farther over center than a standard hammer. What happens is the sear cannot reach the safety notch, or half-cock notch. It's not smart to carry the gun with the hammer at half-cock, but the notch does stop them from going full-automatic.

"Series '80 or Series '70 hammers can be used interchangeably, as the sears are identical.

"After you've checked the sear and disconnector to make certain they move freely, fit the hammer. You're still in the trying-out stage at this point, to make sure you have all the right dimensions. Put in the sear spring, (49), then

Here's a close look at the firing pin plunger and its spring, which fit into the relieved area at the rear of the firing pin (9) in photo above.

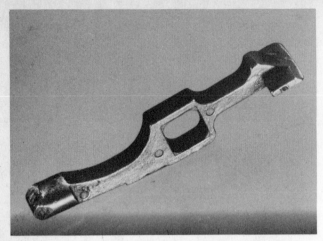

Here's the disconnector (5) and you can see the square "window" to which Tussey refers in his comments.

you can push the regular mainspring housing pin (29) partially into place.

"Then cock the hammer and push the slide partially onto the frame. The grip safety (14) is left off at this point. The important thing is to make sure the slide depresses the cocked hammer as it moves across it. The slide doesn't have to move the hammer much, but it *does* have to touch it, in the fully cocked position. Also make sure the disconnector disconnects properly: with the slide partly back nothing should happen when you pull the trigger. Then let the slide go to its fully closed position and make sure there's good engagement from the disconnector. If there's not enough engagement, the disconnector will slide out from under the ears of the sear and let the sear snap back, which will put it on half-cock.

"Assuming you've got all that to work properly, take the slide off again and try the thumb safety (safety lock, 43), making sure it just touches or just clears the sear. There should be no visible movement when the safety is in the up position.

"It's best not to use used safety locks; use new ones that have to be filed down just a bit to pass behind the sear. Use only a Colt, Pachmayr or Wilson mainspring housing. When pushed into place, with the hammer down, the mainspring housing pin should start into place under finger ten-

the mainspring housing (28). When the mainspring housing is in place, make sure there's tension against the disconnector and trigger; so there's no free play there. What you want is tension at rest. Put a trial pin in to hold the mainspring housing in place. If you don't have a trial pin,

With the barrel held against the frame in its normal relationship, you should be able to see about a 1/32-inch gap between the front edge of the frame feed ramp and lower edge of the barrel feed ramp. This one's okay.

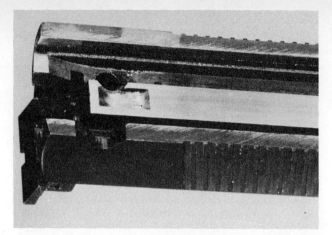

At left is the relief cut that permits the tip of the disconnector to come up when the slide and action are closed and fully into battery. Tussey polished this area.

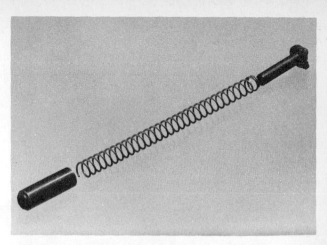

The recoil spring plug (42), recoil spring (40) and recoil spring guide (41) in their normal relationship.

sion, not stopping until it makes contact with the mainspring housing pin retainer (30). What makes this important is that some of the aftermarket mainspring housings are made from castings and not drilled properly. They can break the frame and that's a genuine Excedrin headache. There is nothing wrong with the plastic mainspring housings supplied by Colt. They are dimensionally perfect and they stand up just fine.

"If you assemble with the Series '80 system, there's a handy way to check if everything is functioning properly, after it's all together. Make sure the chamber is empty, hold the muzzle upright, drop a pencil down the barrel, pointed-end-up, cock the hammer and pull the trigger to see if it launches the pencil. If the Series '80 mechanism is put together improperly, nothing will happen and the pencil will remain in place, no matter how many times you

Here's a simple little working tray I find extremely helpful when taking guns apart or putting them back together. The raised outer frame helps prevent loss of small parts. Surface is Naugahyde over padding.

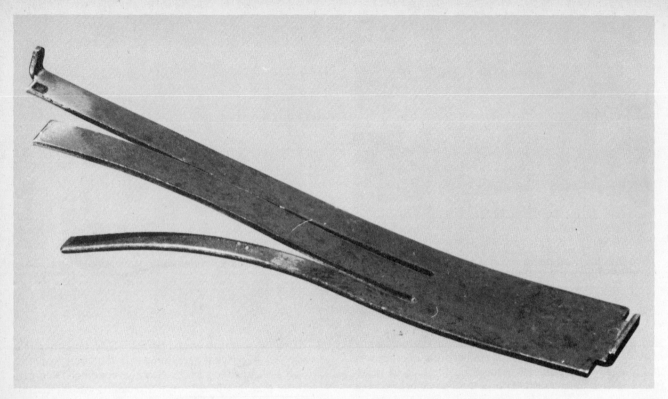

Paraphrasing a soft drink commercial, according to Tussey, things go better with Colt, and this is the sear spring (49) that performs several functions in the assembled pistol, all of them quite important.

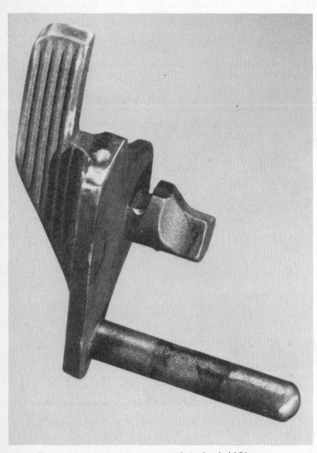

Tussey suggests a new safety lock (43).

cock and snap, even though the hammer drops in a normal manner. The firing pin will remain locked and motionless. Various other modern autoloaders have systems similar to the Series '80 and most, if not all, can be reassembled improperly, so they will not fire. The pencil test is a simple way to verify the firing pin is performing properly — but always make certain the chamber is empty!

"If you use a good quality slide and barrel, the lockup should be precise enough for any ordinary purpose. A neat trick for checking their alignment is to remove the firing pin and spring, as well as the firing pin stop. Then put an *empty, unprimed* case in the chamber and sight through the firing pin port to see how it lines up with the flash hole in the unprimed case. That should identify any serious irregularity in lockup. Take care you do not pull the trigger and drop the hammer with the firing pin and stop removed, as it will damage other exposed parts.

"It's not a simple matter, putting .45s together. The safety mechanisms and systems on the Model 1911 are not simple. *The only thing simple about a Model 1911 is taking it apart.* It is not a simple gun to fit up and I go through about fifty checks and tests in the process of fitting up a .45, testing for safety, engagement and other considerations.

"Apart from receivers by Colt and Para-Ordnance, just about all other receivers require some varying amount of gunsmithing that is not apt to lie within the easy capability of the average person essaying to put a gun together. You will bypass a lot of problems if your hammer, sear, disconnector, sear spring and extractor are genuine Colt parts.

Left, we used a Colt mainspring housing — arched, of course! — and it's shown here with the mainspring housing pin (29) halfway into the hole. Left and right below, the plunger lever (31) comes up when the trigger is pulled, and that, in turn, pushes the firing pin plunger (10) upward to allow the firing pin to go forward. Here you can see both and, perhaps, understand the working relationship a bit better.

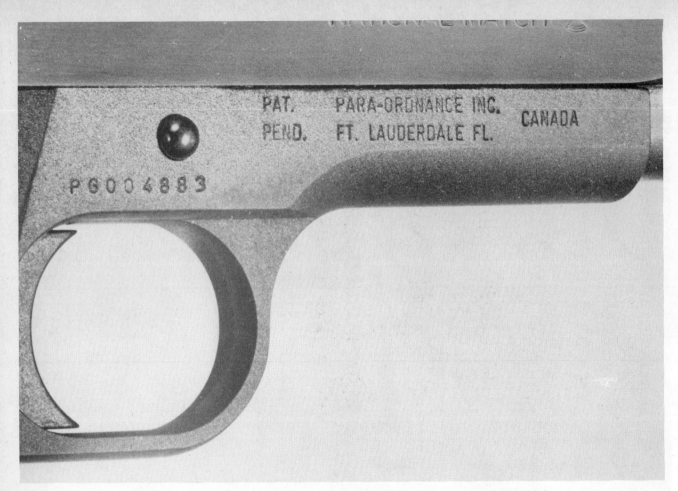

Here's the pertinent printing on the P-O frame and, in view of the serial number, I sometimes think of this pistol as "The Far-sighted Mister P'Goo." I tried to keep from saying that, but was powerless!

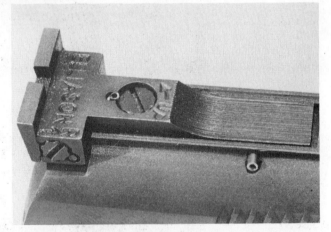

Above, in my humble opinion, there's hardly anything so nice as being able to adjust your rear sight and the Elliason sight that comes with the Gold Cup slide is about as ginger-peachy as such things ever get. Left, shades of Bob Loveless's Old Smoothie! Terry terms this dehorning of the barrel bushing (2) "Tusseyizing."

My old friend, the late Steve Herret, used to be fond of looking at something he'd done and observing it was, "good enough for who it's for." The leatherwork here is by gruff but kindly old Jack Kendall, who can be reached at 1069 Estabrook, Clovis, California 93612 and Herrett's observation comes to mind.!

"Extended safeties and extended slide stops require alteration to the stock slabs on the Para-Ordnance receiver and they may not work at all, due to the thicker frame."

That concludes Tussey's comments. In order to make some of the accompanying photos, it was necessary to take it all apart, piece by piece, then reassemble it again. I managed to do so, but easy it sure as heck wasn't! I'm happy to report that, after reassembly, it passed the Tussey Pencil Test — sort of. Not wishing to have to explain an impaled ceiling to my good lady, I subsituted a fired .223 Remington case, which came out the muzzle and went about three feet in the air. I'd envisioned a little more velocity, hence the caution. Whatever you do, don't use a *live* .223 round!

So how does the Para-Ordnance/Series '80 Gold Cup/ Tussey gun shoot? Quite well, quite reliably and with decent accuracy, by which I mean groups between 2.5 to 3.5 inches off the sandbags at twenty-five yards with most loads. It is a singular experience the first time you sit there and blam fourteen .45 holes in the paper, all sort of lipperty-lipperty. I've fired 9mmPs that held a lot more cartridges, but somehow they weren't the same. I like this pistol and I like it a lot. I even let it go about in my Jack Kendall holster.

Even if you consider yourself adept at detail stripping and reassembling Model 1911s and Series '70s, the Series '80 can bestow more humility than you really felt you needed — at least on the first few encounters.

If you build a pistol, be it M1911, Series '70 or Series '80, I recommend you have it checked over for function and safety by a good, reliable gunsmith or pistolsmith before the first firing of it. If he charges a fee, view it as a bargain in terms of your own safety and peace of mind.

CAUTION! Having no control over components, equipment, assembly techniques and other related factors, the publisher, the author, Terry Tussey and the makers of the various parts and components cannot and do not assume any liability, either expressed or implied, for events, damages, injuries — including fatal injuries — arising from or alleged to have arisen from use of the foregoing text. Any use of such information is clearly and specifically at the individual risk and discretion of the assembler(s) of the pistols and/or the shooter(s) of such pistols and/or any others at or within four miles of the shooting site(s).

CHAPTER

17
CREATING A NEW TYPE OF .45 ACP AMMUNITION

MagSafe Ammo
.45 ACP 103-gr +P Defender #45D
12 pcs #2 Nickel, 5 pcs #4 copper shot
Pellets Penetrate 12" Ballistic Gelatin
S&W 645-1,675 fps/641 fpe; Officers-
1,580/571; Marlin Carbine-1,933/854
85% <u>More</u> Energy than Silvertip!

Zambone uses two .45 autos to test his .45 ACP loads. This is the Colt Officers ACP with the MagSafe +P Defender load, carrying a 103-grain bullet to 1580/571.

Obtaining Controlled Expansion Plus Adequate Penetration Is Not The Simple Matter You Might Think!

THE GOAL FOR .45 ACP MagSafe ammo was to design a frangible (prefragmented) "safety" bullet with better penetration than other such loads already on the market. Many tests had shown me that existing safety slugs didn't have the punch to break through a chest wall and still damage vital organs; they often made shallow "divot" wounds. Policemen I spoke with who'd shot felons with frangible slugs had often had nasty surprises.

After lots of trial and error (mostly error), I created MagSafe's *Controlled-Core* construction, with varying sizes of shot placed in specific places in a projectile jacket. Building a slug this way is as tedious as handknitting the Goodyear Blimp, but the performance is worth extra effort.

MagSafe .45 ACP slugs use Hornady 185-grain JHP bullets with the lead melted out. The conical profile feeds well in stock pistols. The shot core is layered to promote reliable expansion, even after shooting through many layers of heavy clothing; most frangible slugs, and all hollow-point bullets, "clog up" going through clothing. They rarely expand in flesh afterward.

The bottom layer is five pieces of nickel-plated #2 shot (or #2N for brevity). One piece of #2N goes in the middle of that circle as an expander. The middle layer is the same as the bottom one, with another six pieces of #2N shot.

Also used at MagSafe is the five-inch Smith & Wesson Model 645, in which the +P+ load drives its 103-grain bullet to 1900/825 in the five-inch barrel. This load requires a stronger recoil spring, with a rating of about 22 pounds.

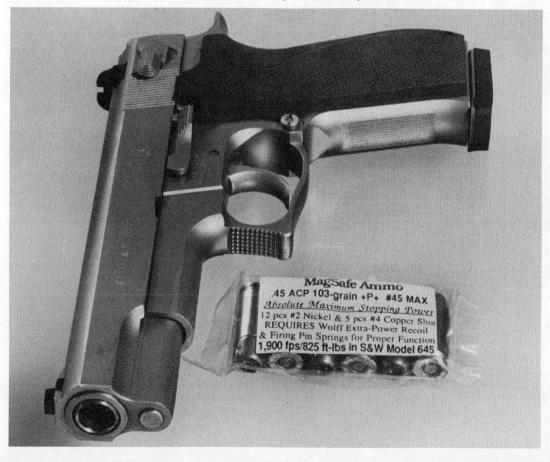

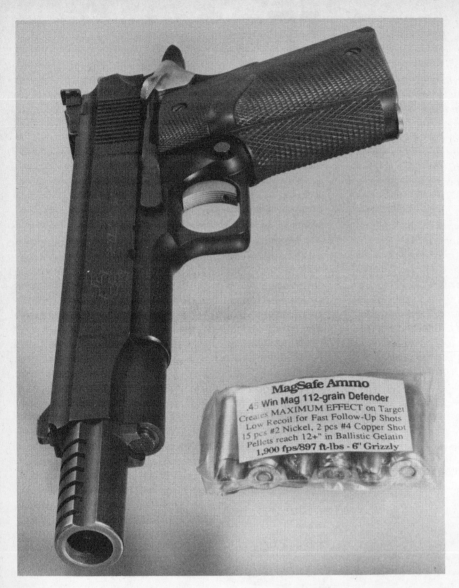

On the packaging label:

MagSafe Ammo
.45 Win Mag 112-grain Defender
Creates MAXIMUM EFFECT on Target
Low Recoil for Fast Follow-Up Shots
15 pcs #2 Nickel, 2 pcs #4 Copper Shot
Pellets reach 12+" in Ballistic Gelatin
1,900 fps/897 ft-lbs - 6" Grizzly

MagSafe has a .45 Winchester magnum load and an L.A.R. Grizzly is their test gun for it. Out of the six-inch Grizzly, the load is good for 1900/897.

The top layer uses five pieces of copper-plated #4 shot.

The cavity is filled with epoxy resin, bringing total weight to 103 grains. The resin seals each shot pellet in place until impact, and buffers the pellets when they hit so the core breaks apart at a controlled rate — rather than all at once.

Sealing the shot in epoxy keeps it from shifting during the slug's trip down the barrel. The loose shot used in other frangible bullets clumps to one side of the projectile jacket as soon as rifling starts. The same thing happens to a bunch of socks thrown in your dryer. Off-balance bullets aren't overly accurate.

We build a standard .45 ACP load called the *Defender* which chronographs over 1675 fps in a five-inch S&W Model 645. Although rated +P in pressure, it recoils like a target load while still packing 641 foot-pounds of energy (fpe). No pistol modifications are needed to shoot this load.

Our extra-effort load is the +P+ "45 MAX," made with shortened .45 Winchester magnum brass for strength. It clocks over 1900 fps in a five-inch barrel, and over 1750 fps in a Colt Officers ACP; the 45 MAX offers 825+ fpe and 700+ fpe respectively. Felt recoil is like standard 230-grain hardball ammo, although the rate of muzzle rise is quicker because initial slide velocity is fast.

An extra-power Wolff recoil spring kit is needed to safely fire this load, but no other modifications are needed to stock pistols. Although pressures are above those of even +P .45 ACP rounds, the rise time, or length of time the brass case and the chamber are subjected to pressure, is near-instantaneous. Light slugs start moving so fast that pressure drops off in a few milliseconds.

During 1988, we shot holes in over $1000 worth of packaged corned beef, testing expansion and penetration of every type of ammo in genuine flesh. Corned beef is extremely tough, muscular tissue, with a "memory" which causes holes to close back up after an object has passed through. The same is true for human chest and stomach walls. Organs like the liver have no memory, and big holes stay big.

Proper testing requires that the test medium be clothed, unless the round is designed for use in a nudist camp. We clothed our corned beef with Levi's jackets, shirts, boot leather or other such items of apparel, looking for valid test results. Note that we didn't shoot phone books — wet or dry — modeling clay, or other such test media, none of which produce results worth analysis.

To simulate the resiliency of a human chest wall, we taped two three-pound packages of corned beef onto gallon plastic milk jugs filled with water. This amounted to about six inches of flesh, with the plastic beef wrappers adding extra surface tension much like skin does. We sought a bullet which would travel completely through the beef, then exit the back of at least one gallon jug of water.

We first found that *no* hollow-point will expand reliably in flesh after it's gone through several layers of clothing. There just isn't enough velocity to cause expansion, no matter what you've heard from the expert gun writers.

Silvertip .45 ACP, for example, usually turns into a hardball after going through clothing. The wound channel in corned beef is less than .45 caliber, because muscle memory pulls the flesh back to close the wound. Silvertips traveled through the beef and three water jugs, with the exit hole in the last jug still no larger than .45 caliber. This was interesting, in light of several ballistic researchers who theorize that Silvertips don't have enough penetration. We found just the opposite; if anything, they'd shoot clean through the average clothed person.

We also learned that other safety slugs often fail to disrupt and dump their #12 shot, because clothing slows them down to where not enough kinetic energy is available to break apart the slug when it finally reaches flesh. But sometimes the same batch of safety slugs disrupted too quickly, making a wide but shallow wound only a few inches deep.

MagSafe's Defender load made a three-inch wide permanent wound channel through the first five to six inches of corned beef. At that point the shot pellets separated and traveled on separate paths rather than in a shot/epoxy cloud; they continued through the flesh and exited the back of the second jug in line.

On impact, the 45 MAX chewed out a three-inch-wide hole so violently that up to a pound of meat was thrown back toward the shooter. The permanent — non-repairable — wound channel was at least six inches deep, with pellets penetrating up to three water jugs.

In December, 1988, we began shooting blocks of 250A — 10 percent formula — ordnance gelatine, a test medium which simulates muscular human flesh. We videotaped each impact in slow motion. These tapes allowed us to see what happens during each one-thousandth of a second while a bullet disrupts gelatine. It's easy to see the temporary wound cavity, which is formed for just a fraction of a second and then shrinks down again.

There's a lot of controversy over what happens when bullets hit flesh. Some researchers think a slug must penetrate at least twenty inches of ordnance gelatine to be capable of stopping an attacker. These are the same experts who shoot naked gelatine; their results are invalid — unless you're attacked by a fat nudist.

Again, we clothed the test medium, and again we found that what looks good at first often fails in valid tests. No JHP slugs expanded well (or at all) in gelatine after going through two layers of a Levi's jacket. Instead, they clog up and turn into wadcutters or hardball slugs. Even specialty designs with posts in the nose cavity clog up, boring through as much as eighteen inches of gelatine and leaving a wound channel smaller than .45 caliber.

Other frangible rounds did poorly. One, tested repeatedly in naked gelatine, went a maximum of five inches: not enough to penetrate a chest wall and reach vital organs. Shot into clothed gelatine, the same safety slug had spotty performance, sometimes dumping shot and reaching barely six inches, other times failing to disrupt and traveling through three of our six-inch gel blocks. In the latter case, the wound channel was no larger than that made by a hardball slug.

Two recent arrivals on the frangible slug scene also were tested. These slugs use a light lead hollow-point nose over a load of #12 shot. The theory is that this hollow-point offers more initial penetration than the plastic ball used on the other safety round. After breaking through the chest wall, the bullet is supposed to dump shot throughout the wound channel and produce a massive wound.

What happens instead is that the lead hollow-point clogs up and penetration is too deep. The shot load doesn't scatter throughout the wound channel as claimed, usually staying entirely within the projectile body. The wound channel is no larger than that made by a Silvertip. Shot into naked gelatine, the same little hollow-point turns into a lead parachute, screeching to a halt within five inches; all the shot backs up behind the wafer of lead formed on impact.

We test ammuniton in two barrel lengths: the five-inch Model 645, and the 3.5-inch Colt Officers ACP. Rounds which performed marginally in long barrels did worse in the Officers ACP, owing to lower impact velocity. Several trick factory rounds, touted by gun writers who think shooting phone books is a good test, do not mushroom whatsoever when shot into clothed gelatine from a short barrel.

MagSafe's 103-grain Defender Load bores through clothing and ordnance gelatine, making a permanent wound channel over an inch wide to a depth of five inches. Then the epoxy drops behind and pellets travel on to a depth of ten to thirteen inches. At the ten-inch mark, pellet pattern is some five inches in diameter, good for multiple organ hits. Such a wide pattern also allows a poorly-aimed torso shot to still connect with vital organs.

The 45 MAX is the only .45 caliber slug we tested which split open a six-inch gelatine cube. The permanent wound channel is some two inches in diameter, with a five-inch temporary wound cavity. Pellets travel a little deeper than with the Defender Load, but the impact energy is greater and gel blocks are ripped apart.

Clearly, a lot of test data that ill-informed gun writers are putting into print is flawed. We've all read about a watermelon blasted into oblivion by this or that wonder bullet, without a dent being made in the cardboard behind the melon. This is written up as though such limited penetration is a good thing. In reality, it isn't enough to reach vital organs and shut down a drugged attacker fast.

Other writers say you can't go wrong with plain ol' GI hardball .45 ammo, if you put the bullet in the right place. That's unrealistic, since most people are scared witless when being attacked, and invariably will throw lead in the general direction of the bad guy in hopes of making him go away.

We spent two years perfecting MagSafe Ammo so it would have no equal in a .45 ACP pistol. I think that goal has been reached. The tests mentioned here can be duplicated at home by anyone with a yen to know which bullets actualy perform. It's a real eye-opener. — *Joe Zambone*

CHAPTER
18

THE PBI
TRI-COMP
MUZZLE BRAKE

Fairly Inexpensive And Quite Easy To Install, It Kills A Lot Of Kick!

THE TRI-COMP recoil compensator is manufactured and sold by Progressive Ballistics, Incorporated (Box 2526, Shawnee Mission, KS 66201). The current price is $120, postpaid, subject to change. It is supplied with an installation instruction sheet that is quite clear, simple and easy to follow.

The Tri-Comp is designed to be installed by replacing the existing barrel bushing of the Colt Government Model, Commander, and all true copies. It cannot be installed on pistols resembling the M1911 that do not have a barrel bushing, such as the Detonics Scoremaster or Colt Officers ACP.

Because of slight tolerances from gun to gun, the Tri-Comp may require a small amount of hand fitting. PBI offers a free fitting service, should the buyer desire it. Just send the Tri-Comp unit, slide, barrel and recoil spring plug, via U.S. mail only. The fitted parts will be returned

The opening in the front of the Tri-Comp is slightly over caliber .60 in diameter, giving the old Remington Rand a remarkably impressive appearance when viewed thus!

within forty-eight hours, not counting weekends and holidays. When sending the parts in for fitting, include $3 return freight or $5 for return by first-class mail.

To install the Tri-Comp yourself, remove the magazine and make a careful check to assure the chamber is empty. Perform the usual field-strip and install the Tri-Comp in the front of the slide in the same way you would replace the barrel bushing. It should fit snugly.

If the Tri-Comp will turn into the final position without undue force, no further fitting is required at this step.

If the Tri-Comp will not turn into the proper vertical position, you must reduce the front-to-back thickness of the lower locking lug by use of a small file. It is important that you remove metal only from the *forward* surface of the lug. The most metal you'll have to remove is .003-inch and that's not much. File with light strokes and try it every few strokes to see if it can be rotated to vertical position. Take care not to remove too much metal. When you are satisfied with the fit, proceed to the next step.

Check the fit of the barrel to the inside of the Tri-Comp. If the barrel will slide through the Tri-Comp, proceed to the next step. If not, the narrow band of steel on the inside of the Tri-Comp must be enlarged by a few thousandths of an inch to accept the barrel. Take a short piece of wooden dowel, one-half-inch in diameter and wrap a small piece of abrasive around it. The Wet-Or-Dry paper or emery cloth, in about the 320- or 400-grit coatings should work well for the purpose.

Sand the inner surface only on the narrow band, lightly and uniformly. Stop frequently, cleaning the sanding grit away with an old toothbrush and check for a smooth slip fit that allows the muzzle end of the barrel to go through the Tri-Comp.

With that done, reassemble the pistol and check to see if the action goes into normal battery without springing or undue resistance. As the action closes, the rear of the barrel is moved upward to engage the locking lugs in the slide. If the Tri-Comp interferes with this movement of the

As noted in the text, the Tri-Comp carries quite nicely in an open-bottom Safariland Sight-Track holster and it definitely reduces recoil, enabling a quicker reacquisition of sight picture.

L.A.R. also has a muzzle brake that replaces the barrel bushing, as shown on page 226. This barrel just has the two vents milled in the portion of the barrel that projects ahead of the barrel bushing, but they were helpful.

barrel muzzle, it will be necessary to remove small amounts from the lower front and upper rear of the of the narrow steel band inside the Tri-Comp. Again, use the wooden dowel and abrasive, pausing frequently to clean away the abrasive and try it for fit.

With all that successfully completed, clean the slide, barrel and Tri-Comp, apply a suitable lubricant and reassemble. The Tri-Comp is the last part to be installed and the first to be removed in field-stripping.

I installed a Tri-Comp on a WWII Remington Rand that serves as a sort of all-purpose test bed for assorted .45 accessories that come along. I didn't stopwatch it to the last second but it hardly took twenty minutes to install it, as it needed little, if any, fitting on that particular gun.

Installed, the Tri-Comp adds a bare 1.034 inches to the overall length of the gun and it carries quite handily in an old Safariland *Sight-Track* holster that's long been a special favorite of mine.

It's a feature to which some would attach more importance than others that the circular opening in the front of the Tri-Comp measures a full .604-inch in diameter: a substantial .153-inch bigger than the usual .45 muzzle. When viewed from up front, it gives the pistol an impressively formidable appearance.

It's my sincere opinion the Tri-Comp mutes down the recoil and muzzle-flip of the .45 auto quite usefully, as compared to firing it before installation.

Assuming a good fit, accuracy with the Tri-Comp is right on a par with that of the same pistol with a conventional barrel bushing. I had a National Match bushing in the RR before, which grouped quite well, but it groups well enough with the Tri-Comp in place that I wouldn't know it was there, were it not for the reduced recoil.

The Tri-Comp is available in a silver finish to match stainless, or nickeled guns. I think it's a neat and useful rig.

CHAPTER 19

Corbin's Series II press can be used for swaging bullets or for reloading. Stand is optional.

MAKING .45 BULLETS

As With Reloading, The Advantages Include Economy Plus Added Versatility!

THERE ARE two basic techniques for producing bullets and they will be discussed under separate headings.

SWAGING

Producing bullets by the swaging process involves cold-forming under high pressure, within a pressure vessel called a *swaging die*. Swaged bullets can be made of lead, various lead alloys similar to those used in making cast bullets, or of lead cores partially enclosed by jackets. The usual material for the jackets is a copper-based alloy called *gilding metal*.

The advantage of jacketed bullets lies in their ability to be driven to high velocities without objectionable fouling of the bore. The primary disadvantage, from the viewpoint of most users, is the substantial cost of the jackets.

On the other hand, swaged bullets are ready to load into the cartridges when completed. You needn't size and lubricate them, as with cast bullets and there is no problem with lube rubbing off to mess up the bullet seating die.

As a further attraction, it is a simple matter to arrive at a desired weight and the weight is subject to considerable variation, if so desired. Once you have everything adjusted, swaged bullets are quite uniform in weight and often

The Silver Press, also new from Corbin, is strictly for bullet swaging and it's much more convenient to use than many other such presses because the reinforcing upper bar is omitted, giving free and easy access.

This sequence of photos illustrates seating the core on the Corbin Silver press. The core has been swaged to size and uniform weight previously and was placed in the gilding metal jacket, with some amount of muscular effort being applied to the handle, as may be clearly apparent in the pair of photos above.

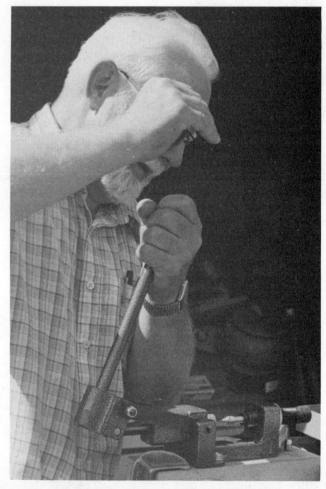

With the press handle having been brought through top-dead-center, the handle is raised to get the bullet back out of the die. This also takes some effort and a few coaxing thumps with the palm of the hand. The pressure exerted in swaging may exceed that developed by most cartridges. The .44 jacket expands to .45.

prove capable of excellent accuracy. By substituting the nose punch, you can produce bullets with other nose configurations, such as soft-points or hollow-points.

There are, on the market, specialized presses designed exclusively for swaging bullets, as well as presses convertible for use in swaging or reloading. In addition, there are dies that can be used to swage bullets in standard reloading presses. Most equipment is designed to be powered by the personal muscles of the operator and the leverage developed by the system is impressive. At the upper end of the price scale, there are swaging presses driven by hydraulic systems.

Cores can be cut from lengths of lead wire, assuming the wire is of suitable diameter, or they can be cast. Using lead wire is convenient and pure lead is softer, easier to form into shape. In casting cores, it is possible to alloy the lead to produce a somewhat harder core, assuming it seems desirable. Casting cores tends to be more economical than using cut lead wire, provided the operator's time is not assigned too high an hourly value.

Typical swaging production consists of four basic operations: (1) Produce the core blanks by cutting lead wire or casting; (2) swage the core blank to final shape and weight; (3) seat the core in the jacket; (4) form the bullet nose to final shape.

In producing the bullets illustrated in the accompanying photos, I used some .44 jackets, .55-inch in length, from Corbin Manufacturing & Supply, (Box 2659, White City, Oregon 97503), a set of the swaging dies for their Mity Mite presses and three of their presses.

Two of the presses are new to the line, the Series II and the Silver Press. I installed the core swaging dies in the Series II, after attaching it to a Corbin bench mount and the mount to a piece of plank. The Silver Press was mounted to a smaller piece of plank and I installed the core-seating die in that, with the nose-forming die in an older Corbin Swaging Press already on hand.

All three of the presses were secured to the portable loading bench in my driveway by means of C-clamps, so I could take a given bullet through all three of the final steps.

Rummaging about for something suitable for use as cores, I came upon a small quantity of cast bullets from the Lyman No. 358156 mould. They never had been gaschecked, sized or lubricated and the average weight was about 153 grains.

I adjusted the core-swaging dies so that only a small amount of metal was extruded through the bleed-holes in the side of the die. Weight of the core, after swaging, was 152 grains, .369-inch in diameter and .530-inch in length. At that diameter, the cores were a snug fit in the .44 jackets.

Using .44 jackets to produce .45 bullets may seem puzzling. As the cores are seated, the jackets are expanded outward to take up the slack in the .451-inch core-seating die and they remain at that diameter through the nose-forming die.

There was a standard hollow-point punch for the core-seating die and my choice of the Lyman 358156 bullets

worked out well, as there was only a small amount of lead exposed ahead of the jacket, after the core had been seated. You need to leave a little exposed, but you don't want a lot.

I adjusted the nose-seating dies to turn in the front of the bullets about .215-inch, measuring back from the tip of the nose. That left a frontal area about .300-inch in diameter and the resulting bullet looked like a good compromise of dimensions: pointed enough to feed well, but blunt enough to offer decent capability at expansion.

Finished weight of the bullet turned out to be 196.5 grains, of which the jacket accounted for 44.5 grains, with the core swaged down to 152 grains, as noted.

Should you desire to produce bullets of weights more commonly encountered on store shelves and handbook/manual listings, it is not a big problem. All that's required is to weigh the jacket and subtract that from the final weight to arrive at the necessary weight for the core. Go on and select a core blank that weighs a little more and remove the excess weight in the core-swaging step. The jacket, plus the swaged core, equals the final weight of the bullet, as nothing is added or subtracted in the remaining operations.

Our unpaid amateur model views his work and finds it good. What's that? You think you've seen him before? You're right, it's Dave Andrews, retired lab chief at Omark/Speer, who just happened to drop by about then.

For the really strenuous, heavy-duty swaging operations, this Model CSP-1 Corbin Swaging Press is capable of handling much greater stresses than the Silver Press, due to its O-frame design although, as noted, the Silver Press is handier, more conveniently accessible. I mount these to a plank for C-clamping to the bench.

Diameter of the finished bullet measured .4515-inch and I regard that as just right for the various .45 handgun cartridges.

The alloy used in casting the Lyman 358156 bullets was moderately hard; about 6 on the Saeco hardness tester's scale of 10.

In a later session I used a four-cavity Lyman mould for their No. 358344 wadcutter bullet and found it made really excellent .45 cores when cast of somewhat softer alloy. The shape of the Lyman 358344 bullet is just about perfect for the purpose, as it's nearly cylindrical, going in.

It's the core-seating punch in the three-die set that forms the basic nose cavity that the nose-forming die turns into a just-right hollow-point and, in addition to the regular seating punch, Corbin has another that forms a cavity with a central post, somewhat in the manner of the *Hydra-Shok* bullet design. I've not, however, figured out how to incorporate that into conventional JHP .45 bullets because the little punch that pushes the nose-formed bullet back out of the die does severe damage to the central post in the process.

When you're swaging bullets for use in revolvers, it's an entirely different ball game. You feed those cartridges into the chambers by hand and thus do not have to worry about a nose shape that will find its way up the feed ramp reliably. That means you can use full wadcutters for the sake of the greater frontal area, or other interesting possibilities.

One such is a hollow-point with a compound angle cavity I dreamed up some while ago and tentatively called the *Spelunker* — because, when it hits, it goes "Spelunk!" and excavates a cave in the process. The outer perimeter of the cavity starts at the outer perimeter of the bullet nose and, at the start, pitches downward at a rather flat angle. About one-third of the way in, it breaks to a much sharper angle. In a typical example, the front cone might have a

120-degree included angle and the rear a 40-degree angle.

The principles behind the design are somewhat akin to that of a variable-pitch aircraft propeller. Upon initial contact with the target material, the broad angle of the front cone initiates expansion at an accelerated rate, opening up the beginning of the rear cone to a broader included angle. As a result, it resembles the celebrated ethnic parachute in that it opens upon impact.

I've experimented successfully with melting down some of the old CCI Red-Jet wax practice bullets and pouring that into the Spelunker cavities to harden. One does that *before* the bullets are seated, please note! That turns the Spelunker into what I call the *Red-Eye Missile* and its impact disruption is slightly better than the original, as the cavity needn't wait to fill up with target material.

Before all that gets your eye to glittering too brightly, let me note that the Spelunkers are best adapted to revolvers, single-shots and the like. They don't feed for bo-diddley in autoloaders. They are relatively simple and easy to swage — it's helpful if you have a lathe and can make your own nose-forming punch — or you can make up cast and lube/sized bullets, then go on to swage the nose cavity. As the lube is incompressible, it has nowhere to go and remains in place.

My old friend and mentor, Massad F. Ayoob, published a recent article warning of the hazards and pitfalls of using any manner of handloaded ammunition in a defensive shooting situation. Ayoob spends a lot of time as a witness in court and knows whereof he speaks. He says using any manner of handload on a fellow human can and will put you at the mercy of the opposing attorney. Under cross-examination, you'll be made to look like the worst public enemy since Jack the Ripper or the guys who invented the call-waiting telephone or plastic popcorn.

A defensive shooting, even though declared entirely justified, usually results in some manner of civil action by the

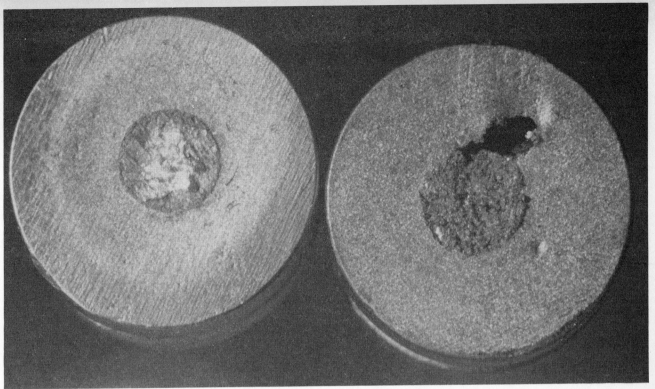

In cast bullets, watch for and reject any with cavities in the base or other irregularities. Toss 'em back in the pot.

RCBS Part No. 82047

BULLET MOULD
45-201-SWC Double Cavity
Caliber: .45 ACP Grains: 201
Bullet Style: Semi-wadcutter
Use Sizer Die .452 and
Top Punch #680

Omark/RCBS now has a line of two-cavity bullet mould blocks and accompanying handles. Some of the other mould makers, such as NEI, market only the blocks, and their blocks are designed for use with RCBS handles.

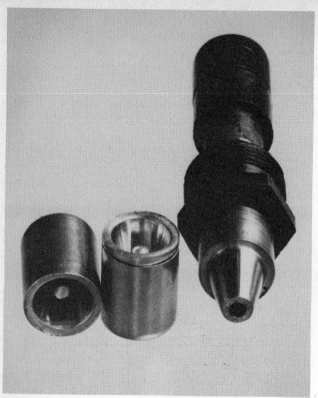

This Corbin core-seating punch leaves a central post in the nose cavity, in the manner of Hydra-Shok JHPs.

behind them on your unsanitary reloading bench. Please explain to the court why you felt you had to violate the Geneva Convention to such an extent!"

It will do no good to protest that the Geneva Convention had nothing to do with or say about expanding bullets. That was covered in the Hague Convention. In the initial screening, any juror who knows anything about firearms will have been screened out and dropped, leaving only those who can be flimflammed nine ways from any given Wednesday.

I don't wish to belabor the point needlessly. If you have a gun that may be used for serious social shooting purposes, put a good commercial load in the magazine and/or chamber. In a .45 ACP, my own preference would run toward the CCI Lawman No. 3965 load, with its 200-grain Speer JHP bullets coming out at a brisk and *uhh* devigorating pace. If you buy a box of these, put them aside and essay to open the package when trouble looms, all I can say is heaven help your hapless *derriere*.

I have commented to my friends at Lewiston, Idaho, that I regard this as one of the world's best handgun loads, put up in one of the world's most absolutely *miserable* packages. If there is anyone who can open a box of the stuff with nothing but his bare hands, that person has my awe-struck admiration. Given a jackknife and plenty of time, one can slit the tough plastic label at each end and pry the lid up. Having done so, you encounter twenty-five cartridges that are stuffed, bullet-down, into a plastic plate that is not attached to the case proper. The noses rest against a layer of foam plastic on the bottom of the box. You can pluck each cartridge from its hole, using great care, going on to stuff it into the magazine or chamber.

If panic drives you to haste, you are quite apt to dump the entire contents of the box onto the ground, leaving you between the aforementioned wok and a horrid place.

I like the CCI No. 3965 load. I like it extremely well. It is my personal favorite .45 ACP factory load. I loathe,

shootee or his/her survivors and, as a Chinese chef might put it, that puts you between a wok and hard place.

"You weren't content with the carnage you could wreak with factory ammunition, even with hollow-point bullets!" the opposing attorney may thunder, with side glances to gauge the effect upon the jurors. "Oh no! You had to concoct these extra-dangerous bullets and then stuff powder

From left, a cast Lyman 358156 SWC bullet; after core-swaging; the .44 by .550-inch jacket; core placed in jacket; after core seating, which expands the .44 jacket to .45 diameter; and after the nose-forming operation.

hate, detest, despise, dislike and *abominate* the package. What I'd suggest, as a way around all this disarming dilemma is to buy two boxes of the CCI load and one of the nice little fifty-round ammo boxes that RCBS offers in the size suitable for .45 ACP and the like. Spread out a blanket or something to catch the spilled rounds and transfer the contents of the two CCI boxes to the one RCBS box. As of that moment, you'll be prepared for onrushing trouble...but not until then!

CAST .45 BULLETS

In the usual course of such things, I discuss cast bullets first and then crank in comments on the swaged variety. I've reversed the customary procedure here. Casting is an economical and eminently practical way of producing a large quantity of bullets. Doing so requires a supply of lead alloy suitable for the purpose, a means for melting and dispensing the molten alloy, some bullet mould blocks and handles, a non-marring mallet for dislodging the cast bullets from the mould cavities and some manner of equipment for sizing and lubricating the cast bullets.

The primary component of casting alloy is lead, but pure lead does not produce bullets that are all that satisfactory for use in cartridges to be fired out of centerfire pistols with smokeless powders. The alloy needs some amount of hardening ingredients, usually antimony and tin, not necessarily in that order, percentage-wise.

There are, or have been, firms that market bullet casting alloy, all ready to use. You can also purchase pure metals and blend them to your personal specifications. Either route is crushingly expensive in these latter days. Ready-made alloy is expensive at the source and the shipping costs will break your financial back.

The alternative is to sniff, scrounge and dicker. I've been doing just that for nearly four decades and can confide it's a *modus vivendi* or way of life for anyone with a yen to do a lot of shooting at modest cost out of pocket.

The Latin word for lead is *plumbum,* which gives us the chemical symbol of Pb for the stuff, as well as the term for plumbers. That leads to my own designation: sort of plumbous, meaning that, if I can melt the stuff, I'll have a try at making bullets out of it.

For a lot of years, bullet casting sort of went hand-in-hand with two other trades: plumbing and printing. Plumbers used pure lead for caulked joints and wiping solder for wiped joints. When they ripped out and replaced an existing installation, the resulting scrap ended up on the floor of their shop and an alert bullet caster could purchase many pounds of the good stuff for trifling sums. Those were (sigh!) the Good Old Days.

During the same era, most printers set quite a bit of their type on an ingenious device called a *Linotype.* It had a keyboard sort of like a typewriter, but with the keys in a different arrangement. The top two lines were ETAOIN and SHRDLU, for example. As one pecked at the keys, brass forms came down to create a mould. When the line was finished, spacers between the words spread it to column-width and a special linotype alloy came gushing down to produce one line of set type, hence the name.

Linotype alloy consisted of lead, antimony and tin, in about that order. After being locked into the forms and put

Lee Precision sells these six-inch dial calipers for about $60 and they are handy as pockets on a shirt! As shown here, the diameter of the core, after going through the core-swaging die, is .369", pretty close.

on the press to run the job at hand, the lines of type became scrap, to be dumped back into the melting pot on the Linotype machine. After some number of cycles through the works, some amount of the tin burned out — as it has an unfortunate habit of doing — and the alloy got "tired," so the printer would replace it with a fresh pig or two with all three ingredients up to snuff.

In those days, the supplier of linotype alloy would make some small allowance for the tired metal in trade against the fresh stuff and, if the bullet caster was sufficiently ingratiating, the printer could be induced to part with the stuff for what the supplier of new alloy would allow, which was an interestingly small number of pennies per pound. Even tired linotype alloy made great bullets and it could be cut with wheel weight metal or vaguely plumbous alloys of unknown pedigree to serve quite well, even then.

Earlier, the day now a-dwindle, I spoke on the phone with Patrick M. Holtz, who runs Lithi-Bee Bullet Lube, (2161 Henry Street, Muskegon, Michigan 49441). He mentioned he'd just located an old printer in the back boondocks of Michigan, who'd sold him a few hundredweight of tired linotype for what amounted to relative petty cash out of pocket. That's why I mention all this. Perhaps there's an interesting trove in *your* locale!

The significant thing about Bre'r Holtz is that he's resumed the production and marketing of lithium-base bullet lube. That good stuff went off the market in December of 1982 when Garth Choate's insurance company advised him he had to cease and desist from making it, due to the fire hazards it presented. Choate, who operated out of Bald Knob, Arkansas, had been brewing it in the same vessel that the family used for cooking catfish. They sent out a form letter at the time, giving their formula to any interested party, noting the good news was that they could settle back to enjoying catfish that didn't taste of bullet lube. I can relate to that.

The first consignment of Lithi-Bee lube arrived last Friday, prompting me to advise Holtz that, as far as I was concerned, 1989 was the year Christmas came on the

I've not cast bullets indoors for more years than I can remember. Paul Hantke used my N8008 camera and SB-24 flash to snap me just as I'd used the plastic mallet to knock the sprue cutter over a Hensley & Gibbs bullet mould. Note the separate cardboard boxes to catch the sprues and finished bullets. That's a small centrifugal fan in the foreground to hasten the cooling of the sprues after decanting the molten alloy.

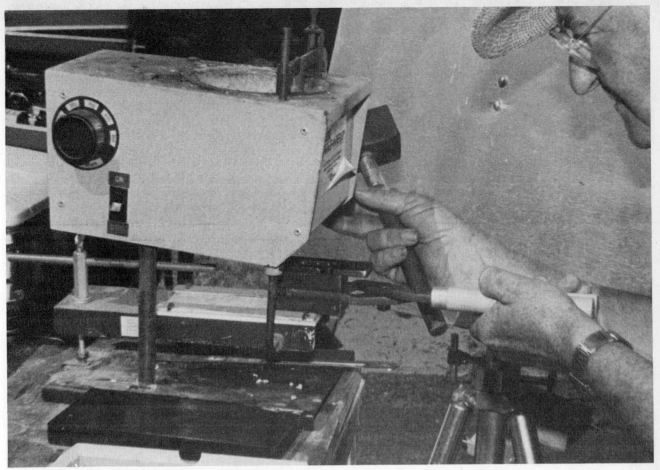

That's an RCBS Pro-Melt casting furnace, with a mould guide from Hensley & Gibbs, both very handy. Though I don't wear glasses ordinarily, I always do so when casting and have had reason to be grateful I did on many an occasion. That's my "solar-powered fill flash" in the background; a square of light plywood, sprayed with silver paint and mounted on a tripod. Usually used for photo work, it also pokes helpful light into the work area.

twenty-eighth of July. I was down to what was left in the faithful SAECO lube/sizer, plus *one* last, final stick of the genuine, clear-quill Choate lube left on a shelf beneath the bench. I was worried and scared mottled-chartreuse.

So what's the big deal with the lithium-base bullet lube? Foosh, I thought you'd *never* ask! It is a blending of lithium-base grease and beeswax. The problems stem from the fact that the lithium grease has an absurdly high melting point that is right up there near the flash-point of the beeswax. The resulting mixture, if properly compounded, will not melt out of the bullet grooves at any ambient temperature much below 160F/71.1C. Despite that, you don't need to apply heat to the lube/sizer to get it into place. It will go into the grooves quite nicely when the mercury is about at 58F/14.4C, or higher.

That's all quite nice, but the stuff has one more endearing trait I've not mentioned, to this point. In the usual course of things, they say you can drive plain-base bullets to up around 1050 fps or so and gas-checked bullets to perhaps 1250 fps or so, maybe a trifle more.

With some of Garth Choate's good stuff in the grooves, I've driven plain-base bullets, made from whatever pot-luck alloy was in the furnace at the time, to velocities in excess of 2000 fps — and had no bore-fouling problems in so doing.

The new supply of lithium-base bullet lube has been on hand for a bit over three days as I write this. I've not had a chance to squeeze any into bullet grooves and blast the resulting slug up-bore to find out how it performs. The thing is, I've got this book to get finished and off the back of my neck. Holtz says it's made precisely to Choate's specifications and I tend to regard that as encouraging.

I tend to regard the lubricant as a really crucial factor in the equation of getting cast bullets to perform in a satisfying manner. I've never had overly gratifying results with the miracle goops that contain alox, though I've had some clip-wave-and-brag groups with the Liquid Alox sold by Lee Precision. That's for use with the *Micro-Band* moulds.

There's another possible application of the Liquid Alox lube that needs to be explored and evaluated. Jim "Blue Laig" Andrews reports he has made up cast bullets, lube/sized them in a conventional manner, then gone on to give them a swozzling-about in Lee Precision's Liquid Alox. Upon setting up, the resulting bullets have been driven to really blistering velocities, without any bore-fouling problems, whatsoever!

All of which leads me to suspect the choice of bullet lube plays a much more critical role in the performance of cast bullets than most of us have suspected.

CHAPTER 20

A FEW PECKS OF POTPOURRI

Bits And Pieces, Fragments And Chunks All Guaranteed To Be Reasonably Pertinent!

IF THE longer word in the title is unfamiliar, it's pronounced about the same as popery and its dictionary definition is, "a confused or heterogeneous mixture; medley; hotchpotch [sic]." I'd've defined it as a Duke's Mixture, ruefully aware I've many words and terms lurking in my vocabulary that are unfamiliar to latterday readers and I try to keep a tight rein on them: the words and terms, not the readers.

The book is getting down into the short rows and I've a number of things I wanted to touch upon and other things I *have* to. Moreover, the copy deadline is only a trifle over a fortnight away. Earlier in the day, I saw a pre-publication proof of an advertisement the publisher is running on the book at hand and it said the book would cover, among other things, the Thompson submachine gun.

Somewhat concerned, I went back and reviewed the outline I'd submitted for the book and it said nothing about tommyguns. Even so, lest someone be disappointed, we'll start with my thoughts on the:

THOMPSON SUBMACHINE GUN

The difference between a real, honest-to-gosh machine gun and a submachine gun is the latter fires cartridges nominally intended for use in handguns, while the former takes rifle cartridges. *Machine pistol* is approximately synonymous with submachine gun and is thus used in some areas.

John Taliaferro Thompson pronounced his middle name "Toliver," it had been his mother's maiden name. He conceived and developed the submachine gun that bears his

surname a bit late for it to prove useful in the mopping-up phases of WWI. His informal term for it was *trench broom.*

Prior to some point around 1933, Thompson submachine guns could be purchased at the more lavishly stocked neighborhood hardware stores and the sad fact is that many were purchased and utilized in adamantly antisocial endeavors. You see, we had the Volstead Act, more commonly termed prohibition. Among other things, it brought into prominence gangsters and other bad-hats, all of whom recognized the strategic advantage of firepower: a concept hardly any other contemporary artifact offered more of than the ubiquitous tommygun.

If you wish to learn more about tommyguns than most people care to know, I refer you to a book titled *The Gun That Made The Twenties Roar,* by William J. Helmer (The MacMillan Co., 1969). Roger Cox did another truly scholarly and exhaustive book on the Thompson and sent me an inscribed and autographed copy. Earlier in the evening, I ransacked my book shelves at the office for it in vain. I have a sneaking Irish hunch where it may have ended up, but that's neither Damon nor yet Pythias, right now. If you've a choice of either book, I'd recommend the one by Cox. It even lists the serial numbers of most of the guns sold between WWI and WWII, including the one John Dillinger bought. If tottery memory serves, his was 6444, but don't bet heavily upon it. I'll never forget what a lousy memory I have.

The concept of full-automatic firing capability tends to set the imagination of many shooting enthusiasts heavily

The Thompson submachine gun is in production at Auto-Ordnance, (William Lane, West Hurley, New York 12491) and they have a semi-automatic version for those who can't own or don't want to own the full-auto model. Even the latter has a selector lever for semi-auto operation, but they fired from an open bolt, which made it quite a challenge to deliver hits with any pretense of precision. I believe the current semi-auto version fires from a closed bolt, however.

aflare. I can confide that, like the kid who went to work in a candy factory, after some given amount of indulgence, one tends to become rather verdantly jaded.

I've related the anecdote before and apologize to any who find it redundant. While serving as a gunnery instructor at Harlingen, Texas, I was one of the instructors on a line of flexible-mounted caliber .30 air-cooled Brownings; perhaps thirty or forty guns on the line. The students had just belted-up one hundred-round belts into the guns and been given the command to open fire on their designated paper targets when a rangy Texas coyote popped out of the sagebrush and went galloping along the line of targets, right to left.

You would have done it. I would have done it. For sure, the students did it, unanimously. Every single one apparently thought to himself to heck with my score for this session. I'm going to get that-there *Canis latrans!* Right, that may not be a literal transcript, hence the absence of quote marks.

As a result, a great many guns, each hosing bullets at a cyclic rate of about eighteen shots per second, zeroed in on the hapless critter and a thick white cloud of pulverized Texas topsoil went blooming into the air.

The popular conviction about full-auto fire is that a hit is made utterly certain by a vague concept termed the law of averages. Hardly anything I can think of actually is farther from the truth. The target is at risk, for sure, but there is no *certain* assurance it will be hit. It is a matter of simple math and logic: The number of paths a bullet may take to score a hit is a finite number and the number of paths that result in a miss is an infinite number; infinity squared, for all I know.

Thus, the coyote — now thoroughly alarmed, with his afterburner cut in — came blazing out of the cloud of white dust and, quite predictably, every gunnery student on the line drew a careful bead and clamped down on the triggers with clenched forefingers.

There was another mushroom of white dust, another emergence of the coyote at a dead-frantic gallop, another burst, another cloud and so on and so forth. They continued their staccato sniping until the 'yote was out of sight or they'd all ran dry on ammo; whichever occurred first. So far as could be determined, not a one of the shooters ever managed to draw a single drop of blood, though I'd not be surprised if the desert dog shifted to some other territory.

I lost the vast bulk of all my fervent faith in the sublime efficacy of full-auto firing, right about as of that episode.

The Thompson was employed fairly extensively in WWII, as well as later armed conflicts and I'm sure there were some who regarded it quite fondly. I am not one of that number. A business associate of mine views the

Smith & Wesson's Model 625-2, discussed on page 244, has a five-inch barrel and I used a B-Square base and Weaver rings to attach this Burris variable handgun scope, capitalizing upon its really impressive level of accuracy. It fires the .45 Auto Rim or .45 ACP loads.

Thompson with considerable cordiality and the M1911A1 Colt with corrosive contempt. So it goes. *De gustibus* and all that.

I will concede I have seen some people employ the Thompson in a remarkably telling manner. About 1969, I saw an officer of the Oklahoma Highway Patrol — I believe his name was Dan Combs — empty an entire fifty-round drum out of a Thompson into a silhouette target at a distance of perhaps twenty to thirty yards, keeping every single, ding-bing hit in an area hardly larger than the palm of a man's hand. That impressed me like you could hardly believe, especially as it was done in one continuous burst.

My distaste is not due to incompetence. I fired the USAAF qualification course and made expert, with some to spare. I can see the utility of the gun in certain applications. I'd incline to favor a short-barreled shotgun and buckshot loads, but the Thompson is sanctioned under the rules of land warfare, while the scattergun isn't. The thing is, one can bring plutonium up to critical mass and flash-fry an

entire city, but it remains a hard-nosed no-no to pink a foeperson with unjacketed lead, and a hollow-point bullet is an outrage to all humanity. Please do not ask me to explain why that is so.

The Thompsons made by Colt between WWI and WWII were among the most handsome examples of the gunmaker's art I've ever seen. I can understand why some people might hanker to own and operate one. If you like such things, I wish you much joy and contentment. Put flatly, they are not my cup of tea.

BEYOND .45

There may be handguns chambered for the .600 Nitro Express or perhaps for the slightly punier .577 Snider. If so, I devoutly hope it never falls within my line of duty to fire the bellowing buggers. The last I heard, Tony Sailer of C-H Tool & Die was retailing .600 Nitro Express cases for sixteen bucks apiece and that was unprimed.

242

Nonetheless, in the midsection of 1989, at least two handguns have come along, firing bullets larger than .458-inch in diameter. I've worked with both and can offer some first hand comments, for such interest as they may afford.

The first to materialize was a Desert Eagle autoloader, commonly encountered in .357 and .44 magnum, more recently in .41 magnum, handling all three cartridges uncommonly well. The pistol I tested was a prototype modified for the .50 Action Express.

Earlier discussions here covered how Evan Whildin, vice president of Action Arms, conceived the .41 Action Express by starting with the head dimensions of the 9mmP and putting that onto a case big enough to accept bullets of .410-inch diameter. He went on to neck it back down to take .355-inch bullets and got the 9mm Action Express. The former is in full production at the moment. The 9mm AE remains somewhere between holding pattern and limbo. Candidly, I hope it comes into full bloom. I regard it as one of the most interesting cartridges to come along in many a moon.

Whildin used the same basic approach to come up with the .50 AE. It has head dimensions the same as the .44 magnum, with a larger case up front to accept bullets of .510-inch diameter, available from Barnes. By simply changing barrel, magazine and recoil springs, you can fire it in a .44 magnum Desert Eagle because the bolt face fits it nicely.

As presently envisioned, the .50 AE, along with Desert Eagle pistols to fire it, will be marketed early in 1990. The cases and ammunition will be produced by Israel Military Industries under the Samson label and headstamp. The final ballistic performance of the load has yet to be established. I've a friend named Tom Hayden, not to be confused with the politician of the same name, who joined me in trying out the .50 AE Desert Eagle. The cases we used had been produced by Brass Extrusion Laboratories Limited and carried a headstamp of A.A.L. over 50 A. EXP.

Although having a case head of nominal .44 magnum dimensions, a few of the cases refused to go into shell holders of that size. Bill Keyes, of the RCBS Custom Shop, fitted me out with an RCBS shell holder stamped 404 J and that accepted all the cases, quite nicely.

Bob Olsen had handled the testing and development of the .50 AE and reported Accurate Arms No. 7 and Hercules 2400 to be the two most promising powders for use with the 300-grain, .510-inch diameter, JSP bullets for it. The test gun had a six-inch barrel but it's a simple matter to install longer barrels in the Desert Eagle. Olsen also had used a ten-inch pressure test barrel in working up his data. Using the 300-grain Barnes bullet, with CCI-200 standard large *rifle* primers, with 26.8 grains of AA-7 powder and

the bullet seated to a cartridge overall length of 1.620 inches, Olsen's ten-inch pressure test barrel averaged 35,030 CUP and 1565/1631. In the six-inch barrel, the same load went 1379/1267.

With other specifications the same, 30.1 grains of 2400 averaged 1604/1714 in the ten-inch, 1295/1117 in the six-inch, with pressures of 38,750 CUP.

The .50 Desert Eagle kicks rather diligently, though I've endured worse on any number of occasions. Hayden, a long-term Desert Eagle fan, was totally delighted with what he saw as its potential. Personally, I rarely encounter targets that fill me with that much anger or alarm, though I can recall occasional instances. All were out of season at the given time, which makes it a bit academic.

The obvious next step, as I've pointed out elsewhere, is to neck the .50 AE case back down to .45, .44, .41, and .357 to breed a whole family of wildcats. The .50 AE necked to .17 should be a real wowser and yes, I'm kidding!

The Wildey gas-operated auto pistol first appeared in the late Seventies, chambered for the 9mm and .45 Winchester magnum cartridges originally designed for use in it. Although the design was excellent, corporate complications cut the original production short — by no means an uncommon occurence in the field of manufacturing innovative new pistols.

More recently, its designer — Wildey J. "Will" Moore, whose first name is pronounced "Will-dee" — refinanced, re-organized and is back in production again with the .45 Winchester magnum version. The 9mm W-mag remains in holding pattern, though Moore voices wistful hopes of getting it launched some day, as well.

In the meantime, he introduced a new cartridge for the Wildey pistol, called the .475 Wildey. It's a wildcat, made from .284 Winchester brass to take .475 bullets from Barnes in weights of 250 and 300 grains. Like the .50 Action Express, its rim is smaller in diameter than the body of the case.

I worked with the loan of a Wildey with a ten-inch .45 W-mag barrel and an eight-inch barrel for the .475 Wildey, plus thirty fired .475 Wildey cases. Case length of the .475 is supposed to be the same as that of the .45 W-mag, namely 1.198 inches. The furnished cases tended to be a trifle shorter, more on the order of 1.186 inches, or so.

The only dies I had available at the time of the test were in something called .475 Linebaugh which as I understand, is a wildcat for a proprietary revolver, based upon the .45-70 case. The same firm also produces single-action revolvers in .50 Linebaugh, but those cases are made from .348 Winchester rifle brass. Happily, the .475 Linebaugh dies loaded the .475 Wildey cases in excellent fashion. Since then, RCBS has made up some loading dies based upon some fired .475 cases I sent to Bill Keyes in their Custom Shop and die sets in the caliber are available from them. I get the word Lyman also can furnish .475 Wildey dies, but have not seen their version.

Like the .50 Action Express, the .475 Wildey takes large rifle primers so I used Federal No. 210M match primers. Peter Hylenski of the Wildey firm said he'd only used Winchester 296 powder in the .475 Wildey to the present, with charge weights from 27.0 to 30.0 grains for the 250-grain Barnes JSP bullet and up to 27.0 grains of 296 for the 300-grain Barnes JSP.

I found 30.0 grains of 296, with the 250-grain bullet, to be a compressed charge at a cartridge overall length of 1.592 inches and it would just barely load into and come back out of the Wildey's magazine. In the eight-inch barrel, that particular load averaged as high as 1552/1337 and grouped quite well off the sandbag benchrest at twenty-five yards. Another five-shot test of the same load averaged only 1524/1290, but three of the five shots went into a neat cloverleaf at that distance.

The Wildey is an interesting pistol, incorporating a knurled and detented control ring that enables the shooter to "dial in" just the right amount of gas-operated motivation for the given load.

The test gun came with a ten-inch .45 W-mag barrel and the eight-inch .475 Wildey barrel. The .45 W-mag has come to be one of my special favorite cartridges, due to its remarkable performance in a ten-inch long slide L.A.R. Grizzly auto I have. Both the ballistics and accuracy of the Grizzly impress me as exceptional. To date, I've not had an opportunity to work with the Wildey in .45 W-mag all that extensively, although I determined the Winchester W45WM load, with its 230-grain FMJ/RN bullet, averaged 1495/1142 and the newer load, with the same bullet, indexed as W45WM2, went 1501/1151, both grouping quite well. With suitable reloads, I've gotten the Grizzly to hitting 1.25-inch aiming pasters four times out of five shots at twenty-five yards, mustering closely comparable ballistics.

Curiously enough, both the .50 Desert Eagle and .475 Wildey pistols showed puckish penchants for caroming the ejected empty cases off the center of the shooter's forehead. Both were prototypes and I'd hope and expect them to be cured of such mischief before they go into production.

A RECENT .45 REVOLVER

After a burdensome number of years of being "a Bangor-Punta Company" and "a Lear-Siegler Company," Smith & Wesson has gone back to being just plain old vanilla-flavored Smith & Wesson, doing what they do best and I, for one, am doggoned grateful for that.

The S&W president, these days, is a genial gent named Steve Melvin, who likes guns, likes shooting and is inflexibly determined that S&W is going to manufacture the best handguns he can lash them into producing. I've had letters from readers who bought a new S&W, encountered some manner of problem with it, called the factory to complain and wound up discussing it with Melvin, himself. Their problem was resolved, *muy pronto* and Melvin saw to it, personally. I respectfully submit you can't hardly get much more dedicated than that.

One of the S&W revolvers introduced recently was their Model 625-2, a six-shooter in stainless steel, with black rubber stocks by Pachmayr, a five-inch barrel and target sights. I borrowed one for evaluation and was so impressed with the groups the open iron sights delivered that I went on to install a Burris 1.5-4-power scope on B-Square's no-gunsmithing base, with Weaver rings. Meanwhile, I stored the rear sight with great care, against the day I'd want to reinstall it.

With the loads it likes, the scoped M625-2 will sizzle five shots into a center-spread of an inch to an inch and a half off the sandbags at twenty-five yards. Before the test gun arrived, I'd been getting reports from various owners that it is one grouping so-and-so. All I can say is that this one is, for sure.

As with the Model 1917s, the Model 1950 and the Model 1955 *aka* 25-2, the 625-2 has a fairly omnivorous appetite for ammo. It works quite well with .45 Auto Rim, or you can put all manner of .45 ACP into half-moon, third-moon or full-moon clips for instant ejection after firing. As a third option, you can simply stuff .45 ACP loads down into the chambers, set them off and pluck forth the empties — provided you have reasonably sturdy fingernails. Or you can use the rim of a spent or loaded round to lever the empties out, assuming you're not under hostile fire at the time.

Unlike the Model 25-2, the 625-2 has a standard-width trigger and I, for one, am grateful for that. The broad target trigger may be great for single-action work. One of the great delights of S&W revolvers, however, is that — with just a bit of practice — one can fire them about as accurately double-action and at a somewhat more rapid rate. That assumes the standard-width trigger. The so-called target trigger scrungles things up for double-action work, eight ways from the jack, in my humble opinion, at least.

For routine shooting and reloading, the .45 Auto Rim is the pluperfectly logical cartridge for the 625-2. For combat or speed competition, the .45 ACP in full-moon clips is decisively indicated but when one is merely punching holes in paper targets or potting the odd tin can of opportunity — split seconds available by the gross — give me the Auto Rim.

The Remington factory load in .45 AR, carrying a 230-grain round-nose lead bullet, is a superb performer in the 625-2, grouping to spreads of 1.5 inches or better at twenty-five yards. It gives the reloader a really challenging level of performance to equal or surpass and that can be at least half the fun of the entire exercise, right?

Speaking as a gunwriter who's been plying the improbable craft for upward of three decades, I've seen test guns come and go. Depending upon the given maker, it may be possible to purchase the gun, sometimes at a cost less than full retail. When I got one of the S&W Model 547s — their remarkable revolver for the 9mmP — in for testing, I was so favorably impressed I put a second mortgage on the house and bought the cute little rascal. I've been glad ever since I did so, as they stopped making it, soon after that and if I'd turned loose of it, I would have hated myself forever.

What I'm saying is the 625-2 shoots like a keeper and it may be time to slap a third mortgage on the old domicile.

By that, you'd be correct in assuming the 625-2 has my seal of approval; the largest size available.

The Smith & Wesson Model 745 was intended as a target version but, for some reason, it had a fixed rear sight. The hammer must be cocked manually for the first shot. Not too many Model 745s were made before it was dropped from production. My Model 645/4506 out-groups this one and has the added advantage of the DA trigger.

SMITH & WESSON .45 AUTOLOADING PISTOLS

Having an impressively tight wrap on the 9mmP auto market, S&W turned its attention to the .45 ACP cartridge or, as they prefer to say, the .45 Auto. Their first two offerings were the Model 645 and the Model 745. In the current S&W system, 4 designates aluminum alloy, 5 is blued steel, 6 is stainless steel and 7 is a combination of blued and stainless steel. Thus the 645 was a .45 Auto in stainless steel and the 745 was a .45 Auto with a blued slide atop a stainless receiver.

The Model 645 featured a double-action trigger and the 745 was a single-action in that the hammer had to be cocked manually for the first shot. Both had fixed rear sights and single-column, eight-shot magazines. The Model 745 is not in current production.

In 1989, Smith & Wesson staged a major upgrading of several models, terming them the Third Generation and the Model 645 was redesignated the Model 4506 in the course of the rearranging of the identifying numbers.

A compact version of the 4506 is called the Model 4516 and, at date of writing, it is not yet into production, nor available for illustration.

Smith & Wesson is involved in development of an auto pistol at the request of the Federal Bureau of Investigation. It will be similar to the Model 4506, but will be chambered for a special loading of the 10mm Auto cartridge. You might assume the FBI would be interested in a +P version of the 10mm Auto, but that's not the way it worked out. What they want is a load that delivers a bullet of about 200 grains at velocities in the 900 fps range. Yes, I guess we could term that a −P load, right?

This is actually a Smith & Wesson Model 4506, although it's rollmarked Model 645, the earlier designation. It boasts a silky double-action trigger and holds eight .45 ACP cartridges plus a ninth in the chamber at the owner's option. The sights are fixed, but quite close with most loads. The metal work is entirely of stainless steel.

I have one of the Model 4506 pistols, though it was produced in the transitional phase and the frame is rollmarked Model 645, making it some manner of a collector item, I suppose. It is a nice pistol and I really enjoy shooting it. Irv Stone of Bar-Sto Precision installed one of their barrels in it and that seemed to bring the groups into helpfully tighter focus.

The feed ramp and chamber of the Model 4506 offer excellent support to the head of the cartridge, rather in the manner of the James E. Clark barrel discussed here earlier. That would seem to make it a likely candidate for +P loads and it handles the Remington +P load quite well, averaging 1150/543 with its 185-grain JHP bullet. I think it would be a good idea to install a stronger recoil spring, if continuing to use such loads, however.

THE DUMMY MODEL 1911

Back in Chapter 8, I included photos of a remarkably realistic but non-firing life-sized duplicate of the Model 1911A1 pistol, but did not include a source for them. They are available from Collector's Armoury, 800 Slaters Lane, Box 59, Alexandria, Virginia 22313 and the current price is quoted as $107, postpaid; subject to change, of course.

I should note their advertisement says the pistols cannot be sent to California addresses unless it is to be used in theatrical work. That probably can be traced back to the man who covered David Horowitz with some manner of air pistol and caused a considerable sensation that resulted in assorted regulations and restrictions on non-firing replicas and similar devices.

Also in Chapter 8, I mentioned possible inclusion of a

photo of the Government Model Colt that Jimmy Cagney tossed onto his boss's desk, along with Cagney's badge. On re-screening my home videotape of the film — which was titled *"G" Men* — I found that particular scene had been edited out for televison presentation. Hence, you were spared the 1934 film that had been put through our television set and then recycled by the video player. It would have been painfully fuzzy, even if it had been available.

BALLISTIC TEST MEDIA

There has been a long-term quest for something into which bullets can be fired to obtain a reasonably accurate evaluation of their post-impact performance. Bullets can be tested in hunting applications, of course, and often have been. There remains, however, the problem of tracking down something that would serve as a realistic analog for human targets; the kind that are apt to shoot back and thus require neutralizing with the least possible delay.

Many different materials have been tried and most of those have been found wanting. One policeman of my acquaintance thought that water-soaked telephone books were just the ticket. The local phone company donated enough to fill the back end of his pickup truck so he hauled them home and, for want of a better place to soak them, dumped the entire load into his swimming pool. I saw your eyebrow go up, there. Yes, in Southern California, it's not uncommon for policemen to own homes with swimming pools.

He went out next morning to check the state of his proposed bullet testing medium and found water had loosened the binding and the entire pool was filled with directory pages, hardly any two still together. It took him the better part of a week to get the pool cleaned out.

The heating and air-conditioning trades use a material variously known as duct seal or duxseal. It's an oil-based clay and it never seems to harden, even over the course of years. It's fairly sticky and can be applied to leaks in duct work to seal them, hence the name. As with many other materials, such as modeling clay, the consistency is governed by the temperature and it softens as it gets warmer. It will stop most handgun bullets inside of a foot or so of penetration and it will expand most bullets capable of expanding.

Duct seal does not resemble flesh to an appreciable extent. For one thing, the holes do not close back down after penetration. You can test bullets in the stuff and it will give you an accurate evaluation of the load's perfomance in duct seal; just that and nothing more. Even so, it can give you a comparison between bullets or between loads.

The current source I know of for duct seal is Uniseal, (1800 West Maryland Street, Evansville, Indiana 47712). I have no information as to quantities or prices.

There has been a trend toward some stuff called *ballistic gelatine* and it's quite different from the familiar table dessert. The official designation is No. 250A Ordnance Gelatine and it can be ordered from the sales office of Kind & Knox, Attention: Donna Richter, (Park 80 West, Plaza Two, Saddle Brook, New Jersey 07662). Joe Zambone uses it for testing his MagSafe loads, discussed elsewhere here. He says he has to buy twenty-five pounds at a time and the last batch cost $113.50, plus shipping and handling.

Zambone uses empty, rinsed one-gallon milk jugs as his moulds, cutting away enough of the top to leave the handle. He fills a two-liter soft drink bottle to the top with cool water and pours that into the jug, then adds 225 grams (not grains) of the gelatine powder. That's 1½ *level* measuring cups or 7.94 ounces. The powder is poured into the water and stirred gently, to avoid unwanted bubbles.

Set it aside for thirty minutes, to let the gelatine absorb the water. Then microwave each jug separately, to bring the temperature up to 104F/40C. Stop and stir gently from time to time to prevent overheated pockets.

Once the solution comes up to temperature, put it in the refrigerator to cool. After thirty minutes, skim the bubbles off the top and discard them.

For shooting, the temperature of the gelatine should not be over 39F/4C. You slit the jug and remove the block before shooting. You may wish to experiment with putting clothing over the test block, as Zambone does.

For extended storage, wrap the exposed surface with Saran Wrap to prevent it from drying out. It will get moldy and useless if stored above 40F/4C for a few days.

All of which would make gelatine the ideal test medium, if you have ample refrigerated space next to your shooting facility. I do not have that convenience and that is one of several reasons gelatine is not practical for my needs. I keep on using duct seal, only because nothing else I know of works as well.

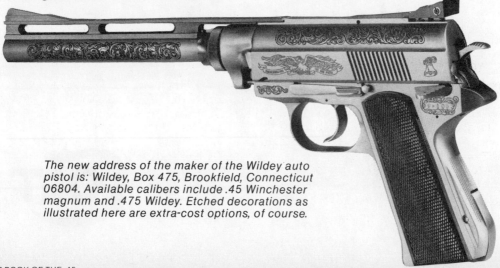

The new address of the maker of the Wildey auto pistol is: Wildey, Box 475, Brookfield, Connecticut 06804. Available calibers include .45 Winchester magnum and .475 Wildey. Etched decorations as illustrated here are extra-cost options, of course.

CHAPTER 21

COLT'S DOUBLE EAGLE

Here Are The Available Facts On The Long-Awaited Double-Action!

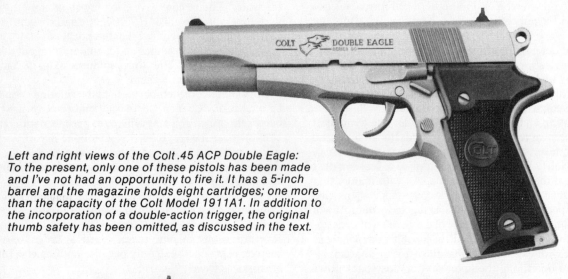

Left and right views of the Colt .45 ACP Double Eagle: To the present, only one of these pistols has been made and I've not had an opportunity to fire it. It has a 5-inch barrel and the magazine holds eight cartridges; one more than the capacity of the Colt Model 1911A1. In addition to the incorporation of a double-action trigger, the original thumb safety has been omitted, as discussed in the text.

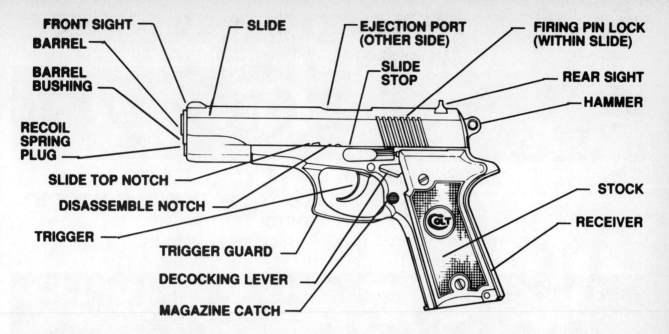

FRONT SIGHT — SLIDE — EJECTION PORT (OTHER SIDE) — FIRING PIN LOCK (WITHIN SLIDE)
BARREL —
BARREL BUSHING —
SLIDE STOP —
REAR SIGHT —
HAMMER —
RECOIL SPRING PLUG —
SLIDE TOP NOTCH —
DISASSEMBLE NOTCH —
STOCK —
RECEIVER —
TRIGGER —
TRIGGER GUARD —
DECOCKING LEVER —
MAGAZINE CATCH —

This drawing is reproduced from the instruction manual that accompanies the Double Eagle and the slide top notch should be spelled slide stop notch. Initially, production of the Double Eagle will be solely in .45 ACP, though it appears fairly probable it may, in time, be offered in other calibers, sizes and with target sights.

A PROJECT that has been under development for a long time at the Colt plant in Hartford, Connecticut, usually was referred to as the "stainless double-action gun." It has been a matter of rumor and conjecture for many years. Finally, it has made its appearance: just one gun, to the present, though it's expected to proliferate.

Aptly christened the Double Eagle, the tool room prototype was on display at the National Rifle Association convention at St. Louis, Missouri, in late April of 1989. To discourage potential souvenir collectors, it was tethered to the exhibit table by a stout length of steel cable, but those so inclined could pick it up, look it over and try the trigger.

I did just that and what came to mind was a favorite all-purpose phrase I've heard repeated uncountable times by my employer: "I've done worse, on a dark night along the Ginza!"

I've encountered revolvers with better double-action trigger pulls and autoloaders with vastly worse trigger pulls. It was, after all, a prototype and those usually resemble the amateur inventor's insect trap in that there are at least a few bugs in them.

Several years ago, L.W. Seecamp devised a system for converting the regular Model 1911A1 Colt to double-action and it worked quite well. Conceivably, Colt could

have cranked it in as an optional improvement on their M1911s, but didn't.

Rather, the Double Eagle bears no more than a casual resemblance to the M1911. There is no grip safety and no thumb safety. Instead, there is a decocking lever located just below the slide stop and above the magazine release. The latter is in the same location as on the M1911. The mainspring housing runs all the way up from the heel of the butt and ends as the tang that projects rearward, replacing the tang of the M1911 grip safety. It is straight in contour until it curves back to form the tang.

The Double Eagle barrel is five inches in length, the same as that of the M1911 and the magazine holds eight rounds of .45 ACP; one more than that of the M1911. There is a fixed front sight blade with a single white dot and a fixed rear sight, with white dots on either side of its notch. The Colt logotype is moulded into the plastic of the stock slabs on either side.

The hammer spur is a rowel type, similar to that of the Commander and Officers ACP. The trigger guard is generously proportioned, with a concave area up front to accommodate the index finger of the non-shooting hand. The metal work is stainless steel and initial chambering is restricted to the .45 ACP cartridge.

With the deletion of the M1911's thumb safety, there is

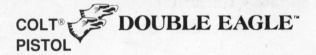
no ready way for the Double Eagle to be carried in the cocked-and-locked mode over a live round in the chamber. Carrying it cocked would be the equivalent of carrying the M1911 loaded and cocked-unlocked: a notably spooky procedure.

Should the owner wish to carry the Double Eagle in a mode most apt to be capable of coping with abrupt trouble, the indicated course would be to disregard the redundant warnings in the manual not to carry it with a load in the chamber. Actually, what they say is, on page 6: "ALWAYS KEEP AND CARRY YOUR PISTOL EMPTY, WITH THE HAMMER FORWARD except when you intend to shoot, so your pistol cannot be fired when you do not mean to fire it."

I guess that leaves you some kind of out. If you're going into a situation where your life might be in sharp peril at an instant's notice, you could say you intend to shoot and thus would be sanctioned to jack a live one into the chamber.

As there is no thumb safety, you will probably want to get the hammer back down — unless, that is, you've reason to fear a *kamikaze* of boojums within the next second or so. Let us turn to page 12-13 of the manual and quote the pertinent paragraphs:

Safety Stop on Hammer

The Safety Stop is a flat, shelf-like surface on the hammer which functions as an automatic fail-safe device. It will engage the sear in the unlikely event of primary sear notch failure. This will prevent the hammer from falling fully forward unintentionally and will insure against uncontrolled automatic fire. It also prevents the hammer from striking the firing pin should your hand slip from the slide or hammer while cocking the pistol, provided the hammer is rotated past the Safety Stop.

The Safety Stop is not a manual safety and should not be engaged by hand other than by the use of the decocking lever.

Decocking Lever

Correct use of the decocking lever minimizes the risk of accidental discharge through mishandling by allowing the hammer to be decocked without touching the trigger. The decocking lever is located on the left of pistol, just below the slide lock. The decocking lever drops the hammer from the cocked position to the safety stop position without the trigger being squeezed. Thus, the firing pin remains locked throughout the decocking function. With the hammer cocked, and fingers clear of the trigger, pushing the decocking lever down momentarily disengages the sear and leaves the hook of the hammer resting against the decocking lever.

Releasing the decocking lever allows the hammer to move forward, and the sear to move back into contact with the hammer before the decocking lever trips out of engagement with the hook of the hammer. The hammer falls forward to be caught by the sear in the safety stop position.

CAUTION: ALWAYS POINT PISTOL IN A SAFE DIRECTION AND KEEP FINGERS CLEAR OF THE TRIGGER WHEN OPERATING THE DECOCKING LEVER TO LOWER THE HAMMER. This will avoid accidental injury in the unlikely event of discharge.

That ends the quotation. I'm glad they said to point the muzzle in a safe direction before operating the decocking lever. I second that motion.

It appears likely the Double Eagle may, in time, be offered in other calibers, such as .38 Super, 10mm Auto or 9mm Parabellum. They may introduce a compact version, in the manner of the Commander or Officers ACP and, quite possibly, a target version comparable to the present Gold Cup. All that, however, is quite a distance down the road ahead. Perhaps I'll be able to include further information on the Double Eagle line in my next book, currently scheduled to be the second edition of *Handgun Digest,* due to appear in early 1991. I hope to see you there.— DAG

Here's the exploded view of the Double Eagle and it may be of interest to compare it to the one for the Series '80 pistol on page 215. I wonder if the term for part No.44 is spelled correctly. It more or less takes the place of the Series '80 part No. 44, and safety lock plunger but, on the Double Eagle, there is no safety lock and thus nothing for the plunger to push against. We'll find out later.

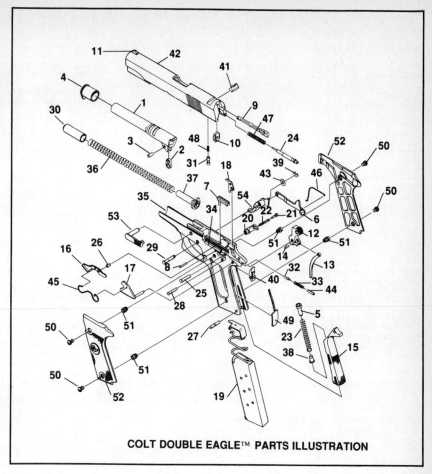

COLT DOUBLE EAGLE™ PARTS ILLUSTRATION

DESCRIPTION

1. BARREL
2. BARREL LINK
3. BARREL LINK PIN
4. BUSHING, BARREL
5. CAP, MAINSPRING
6. DRAWBAR
7. EJECTOR
8. EJECTOR PIN
9. EXTRACTOR
10. FIRING PIN STOP
11. FRONT SIGHT
12. HAMMER
13. HAMMER STRUT
14. HAMMER STRUT PIN
15. HOUSING, MAINSPRING
16. LEVER, DECOCKING FORWARD
17. LEVER, DECOCKING, REAR
18. LEVER, PLUNGER
19. MAGAZINE ASSEMBLY (8 ROUND)
20. MAGAZINE CATCH
21. MAGAZINE CATCH LOCK
22. MAGAZINE CATCH/GATE SPRING
23. MAINSPRING
24. PIN, FIRING
25. PIN, HAMMER
26. PIN, LEVER, DECOCKING
27. PIN, MAINSPRING HOUSING
28. PIN, SEAR
29. PIN, TRIGGER
30. PLUG, RECOIL SPRING
31. PLUNGER, FIRING PIN
32. PLUNGER, SLIDE STOP
33. PLUNGER SPRING
34. PLUNGER TUBE
35. RECEIVER
36. RECOIL SPRING
37. RECOIL SPRING GUIDE
38. RETAINER, PIN
39. RING, RETAINING, TRIGGER
40. SEAR
41. SIGHT, REAR
42. SLIDE, D.A.
43. SPACER WASHER
44. SPIROL PIN
45. SPRING, DECOCKING
46. SPRING, DRAWBAR
47. SPRING, FIRING PIN
48. SPRING, PLUNGER, FIRING PIN
49. SPRING, SEAR
50. STOCK SCREW
51. STOCK SCREW BUSHING
52. STOCK SET
53. STOP, SLIDE
54. TRIGGER

Directory Of Manufacturers

AMMUNITION (Commercial)

Activ Industries, Inc., P.O. Box F, 1000 Zigor Rd., Kearneysville, WV 25430/304-725-0451 (shotshells only)

Atlanta Discount Ammo, P.O. Box 627, Norcross, GA 30091/404-446-2429 (ctlg. $2)

Ballistic Research Industries (BRI), 2825 S. Rodeo Gulch Rd. #8, Soquel, CA 95073/408-476-7981

Cascade Cartridge Inc., (See Omark)

Dynamit Nobel-RWS Inc., 105 Stonehurst Court, Northvale, NJ 07647/201-767-1995 (RWS)

Eldorado Cartridge Corp., P.O. Box 308, Boulder City, NV 89005/702-294-0025

Elite Ammunition, P.O. Box 3251, Hinsdale, IL 60522/312-366-9006

Estate Cartridge Inc., P.O. Box 3702, Conroe, TX 77305/409-856-7277 (shotshell)

Federal Cartridge Co., 900 Ehlen Dr., Anoka, MN 55303/612-422-2840

Fisher Enterprises, 655 Main St. #305, Edmonds, WA 98020/206-776-4365 (Prometheus airgun pellets)

Frontier Cartridge Division-Hornady Mfg. Co., Box 1848, Grand Island, NE 68801/308-382-1390

Hansen Cartridge Co., 244 Old Post Rd., Southport, CT 06490/203-259-7337

ICI-America, P.O. Box 751, Wilmington, DE 19897/302-575-3000

Omark Industries, P.O. Box 856, Lewiston, ID 83501/208-746-2351

PMC-Eldorado Cartridge Corp., P.O. Box 308, Boulder City, NV 89005/702-294-0025

P.P.C. Corp., 625 E. 24th St., Paterson, NJ 07514

Palcher Ammunition, Techstar Engineering, Inc., 2239 S. Huron Ave., Santa Ana, CA 92705/714-556-7384

Precision Prods. of Wash., Inc., N. 311 Walnut Rd., Spokane, WA 99206/509-928-0604 (Exammo)

Prometheus/Titan Black (See Fisher Enterprises)

RWS (See Dynamit Nobel)

Remington Arms Co., 1077 Market St., Wilmington, DE 19898/302-773-5291

Southern Ammunition Co. Inc., Rte. 1, Box 6B, Latta, SC 29565/803-752-7751

3-D Ammunition & Bullets, 112 Plum St., Doniphan, NE 68832/402-845-2285

United States Ammunition Co. (USAC), Inc., 45500 - 15th St. East, Tacoma, WA 98424/206-922-7589

Weatherby's, 2781 E. Firestone Blvd., South Gate, CA 90280

Winchester, 427 N. Shamrock St., East Alton, IL 62024/618-258-2000

AMMUNITION (Custom)

A-Square Co., Inc., Rt. 4, Simmons Rd., Madison, IN 47250/812-273-3633

Accuracy Systems Inc., 15205 N. Cave Creek Rd., Phoenix, AZ 85032/602-971-1991

AFSCO Ammunition, 731 W. Third St., Owen, WI 54460/715-229-2516

Allred Bullet Co., 932 Evergreen Dr., Logan, UT 84321/801-752-6983

Atlanta Discount Ammo, P.O. Box 627, Norcross, GA 30091 (obsolete & wildcat calibers)

Beal's Bullets, 170 W. Marshall Rd., Lansdowne, PA 19050/215-259-1220 (Auto Mag Specialists)

Black Mountain Bullets, Rte.3, Box 297, Warrenton, VA 22186/703-347-1199

B.E.L.L. (See Eldorado Cartridge Corp.)

Russell Campbell Custom Loaded Ammo, 219 Leisure Dr., San Antonio, TX 78201/512-735-1183

Cartridges Unlimited, Rt. 1, Box 50, South Kent, CT 06785/203-927-3053 (British Express; metric; U.S.)

Cor-Bon Bullet Co., P.O. Box 10126, Detroit, MI 48210/313-894-2373

Cumberland Arms, Rt. 1, Box 1150, Shafer Rd., Blantons Chapel, Manchester, TN 37355

Custom Tackle & Ammo, P.O. Box 1886, Farmington, NM 87499/505-632-3539

Eldorado Cartridge Corp., P.O. Box 308, Boulder City, NV 89005/702-294-0025

Elko Arms, 28 rue Ecole Moderne, 7400 Soignies, Belgium/32-67.33.29.34

E.W. Ellis Sport Shop, RFD 1, Box 315, Corinth, NY 12822

Ellwood Epps Northern Ltd., 210 Worthington St. W., North Bay, Ont. P1B 3B4, Canada

Estate Cartridge Inc., P.O. Box 3702, Conroe, TX 77305/409-856-7277 (shotshell)

Jack First Distributors, Inc., 44633 Sierra Hwy., Lancaster, CA 93534/805-945-6981

Freedom Arms, P.O. Box 110, Freedom, WY 83120/307-883-2468

Ramon B. Gonzalez, P.O. Box 370, Monticello, NY 12701/914-794-4515

"Gramps" Antique Cartridges, Ellwood Epps, Box 341, Washago, Ont. L0K 2B0 Canada/705-689-5348

Hardin Specialty Distributors, P.O. Box 338, Radcliff, KY 40160/502-351-6649

Ace Hindman, 1880½ Upper Turtle Creek Rd., Kerrville, TX 78028/512-257-4290

Jett & Co. Inc., RR #3 Box 167-B, Litchfield, IL 62056/217-324-3779

R.H. Keeler, 817 "N" St., Port Angeles, WA 98362/206-457-4702

KTW Inc., 710 Foster Park Rd., Lorain, OH 44053/216-233-6919 (armor piercing for police and military only)

Lindsley Arms Cartridge Co., Inc., P.O. Box 757, 20 Crescent St., Henniker, NH 03242/603-428-3127 (inq. S.A.S.E.)

Lomont Precision Bullets, 4236 West 700 South, Poneto, IN 46781/219-694-6792 (custom cast bullets only)

McConnelistown Reloading & Cast Bullets, Inc., R.D. 3, Box 40, Huntingdon, PA 16652/814-627-5402

Mack's Sport Shop, Box 1155, Kodiak, AK 99615/907-486-4276

MagSafe Ammo, P.O. Box 5692, Olympia, WA 98503/206-456-4623

NAI/Ballistek, Box 535, Lake Havasu City, AZ 86403 (cases f. 25-20 Win. Single Shot)

North American Arms, 1800 North 300 West, Spanish Fork, UT 84660/801-798-7401

Olsen Development Lab. 111 Laveview Ave., Blackwood, NJ 08012/609-228-2786

Patriot Mfg. & Sales, 2163 Oak Beach Blvd., P.O. Box 2041, Sebring, FL 33871/813-655-1798

Personal Protection Systems, Ltd., Aberdeen Rd., RD #5 Box 5027-A, Moscow, PA 18444/717-842-1766 (High-Performance handgun loads)

Precision Ammo Co., P.O. Box 63, Garnerville, NY 10923/914-947-2720

Precision Prods. of Wash., Inc., N. 311 Walnut Rd., Spokane, WA 99206/509-928-0604 (Exammo)

Anthony F. Sailer, see: AFSCO

Sanders Cust. Gun Serv., 2358 Tyler Lane, Louisville, KY 40205

George W. Spence, 115 Locust St., Steele, MO 63877/314-695-4926 (boxer-primed cartridges)

3-D Ammunition & Bullets, 112 Plum St., Doniphan, NE 68832/402-845-2285 (reloaded police ammo)

3-Ten Corp., P.O. Box 269, Feeding Hills, MA 01030/413-789-2086 (44 magnum bulleted shot loads; handgun)

Thunderbird Cartridge Co., Inc., P.O. Box 302, Phoenix, AZ 85001/602-237-3823

R. A. Wardrop, P.O. Box 245, Mechanicsburg, PA 17055/717-766-9663

Zero Ammunition Co., Inc., P.O. Box 1188, Cullman, AL 35056/205-739-1606

AMMUNITION (Foreign)

Action Arms Ltd., P.O. Box 9573, Philadelphia, PA 19124/215-744-0100

AFSCO Ammunition, 731 W. Third St., Owen, WI 54460/715-229-2516

Atlanta Discount Ammo, P.O. Box 627, Norcross, GA 30091/404-446-2429

Beeman Inc., 3440-GD Airway Dr., Santa Rosa, CA 95403/707-578-7900

Chinasports, Inc., P.O. Box 2566, Sante Fe Springs, CA 90670/213-942-2383

Dynamit Nobel-RWS, Inc., 105 Stonehurst Court, Northvale, NJ 07647/210-767-1995 (RWS, Geco, Rottweil)

Fiocchi of America, Inc., Rt. 2, Box 90-8, Ozark, MO 65721/417-725-4118

Gun South, Inc., P.O. Box 129, 108 Morrow Ave. Trussville, AL 35173/205-655-8299

Hansen Cartridge Co., 244 Old Post Rd., Southport, CT 06490/203-259-7337

Hirtenberger Patronen-, Zundhutchen- & Metallwarenfabrik, A.G., Leobersdorfer Str. 33, A2552 Hirtenberg, Austria

Hunters Specialty, Inc., 130 Orchard Dr., Pittsburgh, PA 15235/412-795-8885 (Hirtenberger)

Paul Jaeger, Inc., P.O. Box 449, 1 Madison Ave., Grand Junction, TN 38039/901-764-6909 (RWS centerfire ammo)

PMC-Eldorado Cartridge Co., P.O. Box 308, Boulder City, NV 89005/702-294-0025

PTK International, 6030 Hwy. 85, Suite 614, Riverdale, GA 30274/404-997-5811

RWS (Rheinische-Westfälische Sprengstoff) See Dynamit Nobel; Paul Jaeger, Inc.

AMMUNITION COMPONENTS — BULLETS, POWDER, PRIMERS

A-Square Co., Inc., Rt. 4, Simmons Rd., Madison, IN 47250/812-273-3633 (cust. bull.; brass)

Accurate Arms Co., Inc., (Propellents Div.), Rt. 1, Box 167, McEwen, TN, 37101/615-729-4207/4208 (powders)

Acme Custom Bullets, 2414 Clara Lane, San Antonio, TX 78213/512-680-4828

Alaska Bullet Works, P.O. Box 54, Douglas, AK 99824/907-789-1576 (Alaska copper-bond cust. bull; Kodiak bonded core bullets)

Allred Bullet Co., 932 Evergreen Dr., Logan, UT 84321/801-752-6983 (custom bullets)

American Bullets, P.O. Box 15313, Atlanta, GA 30333/404-482-4253

American Products Co., 14729 Spring Valley Rd., Morrison, IL 61270/815-772-3336 (12-ga. shot wad)

Ammo-O-Mart Ltd., P.O. Box 125, Hawkesbury, Ont., Canada K6A 2R8/613-632-9300 (Nobel powder)

Atlanta Discount Ammo, P.O. Box 627, Norcross, GA 30091/404-446-2429 (bulk brass, primers; ctlg. $2)

Ballistic Prods., Inc., Box 408, 2105 Daniels St., Long Lake, MN 55356/612-473-1550 (shotgun powders, primers)

Ballistic Research Industries (BRI), 2825 S. Rodeo Gulch Rd. #8, Soquel, CA 95073/408-476-7981 (Sabo shotgun slug; Gualandislug)

Barnes Bullets, Inc., P.O. Box 215, American Fork, UT 84003/801-756-4222

Bell's Gun & Sport Shop, 3309-19 Mannheim Rd., Franklin Pk., IL 60131/312-678-1900

Berger Bullets, 4234 N. 63rd Ave., Phoenix, AZ 85033/602-846-5791 (cust. 22, 6mm benchrest bull.)

Bergman and Williams, 2450 Losee Rd., Suite F, No. Las Vegas, NV 89030/702-642-1091 (copper tube 308 cust. bull.; lead wire l. all sizes)

Bitterroot Bullet Co., Box 412, Lewiston, ID 83501/208-743-5635 (Broch.:USA, Can. & Mexico $1 plus legal size env.; intl. $2; lit. pkg.: USA, Can. & Mexico $7.75, intl. $10.75

Black Mountain Bullets, Rte. 3, Box 297, Warrenton, VA 22186/703-347-1199 (custom Fluid King match bullets)

B.E.L.L., (See Eldorado Cartridge Corp.)

Bruno Bullets, 10 Fifth St., Kelayres, PA 18231/717-929-1791 (22, 6mm benchrest bull.)

Buffalo Rock Shooters Supply, R. Rt. 1, Ottawa, IL 61350/815-433-2471

Bullet Swaging Supply, Inc., P.O. Box 1056, 303 McMillan Rd., West Monroe, LA 71219/318-387-7257

CCI, (See: Omark Industries)

CheVron Bullets, R.R. 1, Ottawa, IL 61350/815-433-2471

Colorado Sutlers Arsenal, Box 991, Granby, CO 80446/303-887-2813

Competition Bullets Inc., 9996-29 Ave., Edmonton, Alb. T6N 1A2, Canada/403-463-2817

Cooper-Woodward, 8073 Canyon Ferry Rd., Helena, MT 59601/406-375-3321

Corbin Mfg. & Supply, Inc., 600 Industrial Circle, P.O. Box 2659, White City, OR 97503/503-826-5211 (bullets)

Cor-Bon Custom Bullets, P.O. Box 10126, Detroit, MI 48210/313-894-2373 (375, 44, 45 solid brass partition bull.)

Creative Cartridge Co., 56 Morgan Rd., Canton, CT 06019/203-693-2529

DuPont, (See IMR Powder Co.)

Dynamit Nobel-RWS Inc., 105 Stonehurst Court, Northvale, NJ 07647/201-767-1995 (RWS percussion caps)

Eagle Bullet Works, P.O. Box 2104, White City, OR 97503/503-826-7143 (Div-Cor 375, 224, 257 cust. bull.)

Eldorado Cartridge Corp., P.O. Box 308, Boulder City, NV 89005/702-294-0025

Excaliber Wax, Inc., P.O. Box 432, Kenton, OH 43326/419-673-0512 (wax bullets)

Federal Cartridge Co., 900 Ehlen Dr., Anoka, MN 55303/612-422-2840 (primers)

Fiocchi of America, Inc., Rt. 2 Box 90-8, Ozark, MO 65721/417-725-4118 (primers; shotshell cases)

Fisher Enterprises, 655 Main St., Edmonds, WA 98020/206-776-4365

Fowler Bullets, 3731 McKelvey St., Charlotte, NC 28215/704-568-7661 (benchrest bullets)

Glaser Safety Slug, P.O. Box 8223, Foster City, CA 94404/415-345-7677

GOEX, Inc., Belin Plant, 1002 Springbrook Ave., Moosic, PA 18507/717-457-6724 (blackpowder)

Golden Powder International Sales, Inc., 8300 Douglas Ave., Suite 729, Dallas, TX 75225/214-373-3350 (Golden Powder/blackpowder)

Green Bay Bullets, P.O. Box 10446, 1486 Servais St., Green Bay, WI 54307-54304/414-497-2949 (cast lead bullets)

Grizzly Bullets, 2137 Hwy. 200, Trout Creek, MT 59874/406-847-2627 (cust.)

GTM Co., George T. Mahaney, 15915B E. Main St., La Puente, CA 91744 (all brass shotshells)

Gun City, 212 West Main Ave., Bismarck, ND 58501/701-223-2304

Hardin Specialty Distr., P.O. Box 338, Radcliff, KY 40160/502-351-6649 (empty, primed cases)

Harrison Bullet Works, 6437 E. Hobart St., Mesa, AZ 85205/602-985-7844 (cust. swaged .41 Mag. bullets)

Robert W. Hart & Son, Inc. 401 Montgomery St., Nescopeck, PA 18635/717-752-3655

Hercules Inc., Hercules Plaza, Wilmington, DE 19894 (smokeless powder)

Hodgdon Powder Co. Inc., P.O. Box 2932, Shawnee Mission, KS 66201/913-362-9455 (smokeless, Pyrodex and black powder)

Hoffman New Ideas, Inc., 821 Northmoor Rd., Lake Forest, IL 60045/312-234-4075 (practice sub. vel. bullets)

Hornady Mfg. Co., P.O. Drawer 1848, Grand Island, NE 68802/308-382-1390

Hunters Specialty, Inc., 130 Orchard Dr., Pittsburgh, PA 15235/412-795-8885 (Hirtenberger bullets)

Huntington's, 601 Oro Dam Blvd., Oroville, CA 95965/916-534-1210

IMR Powder Co., Rt. 5 Box 247E, Plattsburgh, NY 12901/518-561-9530 (smokeless powders only)

Jaro Manuf., P.O. Box 6125, 206 E. Shaw, Pasadena, TX 77506/713-472-0417 (bullets)

Kodiak Custom Bullets, 8261 Henry Circle, Anchorage, AK 99507/907-349-2282

Lage Uniwad Co., 1814 21st St., Eldora, IA 50627/515-858-2634

Ljutic Ind., Inc., Box 2117, Yakima, WA 98907/509-248-0476 (Mono-wads)

Lomont Precision Bullets, 4236 West 700 South, Poneto, IN 46781/219-694-6792 (custom cast bullets)

Paul E. Low Jr., R.R. 1, Dunlap, IL 61525/309-685-1392 (jacketed 44- & 45-cal. bullets)

McConnellstown Reloading & Cast Bullets, Inc., R.D. 3, Box 40, Huntingdon, PA 16652/814-627-5402

Mack's Sport Shop, Box 1155, Kodiak, AK 99615/907-486-4276 (cust. bull.)

Magnus Bullet Co., Inc., P.O. Box 2225, Birmingham, AL 35201/205-785-3357

MagSafe Ammo, P.O. Box 5692, Olympia, WA 98503/206-456-4623 (Controlled core bullets f. reloading)

Marshall Enterprises, 792 Canyon Rd., Redwood City, CA 94062/415-356-1230

Mayville Engineering Co., 715 South St., Mayville, WI 53050/414-387-4500 (non-toxic steel shot kits)

Metallic Casting & Copper Corp. (MCC), 214 E. Third St., Mt. Vernon, NY 10550/914-664-1311 (cast bullets)

Michael's Antiques, Box 591, Waldoboro, ME 04572 (Balle Blondeau)

Midway Arms, Inc., 5875 W. Van Horn Tavern Rd., Columbia, MO 65203/314-445-2400

Miller Trading Co., 20 S. Front St., Wilmington, NC 28401/919-762-7107 (bullets)

Necromancer Industries, Inc., 14 Communications Way, West Newton, PA 15089/412-872-8722

NORMA (See Federal Cartridge Co.)

Nosler Bullets Inc., 107 S.W. Columbia, Bend, OR 97702/503-382-5108

Old Western Scrounger, 12924 Hwy A-12, Montague, CA 96064/916-459-5445

Omark Industries, P.O. Box 856, Lewiston, ID 83501/208-746-2351

PMC — Eldorado Cartridge Co., P.O. Box 308, Boulder City, NV 89005/702-294-0025

Patriot Manufacturing & Sales, 2163 Oak Beach Blvd., P.O. Box 2041, Sebring, FL 33871/813-655-1798 (cust. bullets)

Pattern Control, 114 No. 3rd St., Garland, TX 75040/214-494-3551 (plastic wads)

Polywad, Inc., P.O. Box 7916, Macon, GA 31209 (Spred-Rs for shotshells)

Pyrodex, See: Hodgdon Powder Co., Inc. (black powder substitute)

Robert Pomeroy, Morison Ave., East Corinth, ME 04427/207-285-7721 (formed cases, obsolete cases, bullets)

Power Plus Enterprises, Inc., P.O. Box 6070, Colubmus, GA 31907/404-561-1717 (12-ga. shotguns slugs; 308, 45 ACP, 357 cust. bull.)

Precision Ammo Co., P.O. Drawer 86, Valley Cottage, NY 10989/914-947-2710

Professional Hunter Supplies, P.O. Box 608; 660 Berding St., Ferndale, CA 95536/707-786-4040 (408, 375, 308, 510 cust. bull.)

Prometheus/Titan Black (See Fisher Enterprises)

Reardon Products, P.O. Box 126, Morrison, IL 61270/815-772-3155 (dry-lube powder)

Redwood Bullet Works, 3559 Bay Rd., Redwood City, CA 94063/415-367-6741 (cust. bullets)

Remington Arms Co., 1007 Market St., Wilmington, DE 19898/302-773-5291

R.J. Renner Co., P.O. Box 3543, Glendale, CA 91221-0543/818-241-6488 (rubber bullets)

Rubright Bullets, 1008 S. Quince Rd., Walnutport, PA 18088/215-767-1239 (cust. 22 & 6mm benchrest bullets)

Sierra Bullets Inc., 10532 So. Painter Ave., Santa Fe Springs, CA 90670

Scot Powder Co., 1200 Talley Rd., Wilmington, DE 19809/302-764-9779

Southern Ammunition Co., Inc., Rt. 1, Box 6B, Latta, SC 29565/803-752-7751

Speer Products, Box 856, Lewiston, ID 83501

Sport Flite, P.O. Box 1082, Bloomfield Hills, MI 48308/313-647-3747 (zinc bases, gas checks)

Swift Bullet Co., RR. 1, Box 140A, Quinter, KS 67752/913-754-3959 (375 big game, 224 cust.)

Taracorp Industries, 16th & Cleveland Blvd., Granite City, IL 62040/618-451-4400 (Lawrence Brand lead shot)

3-D Ammunition & Bullets, 112 Plum St., Doniphan, NE 68832/402-845-2285

Thunderbird Cartridge Co., P.O. Box 302, Phoenix, AZ 85001/602-237-3823 (powder)

Trophy Bonded Bullets, P.O. Box 262348, Houston, TX 77207/713-645-4499 (big game 458, 308, 375 bonded cust. bullets only)

U.S. Ammunition Co./USAC, 4500 15th Street E, Tacoma, WA 98424/206-922-7589 (bullets)

Vitt/Boos, 2178 Nichols Ave., Stratford, CT 06497/203-375-6859 (Aerodynamic shotgun slug, 12-ga. only)

Ed Watson, Trophy Match Bullets, 2404 Wade Hampton Blvd., Greenville, SC 29615/803-244-7948 (22, 6mm cust. benchrest bull.)

Winchester/Olin, 427 N. Shamrock St., East Alton, IL 62024/618-258-2000

Worthy Products, Inc., R.R.I. Box 213, Martville, NY 13111 (slug loads)

Zero Bullet Co. Inc., P.O. Box 1188, Cullman, AL 35056/205-739-1606

BULLET & CASE LUBRICANTS

C-H Tool & Die Corp., 106 N. Harding St., Owen, WI 54460/715-229-2146

Cienzoil Corp., P.O. Box 1226, Sta. C, Canton, OH 44708/216-833-9758

Cooper-Woodward, 8073 Canyon Ferry Rd., Helena, MT 59601/406-475-3321 (Perfect Lube)

Corbin Mfg. & Supply Inc., 600 Industrial Circle, P.O. Box 2659, White City, OR 97503/503-826-5211

Dillon Precision Prods., Inc., 7442 E. Butherus Dr., Scottsdale, AZ 85260/602-948-8009

Green Bay Bullets, 1486 Servais St., Green Bay, WI 54304/414-497-2949 (EZE-Size case lube)

Javelina Products, P.O. Box 337, San Bernadino, CA 92402/714-882-5847 (Alox beeswax)

Jet-Aer Corp., 100 Sixth Ave., Paterson, NJ 07524

LeClear Industries, 1126 Donald Ave., P.O. Box 484, Royal Oak, MI 48068/313-588-1025

Lee Precision, Inc., 4275 Hwy. U, Hartford, WI 53027/414-673-3075

Lithi-Bee Bullet Lube, 2161 Henry St., Muskegon, MI 49441/616-755-4707

Lyman Products Corp., 147 West St., Middlefield, CT 06455/203-349-3421 (Size-Ezy)

M&M Engineering, 10642 Arminta St., Sun Valley, CA 91352/818-842-8376 (case lubes)

Micro-Lube, P.O. Box 117, Mesilla Park, NM 88047/505-524-4215

Midway Arms, Inc., 5875 W. Van Horn Tavern Rd., Columbia, MO 65203/314-445-2400

M&N Bullet Lube, P.O. Box 495, 151 N.E. Jefferson St., Madras, OR 97741/503-475-2992

Northeast Industrial, Inc., 9330 N.E. Halsey, Portland, OR 97220/503-255-3750 (Ten X-Lube; NEI mold prep)

Pacific Tool Co., P.O. Box 2048, Ordnance Plant Rd., Grand Island, NE 68801/308-384-2308

Ponsness-Warren, P.O. Box 8, Rathdrum, ID 83858/208-687-2231 (case lubes)

Radix Research & Marketing, Box 247, Woodland Park, CO 80866/303-687-3182 (Magnum Dri-Lube)

Redding Inc., 1089 Starr Rd., Cortland, NY 13045/607-753-3331

Rooster Laboratories, P.O. Box 412514, Kansas City, MO 64141/816-474-1622 (Zambini and HVR bullet lubes; case lubes & polish)

SAECO (See Redding)

Sandia Die & Cartridge Co., Route 5, Box 5400, Albuquerque, NM 87123/505-298-5729

Shooters Accessory Supply (SAS) (See Corbin Mfg. & Supply)

Tamarack Prods., Inc., P.O. Box 625, Wauconda, IL 60084/312-526-9333 (Bullet lube)

BULLET SWAGE DIES AND TOOLS

Bullet Swaging Supply, Inc., P.O. Box 1056, 303 McMillan Rd., West Monroe, LA 71291/318-387-7257

C-H Tool & Die Corp., 106 N. Harding St., Owen, WI 54460/715-229-2146

J.A. Clerke Co., P.O. Box 627, Pearblossom, CA 93553/805-945-0713 (moulds)

Mrs. Lester Coats, 416 Simpson Ave., North Bend, OR 97459/503-756-6995 (lead wire core cutter)

Corbin Mfg. & Supply Inc., 600 Industrial Circle, P.O. Box 2659, White City, OR 97503/503-826-5211

Hanned Precision, P.O. Box 2888, Sacramento, CA 95812 (cast bullet tools)

Hollywood Loading Tools (See M&M Engineering)

Huntington Die Specialties, 601 Oro Dam Blvd., Oroville, CA 95965/916-534-1210

M&M Engineering, 10642 Arminta St., Sun Valley, CA 91352/818-842-8376

Necromancer Industries, Inc., 14 Communications Way, West Newton, PA 15089/412-872-8722

Rorschach Precision Products, P.O. Box 151613, Irving, TX 75015/214-790-3487

SAS Dies, (See Corbin Mfg. & Supply)

Seneca Run Iron Works Inc., dba ''Swagease'', P.O. Box 3032, Greeley, CO 80633/303-352-1452 (muzzle-loading round ball)

Sport Flite Mfg., Inc., 2520 Industrial Row, Troy, MI 48084/313-280-0648

CHRONOGRAPHS

Competition Electronics, Inc., 2542 Point O' Woods Dr., Rockford, IL 61111/815-877-3322

Custom Chronograph Inc., 5305 Reese Hill Rd., Sumas, WA 98295/206-988-7801

Paul Jaeger, Inc., P.O. Box 449, 1 Madison Ave., Grand Junction, TN 38039

Oehler Research, Inc., P.O. Box 9135, Austin, TX 78766/512-327-6900

P.A.C.T. Inc., P.O. Box 531525, Grand Prairie, TX 75053/214-641-0049 (Precision chronogr.)

Quartz-Lok, 13137 N. 21st Lane, Phoenix, AZ 85029/602-863-2729

Tepeco, P.O. Box 342, Friendswood, TX 77546/713-482-2702 (Tepeco Speed-Meter)

GUNS (U.S.-made)

A.A. Arms, Inc., P.O. Box 25610-272, Mint Hill, NC 28227/704-545-5565 (AP-9 auto pistol)

AMAC (American Military Arms Corp.), 2202 Redmond Rd., Jacksonville, AR 72076/501-982-1633

AMT (Arcadia Machine & Tool, Inc.), 6226 Santos Diaz, Irwindale, CA 91702/818-334-6629

Accuracy Systems, Inc., 15205 N. Cave Creek Rd., Phoenix, AZ 85032/602-971-1991

American Arms, Inc., P.O. Box 27163, Salt Lake City, UT 84127/801-971-5006

American Derringer Corp., 127 N. Lacy Dr., Waco, TX 76705/817-799-9111

American Industries, 8700 Brookpark Rd., Cleveland, OH 44129/216-398-8300

Armitage International, Ltd., P.O. Box 1099, Seneca, SC 29679/803-882-5900 (Scarab Skorpion 9mm pistol)

Armes de Chasse, 3000 Valley Forge Circle, King of Prussia, PA 19406/215-783-6133

Auto-Ordnance Corp., Williams Lane, West Hurley, NY 12491/914-679-7225

BF Arms, 1123 So. Locust, Grand Island, NE 68801/308-382-1121 (single shot pistol)

BJT, 445 Putman Ave., Hamden, CT 06517 (stainless double derringer)

Beretta U.S.A., 17601 Beretta Dr., Accokeek, MD 20607/301-283-2191

Browning (Gen. Offices), Rt. 1, Morgan, UT 84050/801-876-2711

Browning (Parts & Service), Rt. 4, Box 624-B, Arnold, MO 63010/314-287-6800

Bryco Arms (Distributed by Jennings Firearms)

Bushmaster Firearms Co., 999 Roosevelt Trail, Bldg. #3, Windham, ME 04062 (police handgun)

Calico (California Instrument Co.), 405 E. 19th St., Bakersfield, CA 93305/805-323-1327

Century Gun Dist., Inc., 1467 Jason Rd., Greenfield, IN 46140/317-462-4524 (Century Model 100 SA rev.)

Charter Arms Corp., 430 Sniffens Ln., Stratford, CT 06497/203-377-8080

Colt Firearms, P.O. Box 1868, Hartford CT 06101/203-236-6311

Competition Limited, 1664 S. Research Loop Rd., Tucson, AZ 85710/602-722-6455

Coonan Arms, Inc., 830 Hampden Ave., St. Paul, MN 55114/612-646-6672 (357 Mag. Autom.)

Davis Industries, 15150 Sierra Bonita Lane, Chino, CA 91710/714-591-4726 (derringers; 32 auto pistol)

Detonics Mfg. Corp., 13456 S.E. 27th Pl., Bellevue, WA 98005/206-747-2100 (auto pistol)

E.M.F. Co. Inc., 1900 East Warner Ave. 1-D, Santa Ana, CA 92705/714-261-6611

Encom America, Inc., P.O. Box 5314, Atlanta, GA 30307/404-525-2801

Excam, Inc., 4480 East 11th Ave., Hialeah, FL 33013/305-681-4661

Feather Industries, 2500 Central Ave., Boulder, CO 80301/303-442-7021

Federal Eng. Corp., 2335 So. Michigan Ave., Chicago, IL 60616/312-842-1063

Firearms Imp. & Exp. Corp., P.O. Box 4866, Hialeah Lakes, Hialeah, FL 33014/305-685-5966 (FIE)

Freedom Arms Co., P.O. Box 1776, Freedom, WY 83120 (mini revolver, Casull rev.)

Freedom Arms Marketing (See: L.A.R. Mfg. Co.)

Gilbert Equipment Co., Inc., P.O. Box 9846, Mobile, AL 36609

Gonic Arms Inc., 134 Flagg Rd., Gonic, NH 03867/603-332-8456 (ML)

Grendel, Inc., P.O. Box 908, Rockledge, FL 32955/305-636-1211

Holmes Firearms Corp., Rte. 6, Box 242, Fayetteville, AR 72703

Lew Horton Dist. Co. Inc., 15 Walkup Dr., Westboro, MA 01581/508-366-7400 (sporting firearms wholesaler)

IAI/Irwindale Arms, Inc., 6226 Santos Diaz St., Irwindale, CA 91702/818-334-1200

Interarms Ltd., 10 Prince St., Alexandria, VA 22323/703-548-1400

Intratec, 12405 S.W. 130th St., Miami, FL 33186/305-232-1821

Jennings Firearms Inc., 3656 Research Way, Unit 33, Carson City, NV 89706/702-882-4007

Iver Johnson, see: AMAC

Kimber of Oregon, Inc., 9039 S.E. Jannsen Rd., Clackamas, OR 97015/503-656-1704

Kimel Industries, Box 335, Matthews, NC 28105/704-821-7663

L.A.R. Manufacturing Inc., 4133 West Farm Rd., West Jordan, UT 84084/801-255-7106 (Grizzly Win Mag pistol)

Lorcin Engineering Co., Inc., 6471 Mission Blvd., Riverside, CA 92509/714-682-7374 (L-25 pistol)

Magnum Research, Inc., P.O. Box 32221, Minneapolis, MN 55432/612-574-1868

Marlin Firearms Co., 100 Kenna Drive, New Haven, CT 06473

Maverick Arms, Inc., Industrial Blvd., P.O. Box 586, Eagle Pass, TX 78853/512-773-9007

M.O.A. Corp., 7996 Brookville-Salem Rd., Brookville, OH 45309/513-833-5559 (Maximum pistol)

O.F. Mossberg & Sons, Inc., 7 Grasso St., No. Haven, CT 06473

Navy Arms Co., 689 Bergen Blvd., Ridgefield, NJ 07657

New England Firearms Co., Inc., Industrial Rowe, Gardner, MA 01440/508-632-9393

North American Arms, 1800 North 300 West, Spanish Fork, UT 84660/801-798-7401

North American Specialists, 25422 Trabuco Rd. #105-328, El Toro, CA 92630/714-979-4867

Olympic Arms (See SGW/Safari Arms)

Oregon Arms, Inc., 165 Schulz Rd., Central Point, OR 97502/503-664-5586

Pachmayr, Ltd., 1875 So. Mountain Ave., Monrovia, CA 91016/818-357-7771

Patriot Distribution Co., 2872 So. Wentworth Ave., Milwaukee, WI 53207/414-769-0760 (Avenger pistol)

E. F. Phelps Mfg., Inc. P.O. Box 2266, Evansville, IN 47714/812-423-2599 (Heritage I in 45-70)

Precision Small Parts, Inc., 155 Carlton Rd., Charlottesville, VA 22901/804-293-6124

RPM (R&R Sporting Arms, Inc.), 150 Viking Ave., Brea, CA 92621/714-990-2444 (XL pistol; formerly Merrill)

Rahn Gun Works, Inc., 3700 Anders Rd., Hastings, MI 49058/616-945-9894

Raven Arms, 1300 Bixby Dr., Industry, CA 91745/818-961-2511 (P-25 pistols)

Remington Arms Co., 1007 Market St., Wilmington, DE 19898/302-773-5291

Ruger (See Sturm, Ruger & Co.)

SAM Inc., see: Special Service Arms Mfg. Inc.

SGW/Safari Arms, Inc., 624 Pacific Hwy SE, Olympia, WA 98503/206-456-3471

S/S Sales of Georgia, P.O. Box 94168, Atlanta, GA 94168/404-355-5986

Savage Industries, Inc., Springdale Rd., Westfield, MA 01085/413-562-2361

Sedco Industries Inc., 506 Spring St., Unit E, Lake Elsinore, CA 92330/714-674-5957 (SP-22 pistol)

L.W. Seecamp Co., Inc., P.O. Box 255, New Haven, CT 06502/203-877-3429

Smith & Wesson, Inc., 2100 Roosevelt Ave., Springfield, MA 01101

Sokolovsky Corp., P.O. Box 70113, Sunnyvale, CA 94086/408-245-9268 (45 Automaster pistol)

Special Service Arms Mfg. Inc., 405 Rabbit Trail, Edgefield, SC 29824/803-637-1200

Springfield Armory, Inc., 420 W. Main St., Geneseo, IL 61254/309-944-5631

Steel City Arms, Inc., P.O. Box 81926, Pittsburgh, PA 15217/412-461-3100 (d.a. ''Double Deuce'' pistol)

Sturm, Ruger & Co., Inc., Lacey Place, Southport, CT 06490/203-259-7843

Sundance Industries, Inc., 8216 Lankershim Blvd., #11, North Hollywood, CA 91605/818-768-1083 (Model A-25 pistol)

Super Six Limited, P.O. Box 54, Mequon, WI 53092/414-723-5058

TMI Products, 1010 S. Plumer Ave., Tucson, AZ 85719/602-792-1075

Texas Longhorn Arms, Inc., P.O. Box 703, Richmond, TX 77469/713-341-0775 (S.A. sixgun)

Thompson/Center Arms, Farmington Rd., P.O. Box 5002, Rochester, NH 03867/603-332-2394

Ultra Light Arms Co., P.O. Box 1270; 214 Price St., Granville, WV 26534/304-599-5687

United States Frame Specialists, Inc. (U.S.F.S.), P.O. Box 7762, Milwaukee, WI 53207/414-643-6387

U.S. Repeating Arms Co., P.O. Box 30-300, New Haven, CT 06511/203-789-5000

Varner Sporting Arms, Inc., 100-F N. Cobb Pkwy., Marietta, GA 30062/404-422-5468

Weatherby's, 2781 E. Firestone Blvd., South Gate, CA 90280

Dan Wesson Arms, 293 Main St., Monson, MA 01057/413-267-4081

Wichita Arms, 444 Ellis, Wichita, KS 67211/316-265-0661

Wildey Inc., P.O. Box 475, Brookfield, CT 06804/203-355-9000

Wilkinson Arms, 26884 Pearl Rd., Parma, ID 83660/208-722-6771

Winchester, (See U.S. Repeating Arms)

Wyoming Armory, Inc., Forest Pl., Bedford, WY 83112/307-883-2151

HANDGUN ACCESSORIES

AMT (Arcadia Machine & Tool, Inc.), 6226 Santos Diaz St., Irwindale, CA 91702/818-334-6629

Adco International, 1 Wyman St., Woburn, MA 01801/617-935-1799

Ajax Custom Grips, Inc., Div. of A. Jack Rosenberg & Sons, 11311 Stemmons, Suite #5, Dallas, TX 75229/214-241-6302

Bob Allen Companies, 214 S.W. Jackson St., Des Moines, IA 50302/515-283-2191

American Gas & Chemical Co., Ltd., 220 Pegasus Ave., Northvale, NJ 07647/201-767-7300 (clg. lube)

Armsport, Inc., 3590 N.W. 49th St., Miami, FL 33142/305-635-7850

Baramie Corp., 6250 E. 7 Mile Rd., Detroit, MI 48234 (Hip-Grip)

Bar-Sto Precision Machine, 73377 Sullivan Rd., P.O. Box 1838, Twentynine Palms, CA 92277/619-367-2747 (barrels)

Behlert Precision, RD 2 Box 63, Route 611 North, Pipersville, PA 18947/215-766-8681

Brauer Bros. Mfg. Co., 2020 Delmar Blvd., St. Louis, MO 63103/314-231-2864

Ed Brown Products, Rte. 2, Box 2922, Perry, MO 63462/314-565-3261

Centaur Systems, Inc., 15127 NE 24th, C-3, Suite 114, Redmond, WA 98052/206-392-8472 (Quadra-Lok bbls.)

Central Specialties Co., 200 Lexington Dr., Buffalo Grove, IL 60089/312-537-3300 (trigger locks only)

Clymer Mfg. Co., Inc., 1645 W. Hamlin Rd., Rochester Hills, MI 48309/313-853-5555

D&E Magazines Mfg., P.O. Box 4876-D, Sylmar, CA 91342 (clips)

Detonics Firearms Industries, 13456 SE 27th Pl., Bellevue, WA 98005/206-747-2100

Doskocil Mfg. Co., Inc., P.O. Box 1246, Arlington, TX 76004/817-467-5116 (Gun Guard cases)

Eagle International, Inc., 5195 W. 58th Ave., Suite 300, Arvada, CO 80002/303-426-8100

Essex Arms, Box 345, Island Pond, VT 05846/802-723-4313 (45 Auto frames)

Frielich Police Equipment, 396 Broome St., New York, NY 10013/212-254-3045 (cases)

R. S. Frielich, 211 East 21st St., New York, NY 10010/212-777-4477 (cases)

Glock, Inc. 6000 Highlands Parkway, Smyrna, GA 30082/404-432-1202

Gun Parts Corp., Box 2, West Hurley, NY 12491/914-679-2417

Gil Hebard Guns, 125-129 Public Square, Knoxville, IL 61448

Intratec, 12405 S.W. 130th St., Miami, FL 33186/305-232-1821

Jett & Co. Inc., RR #3 Box 167-B, Litchfield, IL 62056/217-324-3779

Art Jewel Ent., 460 Randy Rd., Carol Stream, IL 60188/312-260-6144 (Eagle Grips)

K&K Ammo Wrist Band, R.D. #1, Box 448-CA18, Lewistown, PA 17044/717-242-2329

King's Gun Works, 1837 W. Glenoaks Blvd., Glendale, CA 91201/818-956-6010

Terry K. Kopp, 1301 Franklin, Lexington, MO 64067/816-259-2636

Lee Precision Inc., 4275 Hwy. U, Hartford, WI 53027 (pistol rest holders)

Liberty Antique Gunworks, 19 Key St., P.O. Box 183GD, Eastport, ME 04631/207-853-2327 (shims f. S&W revs.)

Kent Lomont, 4236 West 700 South, Poneto, IN46781 (Auto Mag only)

Lone Star Gunleather, 1301 Brushy Bend Dr., Round Rock, TX 78681/512-255-1805

Los Gatos Grip & Specialty Co., P.O. Box 1850, Los Gatos, CA 95030 (custom-made)

M.A.M. Products, Inc., 153 B Cross Slope Court, Englishtown, NJ 07726/201-536-7268 (free standing brass catcher f. all auto pistols and/or semi-auto rifles)

MTM Molded Prods. Co., P.O. Box 14117, Dayton, OH 45414/513-890-7461

Magnum Research, Inc., P.O. Box 32221, Minneapolis, MN 55432/612-574-1868

Mag-Pack, P.O. Box 846, Chesterland, OH 44026

Millet Industries, 16131 Gothard St., Huntington Beach, CA 92647/714-842-5575

No-Sho Mfg. Co., 10727 Glenfield Ct., Houston, TX 77096/713-723-5332

Jim Noble Co., 1305 Columbia St., Vancouver, WA 98660/206-695-1309

Omega Sales, Inc., P.O. Box 1066, Mt. Clemens, MI 48403/313-469-6727

Harry Owen (See Sport Specialties)

Pachmayr Ltd., 1875 So. Mountain Ave., Monrovia, CA 91016/818-357-7771 (cases)

Pacific Intl. Mchdsg. Corp., 2215 "J" St., Sacramento, CA 95818/916-446-2737 (Vega 45 Colt. comb. mag.)

Poly-Choke Div., Marble Arms Corp., 420 Industrial Park, Gladstone, MI 49827/906-428-3710 (handgun ribs)

Progressive Ballistics, Inc., Box 2526, Shawnee Mission, KS 66201/816-221-9117 (TriComp muzzle brake)

Ranch Products, P.O. Box 145, Malinta, OH 43535/313-277-3118 (third-moon clips)

Ransom Intl. Corp., 1040 Sandretto Dr., Suite J, Prescott, AZ 86302/602-778-7899

SSK Industries, 721 Woodvue Lane, Wintersville, OH 43952/614-264-0176

Safariland Ltd., Inc., 1941 S. Walker, Monrovia, CA 91016/818-357-7902

Sile Distributors, 7 Centre Market Pl., New York, NY 10013

Robert Sonderman, 735 W. Kenton, Charleston, IL 61920/217-345-5429 (solid walnut fitted handgun cases; other woods)

Sport Specialties, (Harry Owen), Box 5337, Hacienda Hts., CA 91745/213-968-5806 (.22 rimfire adapters; .22 insert bbls. f. T/C Contender, autom. pistols)

Sportsmen's Equipment Co., 415 W. Washington, San Diego, CA 92103/619-296-1501

Turkey Creek Enterprises, Rt. 1, Box 10, Red Oak, CA 74563/918-754-2884 (wood handgun cases)

Melvin Tyler Mfg.-Dist., 1326 W Britton, Oklahoma City, OK 73114/405-842-8044 (grip adaptor)

Wardell Precision Handguns Ltd., Box 4132 New River Stage 1, New River, AZ 85029/602-242-0186

Wilson's Gun Shop, P.O. Box 578, Rt. 3, Box 211-D, Berryville, AR 72616/501-545-3618

HANDGUN GRIPS

Action Products Inc., 22 N. Mulberry St., Hagerstown, MD 21740/301-797-1414

Ajax Custom Grips, Inc., Div. of A. Jack Rosenberg & Sons, 11311 Stemmons, Suite #5, Dallas, TX 75229/214-241-6302

Altamont Mfg. Co., 510 N. Commercial St., P.O. Box 309, Thomasboro, IL 61878/217-643-3125

Art Jewel Enterprises Ltd., Eagle Business Ctr., 460 Randy Rd., Carol Stream, IL 60188/312-260-0040 (Eagle grips)

Barami Corp., 6250 East 7 Mile Rd., Detroit, MI 48234/313-891-2536

Bear Hug Grips, Inc., P.O. Box 25944, Colorado Springs, CO 80936/719-598-5675 (cust.)

Beeman Precision Arms, Inc., 3440-GD Airway Dr., Santa Rosa, CA 95403/707-578-7900 (airguns ohly)

Behlert Precision, RD 2 Box 63, Route 611 North, Pipersville, PA 18947/215-766-8681

Boone's Custom Ivory Grips, Inc., 562 Coyote Rd., Brinnon, WA 98320/206-796-4330

Fab-U-Grip, An-Lin Enterprises, Inc., P.O. BOX 550, Vineland, NJ 08360/609-652-1089

Fitz Pistol Grip Co., P.O. Box 171, Douglas City, CA 96024/916-778-3136

Gun Parts Corp., Box 2, West Hurley, NY 12491/914-679-2417

Herrett's, Box 741, Twin Falls, ID 83303/208-733-1498

Hogue Grips, P.O. Box 2038, Atascadero, CA 93423/805-466-6266 (Monogrip)

Paul Jones Munitions Systems, (See Fitz Co.)

Logan Security Products, Box 16206, Columbus, OH 43216 ("Streetloader" f. K & L frame S&Ws)

Russ Maloni (See Russwood)

Monogrip, (See Hogue)

Monte Kristo Pistol Grip Co., Box 171, Douglas City, CA 96024/916-778-3136

Mustang Custom Pistol Grips, see: R.J. Renner Co.

Nygord Precision Products, P.O. Box 8394, La Crescenta, CA 91214/818-352-3027

Pachmayr Ltd., 1875 So. Mountain Ave., Monrovia, CA 91016/818-357-7771

Robert H. Newell, 55 Coyote, Los Alamos, NM 87544/505-662-7135 (custom stocks)

Olympic Arms Inc. dba SGW, 624 Old Pacific Hwy. S.E., Olympia, WA 98503/206-456-3471

R.J. Renner Co., P.O. Box 3543, Glendale, CA 91221-0543/818-241-6488

A. Jack Rosenberg & Sons, 12229 Cox Lane, Dallas, TX 75234/214-241-6302 (Ajax)

Royal Ordnance Works Ltd., P.O. Box 3254, Wilson, NC 27893/919-237-0515

Russwood Custom Pistol Grips, P.O. Box 460, East Aurora, NY 14052/716-842-6012 (cust. exotic woods)

Jean St. Henri, 6525 Dume Dr., Malibu, CA 90265/213-457-7211 (custom)

Ben Shostle, The Gun Room, 1121 Burlington, Muncie, IN 47302/317-282-9073 (custom)

Sile Dist., 7 Centre Market Pl., New York, NY 10013/212-925-4111

Craig Spegel, P.O. Box 1334, Hillsboro, OR 97123/503-628-1631

Sports Inc., P.O. Box 683, Park Ridge, IL 60068/312-825-8952 (Franzite)

R. D. Wallace, Star Rte. 1 Box 76, Grandin, MO 63943/314-593-4773 (cust. only)

Wayland Prec. Wood Prods., Box 1142, Mill Valley, CA 94942/415-381-3543

Wilson's Gun Shop, P.O. Box 578, Rt. 3, Box 211-D, Berryville, AR 72616/501-545-3618

HEARING PROTECTORS

AO Safety Prods., Div. of American Optical Corp., 14 Mechanic St., Southbridge, MA 01550/617-765-9711 (ear valves, ear muffs)

Bausch & Lomb, 635 St. Paul St., Rochester, NY 14602

Bilsom Interntl., Inc., 109 Carpenter Dr., Sterling, VA 22170/703-834-1070 (ear plugs, muffs)

David Clark Co., Inc., 360 Franklin St., P.O. Box 15054, Worcester, MA 01615/508-756-6216

Gun Parts Corp., Box 2, West Hurley, NY 12491/914-679-2417

Marble Arms Corp., 420 Industrial Park, Box 111, Gladstone, MI 49837/906-428-3710

North Consumer Prods. Div., 2664-B Saturn St., Brea, CA 92621/714-524-1665 (Lee Sonic ear valves)

Safety Direct, 56 Coney Island Dr., Sparks, NV 89431/702-354-4451 (Silencio)

Smith & Wesson, 2100 Roosevelt Ave., Springfield, MA 01101

Willson Safety Prods. Div., P.O. Box 622, Reading, PA 19603 (Ray-O-Vac)

PISTOLSMITHS

Accuracy Gun Shop, Lance Martini, 3651 University Ave., San Diego, CA 92104/619-282-8500

Accuracy Systems, Inc., 15205 N. Cave Creek Rd., Phoenix, AZ 85032/602-971-1991

Accuracy Unlimited, 16036 N. 49 Ave., Glendale, AZ 85306/602-978-9089

Ahlman's Inc., R.R. #1 Box 20, Morristown, MN 55052/507-685-4243

Alpha Precision, Inc., Rte. 1, Box 35-1, Preston Rd., Good Hope, GA 30641/404-267-6163

American Pistolsmiths Guild, Rt. 1, Della Dr., Bloomingdale, OH 43910/614-264-0176

Ann Arbor Rod and Gun Co., 1946 Packard Rd., Ann Arbor, MI 48104/313-769-7866

Armament Gunsmithing Co., Inc., 525 Route 22, Hillside, NJ 07205/201-686-0960

Richard W. Baber, Alpine Gun Mill, 1507 W. Colorado Ave., Colorado Springs, CO 80904/303-634-4867

Baer Custom Guns, 1725 Minesite Rd., Allentown, PA 18103/215-398-2362 (accurizing 45 autos and Comp II Syst.; cust. XP100s, P.P.C. rev.)

Bain & Davis Sptg. Gds., 307 E. Valley Blvd., San Gabriel, CA 91776/213-573-4241

Bar-Sto Precision Machine, 73377 Sullivan Rd., P.O. Box 1838, Twentynine Palms, CA 92277/619-367-2747 (S.S. bbls. f. 45 ACP and others)

Barta's Gunsmithing, 10231 US Hwy. #10, Cato, WI 54206/414-732-4472

R.J. Beal, Jr., 170 W. Marshall Rd., Lansdowne, PA 19050/215-259-1220 (conversions, SASE f. inquiry)

Behlert Precision, RD 2 Box 63, Route 611 North, Pipersville, PA 18947/215-766-8681 (short actions)

Bell's Custom Shop, 3309 Mannheim Rd., Franklin Park, IL 60131/312-678-1900

Bowen Classic Arms Corp., P.O. Box 67, Louisville, TN 37777/615-984-3583

C.T. Brian, 1101 Indiana Ct., Decatur, IL 62521/217-429-2290

Ed Brown Products, Rte. 2 Box 2922, Perry, MO 63462/314-565-3261

Leo Bustani, P.O. Box 8125, W. Palm Beach, FL 33407/305-622-2710

Dick Campbell, 20000 Silver Ranch Rd., Conifer, CO 80433/303-697-0150 (PPC guns; custom)

Cellini's, Francesca Inc., 3115 Old Ranch Rd., San Antonio, TX 78217/512-826-2584

Clark Custom Guns, Inc., 11462 Keatchie Rd., Keithville, LA 71047/318-925-0836

The Competitive Pistol Shop, John Henderson, 5233 Palmer Dr., Ft. Worth, TX 76117/817-834-8479

Custom Gun Guild, 2646 Church Dr., Doraville, GA 30340/404-455-0346

D&D Gun Shop, 363 Elmwood, Troy, MI 48083/313-583-1512

Davis Co., 2793 Del Monte St., West Sacramento, CA 95691/916-372-6789

Leonard Day & Sons, Inc., One Cottage St., P.O. Box 723, East Hampton MA 01027/413-527-7990

Dilliott Gunsmithing, Inc., Rte. 3, Box 340, Dandridge, TN 37725

Dominic DiStefano, 4303 Friar Lane, Colorado Springs, CO 80907/303-599-3366 (accurizing)

Duncan's Gunworks Inc., 1619 Grand Ave., San Marcos, CA 92069/619-727-0515

Dan Dwyer, 915 W. Washington, San Diego, CA 92103/619-296-1501

Peter Dyson Ltd., 29-31 Church St., Honley, Huddersfield, Yorksh. HD7 2AH, ENGLAND

Englishtown Sptg. Gds. Co., Inc., David J. Maxham, 38 Main St., Englishtown, NJ 07726/201-446-7717

Ferris Firearms, Gregg Ferris, 1827 W. Hildebrand, San Antonio, TX 78201/512-734-0304

Jack First Distributors, Inc., 44633 Sierra Hwy., Lancaster, CA 93534/805-945-6981

Fountain Prods., 492 Prospect Ave., W. Springfield, MA 01089/413-781-4651

Frielich Police Equipment, 396 Broome St., New York, NY 10013/212/254-3045

K. Genecco Gun Works, 10512 Lower Sacramento Rd., Stockton, CA 95210/209-951-0706

Gilman-Mayfield, 1552 N. 1st, Fresno, CA 93703/209-237-2500

Gunsite Gunsmithy, P.O. Box 451, Paulden, AZ 86334/602-636-4104

Fritz Hallberg, 240 No. Oregon St., P.O. Box 322, Ontario, OR 97914/503-889-7052

Keith Hamilton, P.O. Box 871, Gridley, CA 95948/916-846-2361

Hanson's Gun Center, 521 So. Circle Dr., Colorado Springs, CO 80910/719-634-4220

Gil Hebard Guns, Box 1, Knoxville, IL 61448

Richard Heinie, 821 E. Adams, Havana, IL 62644/309-543-4535

High Bridge Arms Inc., 3185 Mission St., San Francisco, CA 94110/415-282-8358

Ace Hindman, 1880½ Upper Turtle Creek Rd., Kerrville, TX 78028/512-257-4290

James W. Hoag, 8523 Canoga Ave., Suite C, Canoga Park, CA 91304/818-998-1510

Campbell H. Irwin, Hartland Blvd. (Rt. 20), Box 152, East Hartland, CT 06027/203-653-3901

Paul Jaeger, Inc., P.O. Box 449, 1 Madison Ave., Grand Junction, TN 38039/901-764-6909

J.D. Jones, 721 Woodvue Lane, Wintersville, OH 43952/614-264-0176

Reeves C. Jungkind, 5805 N. Lamar Blvd., Austin, TX 78752/512-442-1094

L.E. Jurras & Assoc., P.O. Box 680, Washington, IN 47501/812-254-7698

Ken's Gun Specialties, Rt. 1, Box 147, Lakeview, AR 72642/501-431-5606

Benjamin Kilham, Kilham & Co., Main St., Box 37, Lyme, NH 03768/603-795-4112

Terry K. Kopp, 1301 Franklin, Lexington, MO 64067/816-259-2636 (rebblg., conversions)

LaFrance Specialties, P.O. Box 178211, San Diego, CA 92117/619-293-3373

Nelson H. Largent, Silver Shield's Inc., 4464-D Chinden Blvd., Boise, ID 83714

Robert W. Loveless, Box 7836, Arlington Station, Riverside, CA 920503/714-689-7800

William R. Laughridge, Cylinder & Slide Shop, 515 E. Military Ave., Fremont, NE 68025/402-721-4277

John G. Lawson, The Sight Shop, 1802 E. Columbia Ave., Tacoma, WA 98404/206-474-5465

Kent Lomont, 4236 West South, Poneto, In 46781/219-694-6792 (Auto Mag only)

George F. Long, 1500 Rougue River Hwy., Ste. F, Grants Pass, OR 97527/503-476-7552

Mac's .45 Shop, Box 2028, Seal Beach, CA 90740/213-438-5046

Mag-na-port International, Inc., 41302 Executive Drive, Mt. Clemens, MI 48045/313-469-6727

Robert A. McGrew, 3315 Michigan Ave., Colorado Springs, CO 80910/303-636-1940

Philip Bruce Mahony, 1-223 White Hollow Rd., Lime Rock, CT06039/203-435-9341

Rudolf Marent, 9711 Tiltree, Houston, TX 77075/713-946-7028 (Hammerli)

Elwyn H. Martin, Martin's Gun Shop, 937 So. Sheridan Blvd., Lakewood, CO 80226/303-922-2184

John V. Martz, 8060 Lakeview Lane, Lincoln, CA 95648/916-645-2250 (cust. German Lugers & P-38s)

Alan C. Marvel, 3922 Madonna Rd., Jarretsville, MD 21084/301-557-6545

Maryland Gun Works, Ltd., TEC Bldg., 10097 Tyler Pl. #8, Ijamsville, MD 21754/301-831-8456

Mountain Bear Rifle Works, Inc., Wm. Scott Bickett, 100-B Ruritan Rd., Sterling, VA 22170/703-430-0420

Mullis Guncraft, 3518 Lawyers Road East, Monroe, NC 28110/704-283-8789

Nastoff's 45 Shop, Steve Nastoff, 1057 Laverne Ave., Younstown, OH 44511/216-799-8870 (1911 conversions)

William Neighbor, Bill's Gun Repair, 1007 Burlington St., Mendota, IL 61342/815-539-5786

Wayne Novak, 1206½ 30th St., Parkersburg, WV 26101/304-467-2086

Nu-Line Guns, 1053 Caulks Hill Rd., Harvester, MO 63303/314-441-4501

Nygord Precision Products, P.O. Box 8394, La Crescenta, CA 91214/818-352-3027

Pachmayr Ltd., 1875 So. Mountain Ave., Monrovia, CA 91016/818-357-7771

Frank J. Paris, 13945 Minock Dr., Redford, MI 48239/313-255-0888

Paterson Gunsmithing, 438 Main St., Paterson, NJ 07502/201-345-4100

Phillips & Bailey, Inc., 815A Yorkshire St., Houston, TX 77022/713-699-4288

J. Michael Plaxco, Rt. 1, Box 203, Roland, AR 72135/501-868-9787

Power Custom, Inc., R Rt. 2 Box 756AB, Gravois Mills, MO 65037/314-372-5684

Precision Specialties, 131 Hendom Dr., Feeding Hills, MA 01030/413-786-3365

Progressive Ballistics, Inc., Box 2526, Shawnee Mission, KS 66201/816-221-9117 (Tri-Comp muzzle brake)

RPS Gunshop, 11 So. Haskell St., Central Point, OR 97502/503-664-5010

Roberts Custom Guns (Dayton Traister Co.), 4778 N. Monkey Hill Rd., Oak Harbor, WA 98277/206-675-3421

Bob Rogers Gunsmithing, P.O. Box 305; 344 S. Walnut St., Franklin Grove, IL 61031/815-456-2685 (custom)

SSK Industries (See: J.D. Jones)

L.W. Seecamp Co., Inc., Box 255, New Haven, CT 06502/203-877-3429

Harold H. Shockley, 204 E. Farmington Rd., Hanna City, IL 61536/309-565-4524

Hank Shows, dba The Best, 1078 Alice Ave., Ukiah, CA 95482/707-462-9060

Spokhandguns Inc., Vern D. Ewer, P.O. Box 370, 1206 Fig St., Benton City, WA 99320/509-588-5255

Sportsmens Equipmt. Co., 915 W. Washington, San Diego, CA 92103/619-296-1501 (specialty limiting trigger motion in autos)

James R. Steger, 1131 Dorsey Pl., Plainfield, NJ 07062

Irving O. Stone, Jr., 7337 Sullivan Rd., P.O. Box 1838, Twentynine Palms, CA 92277/619-367-2747

Victor W. Strawbridge, 6 Pineview Dr., Dover Pt., Dover, NH 03820

A.D. Swenson's 45 Shop, P.O. Box 606, Fallbrook, CA 92028

Ten-Ring Precision, Inc., Alex B. Hamilton, 1449 Blue Crest Ln., San Antonio, TX 78232/512-494-3063

Randall Thompson, Highline Machine Co., 654 Lela Pl., Grand Junction, CO 81504/303-434-4971

"300" Gunsmith Service, 4655 Washington St., Denver, CO 80216/303-295-2437

Timney Mfg. Co., 3065 W. Fairmount Ave., Phoenix, AZ 85017/602-274-2999

Trapper Gun, Inc., 18717 East 14 Mile Rd., Fraser, MI 48026/313-792-0134

Tussey Custom, 223 W. Blueridge Ave., Orange, CA 92665/714-282-8328

Dennis A. "Doc" & Bud Ulrich, D.O.C. Specialists, 2209 So. Central Ave., Cicero, IL 60650/312-652-3606

Vic's Gun Refinishing, 6 Pineview Dr., Dover, NH 03820/603-742-0013

Walters Industries, 6226 Park Lane, Dallas, TX 75225/214-691-6973

Wardell Precision Handguns Ltd., Box 4132 New River Stage 1, New River, AZ 85029/602-242-0186

Wilson's Gun Shop, P.O. Box 578, Rt. 3, Box 211-D, Berryville, AR 72616/501-545-3618

Wisner's Gun Shop, Inc., P.O. Box 58; Hiway 6, Adna, WA 98552/206-748-8942